MARK'S GOSPEL:
A HISTORY
OF ITS INTERPRETATION

MARK'S GOSPEL:
A HISTORY
OF ITS INTERPRETATION

From the Beginning
Until 1979

Sean P. Kealy, C.S.Sp.

PAULIST PRESS
New York/Ramsey

Acknowledgements
The Publisher wishes to gratefully acknowledge the use of the following material. Selections from *Jesus Christ Through History* by Dennis C. Duling and *The New Testament: An Introduction* by Norman Perrin are reprinted by permission of Harcourt Brace Jovanovich, Inc. The excerpt from "Telling Triumph" by Christopher Porterfield © 1978 by Time Inc. is reprinted by permission of *Time,* The Weekly Newsmagazine. Permission to quote from Kummel's *The New Testament* has been granted by Abingdon Press and SCM Press Ltd. Permission to quote from *Explorations in Theology 2* by C. F. Evans has been granted by SCM Press Ltd. Excerpts from *The New English Bible* © 1961, 1970 by The Delegates of the Oxford University Press and the Syndics of the Cambridge University Press are reprinted by permission of Cambridge University Press.

Library of Congress
Catalog Card Number: 81-84384

ISBN: 0-8091-2417-3

Published by **Paulist Press**
545 Island Road, Ramsey, N.J. 07446

Printed and bound in the
United States of America

Contents

"The saint who first found grace to pen the life which was the life of men."

—Laurence Housman

"We may listen to Beethoven's Ninth Symphony knowing no more than that this is sound and melody which thrills the ear and speaks to the heart. We may study the program notes, and we can hear the pattern of music developing, as we listen for the entry of each instrument and the development of each theme. Before we come to the performance, we can learn something of the life of Beethoven and we can become aware that it was out of the prison of total deafness that Beethoven wrote that symphony, and that he never heard it except in the mind. To know that will make listening to that symphony one of the most moving experiences that music can bring."

—William Barclay

"Historians are people who spend a lifetime attempting to discover facts about Roman life that any illiterate serving girl in Cicero's time knew well."

—R. Descartes

"Pure experiencing does not exist; to however minimal an extent it is articulated and in that respect interpreted."

—E. Schillebeeckx

"Action expands to fill the void created by human failure."

—C. N. Parkinson

"All works which describe manners require notes in sixty or seventy years or less."

—Dr. Johnson

"Knowledge of a thing engenders love of it; the more exact the knowledge, the more fervent the love."

—Leonardo da Vinci

Introduction[1]

The gospel of Mark is the most widely translated book in the world, found in more than eight hundred languages and dialects. Mark has even been a success on the modern stage. In 1969 it was restored to a prominent place in the Church's liturgy. In biblical studies it has exercised a special attraction for more than a hundred years.[2] The gospels have received the major share of scholars' attention in modern times, and Mark has been at the center of this interest and in particular of the search for the historical Jesus.[3] The story of its ups and downs in the history of the Church is a fascinating one and of itself is an excellent introduction to modern biblical and in particular gospel studies. None of what we call the major Fathers of the Church wrote a commentary on Mark. They did not in general consider it to be an original work but that it was almost entirely contained in Matthew and Luke who further included much of Jesus' teaching which Mark omitted. Yet Mark survived and this lacuna has been more than adequately compensated for by the modern, almost fanatic interest his gospel has aroused. The evolution of interest in Mark has progressed from

> the period of "simple" Mark (Papias to Wrede) to the period of "tricky" Mark (Wrede to Marxsen) on to "subtle" Mark (Marxsen to Minette de Tillesse) and finally in recent years to "theological" Mark.[4]

An historic, survey-approach, although somewhat untidy of necessity, has many advantages over the systematic approach to the Bible which is all too often based on a flight from history and humanity into the realm of abstraction. As with the Bible itself it is only when we see the modern approach to a gospel in its historical development that we can gain an adequate understanding of the philosophical and cultural reasons behind it. Albert Schweitzer, in his autobiography,

1

My Life and Thought (p. 109), describes how a reading of Aristotle's metaphysics showed him the necessity of trying to grasp

> . . . the nature of a problem as it is in itself, but also by the way in which it unfolds itself in the course of history.

Indeed some such historical survey of the immense literature involved is essential. In the preface to the first edition of his classic commentary on Mark written in 1950, Vincent Taylor pointed out:

> The literature on questions of introduction, text, language, theology and exegesis in English, German, French and Swedish, in encyclopedias, monographs and learned journals is immense. Indeed a would be commentator might easily spend the whole of his life in reading and evaluating these contributions . . . he must follow the history of criticism in general and the development of modern theology, the exegesis of the Old Testament, the Apocrypha and Pseudepigrapha, the Rabbinical writings, the main currents of Hellenistic thought, the history and fortunes of primitive Christianity, the problems of science, religion and philosophy. No knowledge, in fact, is out of place in such an understanding.

Thirty years have elapsed since Taylor wrote, and the position has become even more complicated since. An historical survey, the present writer feels, is a basic tool, the minimum required for a fruitful reading of Mark. In a world where so much biblical study is an "analysis of less and less" the need for a synthesis, an overview, is self-evident. Even in a limited area of knowledge to maintain an up-to-date grasp of a subject is difficult. It is a warning against taking too seriously such concepts as the "assured results" of scholars and is an indication of the importance of going over the whole development of a subject from the beginning. Such a history shows how sketchy our historical knowledge really is and how careful one must be with philosophical approaches to history which tend to prove too much. Thus, the famous Hegel, who dominated nineteenth century German intellectual life, once remarked when asked what he did with those uncomfortable facts which did not suit his theories: "So much the worse for the facts." This historical survey is a mark of respect for the many dedicated scholars who have struggled to make Mark alive and speak once again. It not only helps to avoid the mistakes of the past, indicating many of the blind alleys which scholars pursued from time to time, but it is also a challenge to our generation to carry forward the torch of scholarship.

Such a survey shows how the scholars struggled to discover precisely what kind of evidence we actually possess in a gospel, and to what modern questions the nature of the evidence does not allow solutions. It is a warning about the lack of absolute certainty, a fundamental aspect of the human condition and in particular of biblical scholarship which deals with such a mysterious, intangible faith. As has been aptly said, if one has the definite answer to the problems of Mark, "it is not flesh and blood which has revealed it but my Father who is in heaven."

A history like this is obviously incomplete, quite selective and open to revision and development. Frequently only the extreme views are mentioned, and it ignores how the many ordinary believers have interpreted and lived a gospel like Mark.[5] On the other hand a history of interpretations helps to avoid superficiality in reading, widens one's horizon in studying a gospel, and opens up the unsuspected depths of a profound many-sided work like Mark. It provides access to the ideas of many scholars and points out what one all too easily overlooks. All too often education today consists in the reading of only those books with whose point of view the professor or student is in complete agreement. The advice to read books from time to time, books both biblical and others, with whose point one is in complete disagreement is very salutary. While it is true to say that historical writing and thinking begins with the realization that the past is quite different from our own time, nevertheless an historical investigation often teaches us how similar are the fears and problems of man today and yesterday.

Western scholarship has of course always tended to a superiority, a confidence in its own ideal of objectivity, its scientific interpretation as *the* interpretation while ignoring vast areas of Christianity such as the Orthodox, the Coptic, and the Ethiopian whose approach may often be quite close to the biblical culture and mentality which are all too remote from the thinking of Western scholars. Today with the growing numerical superiority of the Church in the third world in succession to the Early Greek Church and the Western dominated Church, new interpretations of the gospel, such as those offered by liberation theology, are showing just how culturally bound Western theology was. History is a reminder that the Holy Spirit speaks in every age and people and not just in our own. Very often the aim of scholars seems to be to arrive at a confrontation of the biblical writers with our modern times and ideas while ignoring the important developments which went on in between. On reflection, no scholar would accept the Bible or even a gospel as a complete blueprint for our life in the complicated world of today. Frequently the result of our inquiry is what Augustine called the state of "educated ne-science," an awareness of what we do not know or what John Keats described as "negative capability," a state of mind and heart in which we are "capable of being in uncertainties, mysteries, doubts, without any irritable reaching after fact and reason."[6]

One can often only echo the lament of R. H. Lightfoot who sus-pected that New Testament scholars tend to have a false sense of ob-ligation to decide definitely one way or the other even when the evidence does not really allow such a decision. "They are so hot for certainties," he used to quote from Meredith, adding, "If only they would freely admit: 'We do not know.' "[7] This reminds one of the caution in avoiding dogmatism in expressing views such as the great scholar Origen exercised as he endeavored to leave the door open for further debate and clarification. C. H. Dodd struck a blow at schol-ars' vanity in a letter to John A. T. Robinson on the dating of the New Testament:

> I should agree with you that much of this late dating is quite arbi-trary, even wanton, the offspring not of any argument that can be presented, but rather of the critic's prejudice that if he appears to assent to the traditional position of the early Church he will be thought no better than a stick-in-the-mud. The whole business is due for radical re-examination, which demands *argument* to show, e.g., that Mark *must* be post-70—or must be so because anything earlier than that could not present such a plain, straight-forward story; that would be to neglect the findings of the fash-ionable *Redaktionsgeschichte*. It is surely significant that when historians of the ancient world treat the gospels, they are quite un-affected by the sophistication of *Redaktionsgeschichte,* and handle the documents as if they were what they professed to be (Sherwin-White, with all his limitations, is the latest instance). But if one approaches them in that way, does not the case for late dating col-lapse?[8]

The story of Mark in the hands of the scholars is a fascinating one with its ups and downs, with no questions barred in the ceaseless quest to penetrate the relevance of Mark. So often the quest in mod-ern times has been conducted with dogmatic assumptions and nega-tive prejudices, with an obsessive pre-occupation with historical questions. Yet who can deny that genuine progress has been made in gospel studies, especially in clearing away inadequate approaches and in demanding of the exegete a self-questioning and more cautious attitude toward repeated theories which too easily become dogmas? Today there seems to be a more healthy return to the theological and pastoral understanding of the gospels, their original function. For it is only when the gospel is approached from a pastoral point of view, its original purpose, as the Fathers of the Church so well realized, that it can be properly understood.[9] Interestingly, the recent emphasis on the gospels as literature has come to a rather similar conclusion. Thus Tannehill is impressed with

> the large amount of forceful and imaginative language in the Synoptic Gospels. The shapers of these words evidently wished to speak with strong personal impact. They wished not merely to inform but to challenge. They called for change in basic commitments, values, attitudes. . . . The author anticipated, I believe, that his readers would identify with the disciples and encouraged this identification by his positive portrait of the disciples early in the Gospel so that the negative turn in the disciples' story would lead the readers to reexamine their own discipleship. Thus the purpose of the author of Mark was not merely to present certain ideas about Jesus or to warn his readers against some group distinct from themselves but to lead his readers through a particular story in which they could discover themselves and thereby change. If this is true, the tension between Jesus and the disciples, internal to the story, mirrors an external tension between the church as the author perceives it and the discipleship to which it is called.[10]

This survey is divided for convenience into seven parts of varying extent based on the knowledge available and the writer's competence. The aim is comprehensiveness, despite the fact that sometimes only a title is known, to provide at least a basis which, it is hoped, other scholars and students may develop. It is recommended that a course on Mark's gospel should include a study of at least one pre-eighteenth century commentary.

Part One: The First Five Centuries.
Part Two: The Decline of Mark: The Middle Ages to the Eighteenth Century.
Part Three: Mark the First Gospel: Reimarus and the Nineteenth Century Liberals.
Part Four: Mark the Theologian: Wrede and the Twentieth Century.
Part Five: The Form Critics.
Part Six: Marxsen and the Redaction Critics.
Part Seven: Mark Restored: 1969 Onward.

A "Marcology" like this is obviously the fruit of widespread reading and the labors of many scholars. However, the footnotes have been kept to what is hoped is a helpful minimum, not out of ingratitude but so as not to overburden the reader.

A recent preface ended by listing those who helped the author, saying: "If you are not totally satisfied with this book, don't blame me, for I did what I could—blame them."

The opposite is true here. Sister Tina Heeran, H.R.S. strove valiantly to bring order out of a chaotic manuscript, and with the helpful criticisms of my confreres Fathers Frank Comerford, Basil de Winton, Tom Farrelly, Michael Cahill, Sam Otto and Francis Malinowski, the author received encouragement without which this book would never have been completed.

1
The First Five Centuries

A.D. 30, April 7:		Death and resurrection of Jesus.
c.	*32–34:*	Conversion of St. Paul.
c.	*34–38:*	Beginning of Gentile mission in Antioch.
c.	*41:*	Herod Agrippa I, appointed king of Judea, executes James, the son of Zebedee, and imprisons Peter. James the brother of the Lord seems to have been executed in A.D. 62.
	49:	The Edict of Claudius expels the Jews from Rome; the Apostolic Council in Jerusalem.
	60s:	The writing of the Marcan tradition.

John A. T. Robinson has reminded us in his *Redating of the New Testament*[11] how little basis there is for many of the dates confidently assigned to the books of the New Testament. His own survey of major studies—English, American and Continental, Protestant and Catholic—published over the twenty years following 1950 gives the approximate date of A.D. 70 for Mark. Two notable events took place in the decade of the 60's. In July 64 Rome was burned and a Christian persecution began as the Christians were made the scapegoat by Nero. Peter and Paul were martyred in this persecution. Secondly, the Jewish War of 66–70 sparked off by Zealots and some aristocratic patriots ended in the destruction of Jerusalem, 10 August 70, by the Romans. The Roman general Titus, son of Vespasian, destroyed the temple and razed the city, a dreadful catastrophe which must have seemed an act of God himself to both Jews and Christians. The Jerusalem Christians had fled to Pella in 66.

There is a growing agreement among scholars that the author of the shortest gospel, which appears to be an "uncomplicated, even simplistic narrative" by a rather dull-witted writer who allowed so many uneven and awkward transitions and unresolved tensions in his work, was "a person of considerable creativity and theological insight" facing serious and complex problems in his community.[12] Mark's narrative is the third stage in the gospel tradition.

The first stage is formed by the actual living words and deeds of the historical Jesus, the scandal of particularity as it is called, i.e., revelation coming, not through abstract and universal ideas but through the seemingly arbitrary choice of God, of a particular people and a particular person, Jesus of Nazareth.

In the second stage the memory of Jesus is interpreted, applied and handed on through the faith-life, preaching and teaching of the early Christians. Of itself without the Christian interpretation, the crucifixion of a Jew some nineteen and a half centuries ago is just another of many sad stories which does not make sense or explain human history.

The third stage, which is at least a generation distant from the historical Jesus, consists in the literary activity, the selection from tradition, the synthesis made by the evangelists each for a particular community who already had a good knowledge of the historical Jesus but who needed some particular teaching and emphasis. Today it has become increasingly clear that an adequate appreciation of a work like Mark's demands an appreciation of the community in which he lived and to whose traditions he was heir and to whose problems he addressed himself. The community, it should be remembered, would have acted as a critic and a guarantee of his work.

Only in our time is Mark's achievement being fully appreciated. In some sixteen brief chapters he has amazingly distilled his Christian experience not unlike a great poet compressing a deeply felt emotion into words. Mark did not produce or try to produce a full description of the Jesus experience but an action document or manifesto or, to use a modern phrase, "an experience causer" destined to change people's lives. But an artistic work like Mark's gospel, once written, takes on a life of its own which even the original author cannot control as it is handed on from generation to generation in a variety of contexts—a point which is perhaps only fully appreciated in modern studies on literature. Mark could well echo the lines of Tennyson's Ulysses:

> I am a part of all that I have met . . .
> though much is taken, much abides. . . .

The relevance and the message of a text depends not only on the text but on the situation of the reader.

At the Nairobi Council of Churches 1975 Meeting, Robert McAfee Brown explained that the key question "Who do *you* say that I am?" is not only a question about Jesus but forces us to examine ourselves.

> Who am I to whom this question is addressed? If the "I" is a black African the nuances of the answer will be different than if the "I" is a white African; if the "I" is in prison, the answer will not be identical with that of the "I" who works on a university campus; if the "I" is a woman, we will learn some things about Jesus that are denied to us as long as the "I" is a man. This is why, as we hear one another's answers throughout this assembly, we need to know as much as possible about the "I" who is answering.

The same is true if we want to understand the varying answers of biblical scholars down the centuries since Mark was written.

A recent theoretician of interpretation, Paul Ricoeur,

> has given a careful account of what happens when speech is put into writing: the entire context of the language changes, for the text becomes an object in its own right, which can create audiences the writer never imagined, and the discourse in the text can no longer be governed by the situation of a speaker and a listener, in which meaning is controlled by countless refinements of gesture, intonation, and by the fact that speaker and hearer share the world immediately around them.[13]

Thus by committing what they have "to say" to "writing," authors in fact set up a barrier to our understanding what the original discourse meant as they have cut it from its original situation and let it create a new world of its own. For Ricoeur our inability to give a final and complete interpretation, our incompleteness and our need to continually revise our opinions are not merely the unfortunate results of our limited knowledge and sources but are actually built into the very activity of understanding a text. He concludes that the moment we know exactly what a particular text means, the text's meaning vanishes.

Although one cannot be certain about the material used it seems likely that originally Mark was probably written on a series of sheets of papyrus, about 5" × 10" each, glued together to form a scroll about nineteen feet long which could be rolled up for convenient storing. We do not possess Mark's autograph copy. But with our present knowledge we can go back to within some one hundred and fifty years of the original, although with no knowledge of the number of copyists involved in the intervening period. Our earliest copy is the Chester Beatty Papyrus (p[45]) in Dublin. This dates from the early third century or perhaps even the second century, as recent dating of papyri tends to place them earlier than Kenyon's dates. It contains six fragmentary leaves of Mark (Mk 4:36–40; 5:15–26, 38—6:3, 16–25, 36–50; 7:3–15, 25—8:1, 10–26, 34—9:8, 18–31; 11:27—12:1, 5–8, 13–19, 24–28). Scholars describe its text as a Caesarean type of text which arose in Egypt in the second century.[14a]

Today with our easy access to cheap and often subsidized and mass produced copies of Mark we have little real understanding of the difficulties of producing and transmitting books in antiquity. To quote a modern scholar:

> As a rule, for technical reasons alone, an author was compelled to keep his material within strict limits. He had to make careful plans in advance so that his work would be the right length, since there was comparatively little room on papyrus scrolls and they were very expensive indeed, given the wages earned by the majority of the population. By and large, only rich people could afford a large number of books, i.e., a real library. So, for example, it is very doubtful whether the early Christian Churches always owned the texts of all the books of the Old Testament; indeed we cannot even take it for granted that in the early period everyone had access to the writings which were collected together towards the end of the second century to form the New Testament canon. For this reason people were fond of using collections of testimonies and extracts, or even simply quoted from memory—which at that time still tended to be very good.[14b]

William Barclay has some interesting deductions on the cost of a properly scribed book.[15] The standard of measurement of a book was the "stichos" which was the average length of a Homeric line of poetry, a hexameter of about sixteen syllables. The Codex Claromontanus gives the number of stichoi as Mark (1,600), Matthew (2,600), Luke (2,900), and John (2,000), with a total of more than 18,000 in the whole New Testament. Barclay also notes that in A.D. 310, at a time of severe inflation, the emperor Diocletian issued a wide-ranging price-fixing edict. A good scribe was to receive 20–25 denarii per

100 stichoi, whereas a laborer's or a mule driver's wage was 25 denarii a day and the wage of a skilled craftsman, a mason or carpenter or smith was 50 denarii per day. Barclay concludes:

> ... a properly scribed copy of the four gospels would cost the equivalent of a craftman's wages for about six weeks. There is little wonder that there was no haste to commit things to writing.[16]

70s–80s

The rewriting of the Markan tradition by Matthew and Luke for their own communities, inasmuch as they were evidently not satisfied with Mark's tradition as an adequate solution to their problems.[17] Mark can be described not only as the first interpreter of the Jesus tradition which we possess in writing but also the first commentator. Witness his numerous explanations of Jewish practices, beliefs and Aramaic phrases for his at least partly non-Jewish audience (1:9; 3:17; 5:41; 7:3f, 11, 34; 12:18; 14:12; 15:22, 42). Matthew and Luke continued this essential process of reinterpretation and commentary, a process which could have continued indefinitely but for the closing of the New Testament twenty-seven book canon by the Church and its recognition that this canon was produced under the mysterious concept of "inspiration." In fact of course the process continued to this day in the biblical and theological interpretations and commentaries which have been produced without ceasing.

c. 130

Exposition of the Oracles of the Lord, a five volume work by Papias, bishop of Hierapolis in South Phrygia in the province of Asia. This is perhaps the first gospel commentary to be written.[18] The Church tradition about Mark's gospel begins with the evidence of Papias whose association of the gospel with Mark and Peter is dominant in the early centuries and is found in such widespread authors as Irenaeus, Clement of Alexandria, Origen, Jerome, Tertullian, and the Muratorian Canon.

Writes John A. T. Robinson:

> It is a curious phenomenon that for the gospel that was least read or esteemed in the early church there is more tradition relating to its date of composition than any other.[19]

Thus, neither Papias nor Justin mentions Paul's letters which Luke himself does not appear to have known. Papias' work has unfortunately not survived, and so we must rely on Eusebius' account of his information. Eusebius questioned Papias' intelligence but not his honesty and integrity.[20] Irenaeus described Papias as "a hearer of John and a companion of Polycarp, a man of primitive times.[21] Papias describes his methods of investigation as follows:

> I will not hesitate to give a place for you, along with my interpretations, to everything that I learned carefully and remembered carefully in time past from the elders, guaranteeing their truth. For, unlike the many, I did not take pleasure in those who have so very much to say, but in those who teach the truth; nor in those who relate foreign commandments, but in those who record such as were given from the Lord to the faith, and are derived from the truth itself. And again, whenever I met a person who had been a follower of the elders, I would enquire about the discourses of the elders—what was said by Andrew, or by Peter, or by Philip, or by Thomas or James, or by John or Matthew, or any other of the Lord's disciples, and what Aristion and John the elder say. For I did not think that I would get so much profit from the contents of books as from the utterances of a living and abiding voice.[22]

Papias is quoted by Eusebius with regard to Mark (before Matthew):

> This also the elder (John) used to say. When Mark became Peter's interpreter, he wrote down accurately, though by no means in order, as much as he remembered of the words and deeds of the Lord; for he had neither heard the Lord nor been in his company, but subsequently joined Peter as I said. Now Peter did not intend to give a complete exposition of the Lord's ministry but delivered his instructions to meet the needs of the moment. It follows, then, that Mark was guilty of no blunder if he wrote, simply to the best of his recollections, an incomplete account.[23]

Many details of Papias' account are not fully clear, but it seems correct to say that he understood Mark's gospel as neither a full biography nor a chronological account but as the product of memory and interpretation yet with a solid historical basis in Peter himself. While he insists that Mark was not an eyewitness he is also concerned to defend his accuracy perhaps against some current critics about whom we can only surmise. But it is amazing how many words in Papias' account are found also in the prologue to Luke's gospel. Perhaps he is suggesting that Mark with his Petrine background is at least as well founded as Luke.[24] T. W. Manson suggested that the Greek term translated "interpreter" meant a function like a modern "private secretary" and "aide-de-camp."[25] One can conclude from Papias, especially from his remarks about the different translations or interpretations of Aramaic Matthew in the Greek language, that the difference between the various gospels was something of a problem. It should be noted that Papias is contradicted by the fourth century writer Epiphanius who says that Mark was a disciple of Jesus, one of the seventy whom he sent out (Lk 10:1) but who later abandoned him (Jn 6:66).

c. 150

But Mark although rewritten by Matthew and Luke was not discarded by the Christian community but included in its canon of four gospels. The controversy with Marcion who only accepted Luke's gospel was probably influential in the Church's preservation of the four gospels. About A.D. 144 Marcion was expelled from the church at Rome for proposing in his *Antitheses,* a work no longer extant, his own list of genuine Christian writings. Marcion disapproved of the scanty treatment of Jesus' words in Mark's gospel. He believed that Paul alone with his distinction between gospel and law appreciated the radical message of Jesus. But even Paul and Luke had to be purged of their Judaizing tendency according to Marcion who, it seems, could claim as his followers nearly half the Christians of his day.

However, Papyrus Egerton 2 which dates about this time seems to combine as of equal value material from all four gospels with non-canonical material.

About this time also Justin Martyr in his *Dialogue with Trypho* (106) mentions that Jesus described James and John as "sons of thunder" and says that his information comes from the "Memoirs" of Peter. As the episode is found only in Mark 3:17 he seems to be describing Mark's gospel as Peter's Memoirs. This is the only use of the word ("Apomnemoneumata") in Christian writings to describe a gospel. However, Victor of Antioch uses a similar word, "hypomneumata," in the fifth century.

c. 160–180

The so-called *Anti-Marcionite Prologue*[26] which may date from this time or perhaps much later says of Mark:

> He was the interpreter of Peter. After the death (post excessionem) of Peter himself he wrote down this same gospel in the regions of Italy.

It describes Mark as "colobodactylus" ("stumpy-fingers" or "deformed in the finger") which it explains as having short fingers in comparison with the dimensions of his body, a point which must have been due to an authentic remembrance, since it would scarcely have been invented. The same word is applied to Mark by the third century Roman theologian Hippolytus.[27] It can be taken metaphorically, suggesting that Mark was no stylist. It can also be taken literally, with the suggestion that Mark deliberately mutilated himself to avoid serving as a priest who must be without physical flaw or to avoid military service.

c. 170

Tatian's Diatessaron: i.e., One through Four, an attempt to present in one narrative the total material about Jesus. Tatian, it should be remembered, continued the earlier tradition of a Matthew and a Luke by compiling his gospel from material available at his time. It seems evident that only four were available to him, and, taking the outline of Matthew for the events up to the trial and John for the events from the trial on, he wove into them the additional information from the other gospels, often ingeniously, for he wished to omit nothing from his popular harmonization.[28] His work was an incredible success not only in the East but also in the West, especially from the Middle Ages onward to modern times when it was the basis of many of the Lives of Jesus—e.g., Gerson (d. 1429) published a Monotessaron which accounted for the differences between the gospels as due to different points of view. It was translated from the original Syriac (or Greek?) into Greek, Armenian, Arabic, Persian, Latin, Georgian and many other languages, showing the obvious widespread need for a harmony of the differences among the gospels. Most Christians have functioned with some kind of harmonization of the gospels, e.g., the Christmas crib composed of Luke's shepherds and Matthew's magi. But the Church, afraid that an inspired text would be replaced by a human one, preferred to keep four gospels, and only in the Syrian church did it replace the four gospels in Church usage. Bishop Rabbula of Edessa (c. 411) issued a decree in favor of four gospels. Somewhat later Theodoret, bishop of Cyrrhus (c. 423–458), on discovering that it was used by about a quarter of his churches, had it replaced by the four gospels, since "the faithful did not perceive the malice of this composition."[29]

Thus one can see the early Church development of the gospels as a process which involved a struggle on two fronts. There was the tendency of a Marcion and in a different way of a Tatian to reduce the number of the gospels to one. Yet on the other side one should remember that we possess fragments and references to over fifty Christian gospels which were also excluded in the growth of the orthodox Christian New Testament canon.

c. 180–200

Irenaeus: About this time Irenaeus in his work *Against Heresies* (3.1.1) wrote:

> After their death [i.e., the death of Peter and Paul] Mark, the disciple and interpreter of Peter, also handed down to us in writing the things preached by Peter.

By his time the four gospels are solidly established, as he argues 3. 11. 8):

> As there are four quarters of the world in which we live, as there are four universal winds, and as the Church is scattered all over the earth, and the gospel is the pillar and base of the Church and the breath of life, it is likely that it should have four pillars breathing immortality on every side and kindling afresh the life of men. Whence it is evident that the Word, the architect of all things, who sits upon the cherubim and holds all things together, having been made manifest to men, gave us the gospel in a fourfold shape, but held together by one Spirit.

Irenaeus can be said to give the oldest clear evidence about the date of Mark, i.e., after the deaths of Peter and Paul.

As regards the knowledge of Mark in the earliest writings the Epistle of Clement of Rome seems to refer to the Corinthians (c. 96), i.e., 1 Cl 15:2, the Epistle of Polycarp (d. 156) to the Philippians (c. 107), the Epistle of Barnabas (c. 130), the Shepherd of Hermas (c.

100–145), i.e., Hermas Sim 5:2. However, these indications are rather difficult to establish. B. W. Bacon (1919) has pointed out that 1 Clement quotes Isaiah 29:13 in the same form as found in Mark 7:6. However, the sobering words of Westcott's conclusion (Canon of the New Testament, p 13) after careful research are still valid:

> No Evangelic reference in the Apostolic Fathers can be referred certainly to a written record.

Irenaeus has been described as the father of authoritative exegesis in the Church. He was convinced of the importance of apostolic tradition. The one standard of correct interpretation against heretics is the rule of faith as preserved in churches in the apostolic succession.[30] Further, Irenaeus' view of the evangelists as

> "primarily theologians not concerned to present biographies of Jesus, but to drive home theological claims about him" has been described as "a striking anticipation of a 'discovery' which shaped all study of the Gospels in the last hundred years."[31]

On Mark in particular, he remarks:

> Those who separate Jesus from the Christ, saying that Christ remained unsubjected to suffering and that it was Jesus who suffered, would be able to correct their error if they would make use of the Gospel of Mark and read it with a love of truth.[32]

It is very interesting to read some of the interpretations which the early writers like Irenaeus give to the parables of Jesus. Thus Mark's famous parable in chapter 4 speaks of "the mystery of the kingdom" but does not give plain explanations until the second half of his gospel. Irenaeus explains the mustard seed in terms of the resurrection. Jesus is the heavenly word sown like seed in the field of the world, hidden in the earth in a tomb and after three days born a mighty tree whence the branches, the twelve apostles, spring, giving shelter to the Gentiles as birds of the heaven. 1 Clement (24:1ff; 23:3ff; 26:1) which seems to be commenting on Mark's parable of the Sower tradition interprets it as an illustration of the resurrection. The tradition of these early writers who see all the seed and growth parables as resurrection teaching gives probably the best interpretation of this difficult chapter in Mark.

With Irenaeus[33] begins the popular tradition of likening the four evangelists to the four cherubim of Ezekiel and the four living creatures of Apocalypse 4. He identified Mark with the eagle, for he begins with the prophetic spirit (Isaiah) coming down from on high to men. Interestingly, the tradition is never consistent about Mark unlike the other three evangelists, and we find him depicted in successive patristic writing as eagle, lion, man and ox as if to say that the Fathers could not quite agree on Mark's characterization. The symbols which won the widest acceptance in Christian art—the lion (Mark), the man (Matthew), the ox (Luke), and the eagle (John)—are first found in the third century commentary of Victorinus of Pettau on Apoc 4:7 and again in Jerome's Prologue to his Commentary on Matthew. An old Latin distich which uses these symbols in speaking of Christ curiously applies the lion symbol to the resurrection because of the ancient belief that a lion was born inanimate and only roused to life after three days by the roar of its father who brought it food.

> Fuit homo nascendo, vitulus moriendo,
> leo renascendo, aquila ascendendo.

It is interesting to note Augustine's insight *On the Agreement of the Evangelists* (1:6) that Mark is best represented by the man since he gives the most human picture of Jesus—Matthew presents Jesus as the Lion of Judah, Luke's ox signifies the Savior of the world, and John's eagle represents the one who looks straight at the sun. This fourfold symbolism is a kind of theology in picture, in miniature, which has served as a continuing reminder to the Church of the pluralism available in the gospels. It is a variety, however, which has only been adequately investigated in recent years.

c. 180

Clement of Alexandria according to Eusebius[34] inserted into his Hypotyposes

> a tradition of the primitive elders [that] those gospels were first written which include the genealogies [i.e., Matthew and Luke].

But for Clement this does not mean that Mark was a literary conflation of Matthew and Luke omitting such parts as the infancy narratives where Matthew and Luke did not agree, because Clement continues:

> When Peter had publicly preached the word at Rome, and by the Spirit had proclaimed the Gospel, those present, who were many, exhorted Mark, as one who had followed him for a long time and remembered what had been spoken, to make a record of what was said: and that he did this, and distributed the Gospel among those that asked him. And that when the matter came to Peter's knowledge he neither strongly forbade it nor urged it forward.

Earlier, in fact, Eusebius had quoted Clement as saying that Peter had authorized Mark's gospel to be read in the churches, for when he "learned by revelation of the spirit what was done, he was pleased with the man's zeal."[35]

Another passage from Clement preserved only in a Latin translation describes Mark as writing while Peter was still in Rome:

> Mark, the follower of Peter, while Peter was preaching publicly the gospel at Rome in the presence of certain of Caesar's knights and was putting forward many testimonies concerning Christ, being requested by them that they might be able to commit to memory the things which were being spoken, wrote from the things which were spoken by Peter the Gospel which is called according to Mark.[36]

But in 1958 a rather fascinating discovery of what seems to be an authentic letter of Clement describing another "secret gospel" of Mark and referring to "notes of Peter" was made by Professor Morton Smith of Columbia University. He was working among old manuscripts in the ancient monastery of Mar Seba in the wilderness of Judaea, about twelve miles southeast of Jerusalem, when he discovered a letter copied into the back of an edition of the letters of Ignatius of Antioch published in Amsterdam in 1646. This seventy-two line fragment according to Smith is a copy of an authentic letter written between A.D. 175 and 200 by Clement, an important leader of the Alexandrian Catechetical school who was forced out of Egypt in the persecution c. A.D. 202. In this letter the author attacks some libertine Christians, the followers of Carpocrates who "boast that they are free but have become the slaves of lust." He insists that their false version of Mark's gospel must be distinguished from Mark's "secret gospel":

> As for Mark, then, during Peter's stay in Rome, he wrote an account of the Lord's doings, not, however, declaring all of them, nor yet hinting at the secret ones, but selecting what he thought most useful for increasing the faith of those who came over to Alexandria, bringing both his own notes and those of Peter, from which he transferred to his former book the things suitable to whatever makes for progress towards knowledge. Thus he composed a more spiritual Gospel for the use of those who were being perfected. Nevertheless, he yet did not divulge the things not to be uttered, nor did he write down the hierophantic teaching of the Lord, but to the stories already written he added yet others and, moreover, brought in certain sayings of which he knew the interpretation would, as a mystagogue, lead the hearers into the innermost sanctuary of that truth hidden by seven veils. Thus, in sum he prepared matters, neither grudgingly nor uncautiously, in my opinion, and, dying, he left his composition to the Church in Alexandria, where it even yet is most carefully guarded, being read only to those who are being initiated into the great mysteries.

Scholars are particularly interested in a narrative which Clement quotes from the Secret Gospel and which was added to Mark 10:34. It describes Jesus raising a young man from the dead at Bethany and says that the young man came to Jesus by night six days later and was taught "the mystery of the kingdom of God." While some scholars have pointed out examples of Clement's credulity in accepting dubious writings and that such expansions are an obvious pastiche from our Mark and our John, the consensus is that the letter is from Clement and that he approved this esoteric gospel.[37] The passage from the Secret Gospel reads as follows:

> Immediately after the section which begins "And they were on the road, going up to Jerusalem" and continues to "after three days he will rise" (Mk 10:32–34) there follows, as the text goes, "And they come to Bethany, and there was a woman there whose brother had died. She came and prostrated herself before Jesus and said to him, "Son of David, pity me." The disciples rebuked her, and Jesus in anger set out with her for the garden where the tomb was. Immediately a loud voice was heard from the tomb, and Jesus approached and rolled the stone away from the entrance to the tomb. And going in immediately where the young

man was he stretched out his hand and raised him up, taking him by the hand. The young man looked on him and loved him, and began to beseech him that he might be with him. They came out of the tomb and went into the young man's house, for he was rich. After six days Jesus laid a charge upon him, and when evening came the young man came to him, with a linen robe thrown over his naked body; and he stayed with him that night, for Jesus was teaching him the mystery of the kingdom of God. When he departed thence, he returned to the other side of the Jordan.

After this there follows "And James and John came forward to him" and all that section (Mk 10:35–45). But as for "naked to naked" and the other things about which you wrote, they are not to be found. After the words "And he comes to Jericho" (Mk 10:46a) it adds only, "And there was the sister of the young man whom Jesus loved and his mother and Salome; and Jesus did not receive them." But as for the many other things which you wrote, they are falsehoods both in appearance and in reality. Now the true interpretation, which is in accordance with the true philosophy. . . .

In 1978 Smith developed his interpretation of Clement's letter in a book significantly called *Jesus the Magician* (Gollancz). He tries to show that Jesus was primarily a magician rather than a prophet or a teacher. The nocturnal meeting described in the fragment was the young man's initiation into the esoteric and libertine circle of Jesus, an initiation which may have included sexual contact. Jesus he describes as a divine magician who saw himself above all human restrictions and who admitted his followers to this freedom from all rules and restrictions by a mystical union with himself through baptism. However, the secret magical tradition was lost by the Jerusalem church under James and by the Gentile Church under Paul. It was only for the few and survived in such groups as the Carpatians.

c. 200

By this time, as Origen put it, there were four gospels

which are alone undeniably authentic in the Church of God on earth.[38]

Origen himself knew of five other gospels which were not guided by the Spirit. According to Eusebius, Origen says:

> The second gospel is by Mark, who composed it according to the instructions of Peter, who in his catholic epistle acknowledges him as his own son.[39]

Thus he confirms the Papias tradition and identifies Mark with 1 Peter 5:13.

Origen was the first to compile scholarly and systematic commentaries on all the books of both the Old and the New Testament. With his unrivaled linguistic textual knowledge, his mastery of contemporary learning which he used in his exegesis, he has been described as bringing

> the truth of a master to what had hitherto been nothing much more than the exercise of amateurs.[40]

Yet Origen was typical of many later scholars whose own presuppositions would influence their interpretations. All too often Origen failed to appreciate the New Testament authors' intentions and historical sense while making them teach Platonism instead of their own concerns.[41] In the fourth book of his *De Principiis*, the first comprehensive Christian theology, he applied Plato's threefold distinction of body and soul and spirit to produce three senses of Scripture.

(a) the corporeal or literal and historic sense which was directly conveyed by the Bible and was sufficient for the ordinary needs of the faithful;

(b) the psychic or moral sense;

(c) the spiritual sense.

Origen recognized such problems as the different placing of the cleansing of the temple in the synoptics and John but attempted to deal with such problems not through harmony or historical criticism but through allegorization, i.e., the temple is the soul skilled in reason to which Jesus ascends from Capernaum to purify it. Through allegory Origen made the Bible relevant and contemporary rather than a remote record of the past. He had the evident precedent of Paul (e.g., Gal 4:24) and the symbolism of John as authorities for the method. Yet Origen recognized the danger of cutting the Bible loose from history altogether and late in his life insisted that the four evangelists used straightforward narrative prose in telling the things that happened in the life of Jesus. Origen in fact saw that the historicity of Jesus was a necessary guarantee against an arbitrary Christian faith.[42]

Writing about the same time as Origen in North Africa, Tertullian in *Against Marcion* (4.5) remarks that Mark's gospel could be called the Gospel of Peter.

> That gospel which Mark edited may be affirmed to be of Peter, whose interpreter Mark was.

Tertullian in *Adversus Praxeas* (21:23) and the Roman Hippolytus in *De Antichristo* (56) seem to have been the first writers to apply the term "evangelist" to the writers of the four gospels.

What has often been thought to be our earliest New Testament list of books, the Muratorian Fragment from Rome about the end of the second century, is unfortunately mutilated. It seems to refer to Mark but contains only some words which probably apply to Peter or his preaching: "At some things he was present, and so he recorded them." However, more recent studies put the dating of the Muratorian Fragment in the fourth century.[43]

323

This is the year of the final edition of Eusebius' *Ecclesiastical History* in which he provided a considerable amount of valuable earlier information about the New Testament and its authors. Following Origen, he divided the books of the Church into three categories— the universally accepted (Four gospels, Acts, Paul's letters including Hebrews, 1 John, 1 Peter), disputed (James, Jude, 2 Peter, 2 and 3 John; Apocalypse hovered between accepted and disputed), and spurious (many would put James' letter here, he says). According to Eusebius:

> It is said that this Mark journeyed to Egypt and was the first to form churches at Alexandria itself.[44]

He describes Annianus as succeeding Mark at Alexandria but does not say that it was due to Mark's death as Jerome does.

Eusebius[45] noted that the "accurate" Mss of Mark end with 16:8 and that 16:9–20 are missing from "almost all Mss." Writers like Origen, Tertullian, Cyprian, and Cyril of Jerusalem do not seem to know the long ending. It is missing from the important Codices B and S. However, Irenaeus quotes Mark 16:9, and the long ending is found in an Arabic version of Tatian, showing that it was in existence in the mid-second century.

Eusebius developed the work of the Alexandrian Ammonius (c. 220?) in numbering the section of the gospels. Further he classified his divisions into ten canons or tables to show by numbers at a glance the corresponding passages between the four gospels, e.g., his tenth section contained the sections proper to each evangelist alone. His divisions are found in the margins of nearly all Greek and Latin manuscripts. They were invaluable in identifying passages before the gospels were divided into chapters and verses. These canons are reproduced in the Greek New Testaments of Tischendorf and Nestle.

367

Only with lists of the late fourth century, especially those found in Athanasius, Augustine and the Councils of Hippo (393) and Carthage (397), do we find the twenty-seven Testaments of Tischendorf and book canon of the New Testament listed exactly as we have them today and can speak of fairly common agreement in the Church. The first listing is found in the Easter Letter of St. Athanasius to his people in 367:

> There must be no hesitation to state again the books of the New Testament, for these are: Four Gospels, according to Matthew, according to Mark, according to Luke and according to John. . . .[46]

386–398

From this time date the Homilies of John Chrysostom on Matthew. In the preface he says that Mark wrote in Egypt at the request of the disciples. This unique opinion may be based on a misunderstanding of Eusebius and his tradition or perhaps on the opinion of Clement that Mark wrote a second gospel. Chrysostom (4:1) considered that Mark reproduced the brevity of Peter while Luke reproduced the abundance of Paul, an opinion also found in Ambrose (Lk 1:11).

c. 393

In Jerome ten homilies on Mark are extant (C.C. 78, 451–500) which consist mainly of moral exhortations but with occasional critical reflections such as the following on 1:2 ("as is written in the prophet Isaiah . . ."):

> But as far as I remember, as much as I search in my mind, examining carefully both the works of the seventy translators (i.e., the Greek Septuagint) and the Hebrew books, I have not been able to discover that Isaiah wrote these words. "Behold I send before you my angel who will prepare the way for you" is written at the end of the book of Malachi. But if they are written at the end of Malachi why does Mark say that they are written in the prophet Isaiah? The evangelists spoke under the inspiration of the Holy Spirit and Mark here no less than the others. In fact the apostle Peter says in his epistle: "Our church chosen along with you greets you as does Mark my son." O Apostle Peter, your son Mark, son in the Spirit not in the flesh, expert in spiritual matters, has made a mistake here.

Jerome goes on to refer to Porphyry's attack against the evangelists, using such texts to show they were unskilled not only in the things of this world but also in the Scriptures. Jerome solves the problem by concluding that according to Mark only verse 3 is written in Isaiah. However, wishing to show that it was the voice of an angel who was commanded, Mark added the other words.

Another reflection of Jerome's on the end of the transfiguration scene in Mark 9:8 ("Suddenly looking around they no longer saw anyone") gives an interesting view of Jerome's exegesis.

> When I read the Gospel and find there testimonies drawn from the Law and some drawn from the Prophets, I think only of Christ, that is, I see Moses, I see the Prophets but only to understand that they speak of Christ. And when I have arrived at the splendor of Christ and when I see him like the glorious light of the sun I cannot look at the weak light of a lamp. For if one lights a lamp by day, does it give light? If the sun shines the light of a lamp is not seen. Similarly when Christ is present the Law and the Prophets do not give light. I do not undervalue the Law and the Prophets; rather I praise them with all my power because they announce Christ. But I read the Law and the Prophets with the intention of not remaining with them but with the aim of arriving, through them, at Christ.

In the preface to his *Commentary on Matthew* written in the last decade of the fourth century Jerome comments:

> Mark, the interpreter of the apostle Peter, and the first bishop of the Church of Alexandria, who himself had not seen the Lord, the very Savior, is the second who published a gospel; but he narrated those things he had heard his master preaching more in accordance with the trustworthiness of the things performed than in order.

The new point here is the connection of Mark with Alexandria, a point not found in Papias, Irenaeus, Clement or Origen. In Jerome's *Commentary on Philemon* 24 he seems to make the first identification with Mark the writer of the gospel, i.e.,

> who I think (*puto*) is the author (*conditorem*) of the gospel.

But Philemon was an unusual work rarely commented upon and so no inference can easily be drawn.

In his book *On Famous Men,* written between 393–395, Jerome echoes Clement and Papias when he writes:

> Mark, the disciple and interpreter of Peter, when asked by his fellow Christians at Rome, wrote a short gospel according to what he had heard Peter reporting. When Peter heard of this he approved it, and authorized it to be read in the churches.

He adds that Mark,

> taking the gospel which he had completed came to Egypt, and proclaiming Christ first in Alexandria, established the Church in such doctrine and continence of life that he induced all the followers of Christ to follow his example.

There is also mention somewhat surprisingly that Mark died at Alexandria in the eighth year of Nero's reign (54–68) which would be before the traditional dates for the deaths of Peter and Paul whom Mark outlived according to Irenaeus. In fact in one of his letters[47] he describes Mark writing as Peter narrates. Jerome, probably following Eusebius, noted[48] that the long ending of Mark is in very few Mss and is missing from almost all Greek Mss. Jerome[49] quotes the first half of the so-called Freer Logion, an addition found in the fifth century Codex W between vv 14 and 15 which softens the condemnation of the Eleven in v 14.

c. 400

Augustine in his work *On the Agreement of the Evangelists* sought to demonstrate the basic agreement of the gospels despite their apparent inconsistencies and inaccuracies.

> Whenever we find the evangelists inconsistent in their accounts of anything said or done by our Lord, we are not to suppose them to be speaking about the same thing but of some other very like it, said or done at a different time. For it is a sacrilegious vanity to calumniate the gospels rather than to believe the same thing to have been twice performed, when no man can prove that it could not really be so. Therefore when this rule fails, the reader's next direction is to take up with any solution rather than allow it as consequence that any of the evangelists had been guilty of an untruth or a mistake.

Thus Augustine expounded the principles which would guide treatment of the synoptic differences for over a thousand years. He had long searched for a proper exegetical method to interpret the Scriptures. In fact the literalism which the Manichees used to discredit the immorality of the Old Testament patriarchs was the main reason for his hesitation in becoming a Christian. However, the discovery of allegory solved his problem when he heard Ambrose the bishop of Milan expounding 2 Cor 3:6: "The written law kills but the Spirit gives life." Augustine concluded that any interpretation of Scripture must be faithful to the authoritative teaching and tradition of the Church, the mind of the original writers and especially the primacy of the law of love as expounded by Jesus.

> If it seems to anyone that he has understood the divine Scriptures, or any part of them, in such a way that by that understanding he does not build up that double love of God and neighbor, he has not yet understood.[50]

In his *On Christian Doctrine* Augustine set forth his exegetical principles. To read the Bible correctly one should be skilled in Hebrew and Greek, in history, science, and local culture. An interpretation should try to bring out the true sense of each text as faithfully as one can, explaining the Bible through the Bible as far as possible and using allegory to smooth out inconsistencies, difficulties and apparent errors.

The Reformation, for example, would see an even more rigid application of Augustine's principles on the relation between the synoptics due to their theory of verbal inspiration, e.g., the harmony published by the Lutheran Reformer A. Osiander of Basel in 1537 which established the style of Protestant harmonies for the following centuries. Calvin, when he wrote on the synoptics, actually based his commentary on a harmony of all three. Writing his *Examination of the Gospels* in 1880 the Russian novelist Leo Tolstoy used Grechulevich's Harmony because it included John's Gospel.

But Mark seems to have received a devastating blow from Augustine's new theory that while Mark had nothing in common with John, and little with Luke, he was an abridgement of Matthew: "Marcus eum subsecutus tanquam pedisequus et breviator ejus videtur" (i.e., Mark followed him like a slave and seems [to be] his summarizer).[51] Yet it was the authority of Peter which seems to have enabled Mark's work to survive. But as a result of Augustine's idea Mark barely survived in the shadow of Matthew until his revival in the nineteenth century. This new theory of Augustine contradicted all the patristic evidence hitherto that Mark was Peter's interpreter. But whether Augustine was aware of this is not clear. As Leon-Dufour points out:

> Other passages of St. Augustine prove that it would be an anachronism to construe him into saying that Mk shows a literary dependence on Mt. He says also that Mt or Mk has omitted what their successors have narrated (2, 14.16.33.98), that Mk or Lk has omitted what their predecessors had (2, 14;3, 52. 73), and even that each evangelist was acquainted with the entire tradition, and has been guided in his selectivity by the Holy Spirit (2, 27. 28. 31. 44. 90).[52]

The function of the Holy Spirit was not only to arouse the memories of the evangelists but to prevent them from errors. If anyone thought he detected an error Augustine's advice was "Aut codex mendosus est, aut interpres erravit, aut tu non intelligis" (Either there is a mistake in the codex, or the interpreter went wrong, or you do not understand). In support of the view that for Augustine Mark only "seems" to be a summary of Matthew one could adduce the brief introduction to Mark's gospel by Isidore (c. 560–636) who is known as the schoolmaster of the Middle Ages (Migne, P. L. 83. 175). Isidore describes Mark as the "abbreviator" of Matthew who gives Peter's teaching in a "rapid style." Mark, according to Isidore, steers a middle course between Matthew and Luke while recalling more from Matthew and keeping not only his order of events but also his order of words.

Fifth Century

In the late fifth century Victor of Antioch complained of the total lack of a commentary on Mark.[53a] He remedied this by a Greek compilation from the earlier writers on the other three gospels who incidentally commented on Mark, e.g., Origen, Titus of Bostra, Theodore of Mopsuestia, Chrysostom, and Cyril of Alexandria. His commentary was very popular in the East and has survived in more than fifty codices of the gospels.[53b] A Latin version was published by Theodore Peltanus in 1580. The Greek text was published by P. Possinus (Catena Graecorum Patrum in Evangelium secundum Marcum, Rome 1673) and again by Matthai (1775) and finally by J. A. Cramer in his Catenae of the Greek Fathers on the New Testament (8 Vols: 1838–1844).

The following selection from his commentary on Jesus' taking aside the deaf and dumb man to heal him (Mk 7:31–37) gives an example of Victor's commentary:

> He takes the deaf and dumb person brought to him "apart from the multitude" not to perform his divine wonders openly; teaching us to put away vain glory and pride: for there is nothing through which a man works wonders more than by giving himself to humility and observing modesty. "He first put his fingers into his ears" who could heal by a word, to show that the body united to his divinity, and to its operation, was endowed with divine power. Because of the sin of Adam human nature had suffered much, and had been wounded in its senses and in its members. But Christ coming into the world revealed to us, in himself, the perfection of human nature; and for this reason he opened the ears with his fingers and gave speech by moisture of his tongue. And so we read: "he put his fingers into his ears, and spitting, he touched his tongue." . . . He also groaned as taking our cause upon himself, and as having compassion on human nature, seeing the misery into which humanity had fallen. . . . He also told them to keep the miracle secret, lest the Jews through envy should put him to death before due time.

The influence of Victor's commentary can easily be seen in later expositors such as Gregory the Great. Gregory in fact did not compose a Marcan commentary, but in Migne (P. L. 79) there are two commentaries on Mark which his disciples Paterius and Alulfus compiled from such works of Gregory as his commentary on Job and his homilies on Ezekiel. Thus a comparison shows that, for example, many of Victor's applications of the parable of the Seed Growing of Itself (Mk 4:26–29) are repeated. For Victor the sleep of the sower recalls the ascension, the succession of day and night, and the bringing forth of fruit by the practice of justice and by patience in time of affliction. The sower's ignorance of the manner of the growth and the sprouting of the seed of itself allude to the free will of man who has to do good works. Blade, ear and corn are images of the different stages of the Christian life which is meant to sprout and blossom forth not merely through obedience but by courage in trials and must strive upward for heaven and carry the sheaves of good works. Lastly, the sickle reminds us of the living trenchant word of God which penetrates to the division of soul and spirit (Heb 4:12) and by which the just shall be summoned to the heavenly granaries. This parable refers only to the just, who all bear fruit but not in the same measure.

This interpretation not only influenced Gregory but also Bede (M. 92.172), Theophylact (M. 123.533) and Euthymius Zigabenus (M. 129.796) with little change. According to Theophylact the kingdom of God suggests the incarnation of God's Son for our sakes, because the man is God himself become man for us. The scattering of the seed over the earth is his proclamation of the gospel, until he slept, the ascension. But nevertheless he watches night and day because when God seems to sleep, he still watches both by night when we advance in the knowledge of God through trials and by day when he grants us a pleasant and happy life. But the seed grows without his knowledge because we have a free will and it depends on our decision whether it grows or not. We are not compelled to bring forth fruit, but we do it spontaneously, of ourselves. At first we let the blades sprout forth and show the beginning of good, and so far we are still small and have not yet arrived at the full perfection of the Christian life. Then the ear comes when we stand in trials. Next the ear is surrounded by buds and stands upright and is soon full. Finally, there is ripe corn in the ear, when anyone brings forth fruit. When summertime allows, the sickle gathers the crop. By the sickle he understands the word of God, and by the harvest the end of the world. Later exegetes such as Jansenius Gandavensis (Lugduni, 1580, p 388), Maldonatus, Calmet, and Patrizi apply the parable to any preacher of the gospel but carefully distinguish the application from the real interpretation.

One can also trace back to Victor the interpretation that the objective of the parables ("seeing they may not see": Mk 4:12) is the sense of a just punishment by God on the Jews because of their unworthiness due to their non-observance of the law. Later authors such as Euthymius would add also the merciful goodness of God who would humble the broad unbelief of the Jews through the disguise of parables while at the same time saving them from still heavier punishments which they would have incurred if they rejected the undisguised truth. Commentators like Jansenius, Gandavensis and Cornelius à Lapide would give a more kindly interpretation in terms of a simple effect, translating the Greek conjunction as "because." Julicher will reject the theory that the purpose of parables is to disguise the truth and to harden hearts which he admits is in keeping with the words of the evangelists, as "in irreconcilable contradiction to all historical possibility" and as reaching "the climax of unnaturalness" (1.127).

Fifth Century Codices

From the fifth century come two famous biblical codices, Washingtonianus (W) and Bezae (D), which give the gospels in what is called the Western order of Mt-Jn-Lk-Mk. This order seems to have been common in Western Europe—the fourth century Codices Vaticanus and Sinaiticus which give the best textual (Alexandrian) tradition for Mark have the more familiar order of the gospels. The Codex Washingtonianus which dates from about 400 was acquired in Egypt by C. L. Freer in 1906. It represents the Caesarean textual tradition. It has an unusual text like the Old Latin version in Mark 1:1—5:30. Also it has an unusual ending to Mark after 16:14. The fifth century Codex Bezae which perhaps comes from North Africa was given by Theodore Beza to the Cambridge University Library in 1581. This rather eccentric text which has long additions to Acts not found elsewhere is the chief representative of the Western textual tradition of the gospels which has a liking for paraphrase. The differences are found especially in 8:26; 10:27; 11:3; 14:4. Only in 13:2 is there a different meaning where the Western text adds "and in three days another shall arise without hands." The eighth century Codex Regius (L) is interesting because it gives two endings to Mark, both the traditional 16:9–20 and the shorter ending. Significant (Caesarean) readings for Mark are also found in the ninth century Codex Koridethianus.

2
The Decline of Mark:
The Middle Ages to the
Eighteenth Century

Since this is an unfamiliar period to many, some general remarks are in order here. The impression is often given that Mark was almost completely ignored. However, a modern survey of the Early Middle Ages from 650 to 1000 shows thirteen commentaries on Matthew with four each on Mark and Luke and seven on John.[54] On reflection the lack of use of a book for a period in the Church should not cause too much surprise since there has always been "a canon within the canon." St. Paul's epistles were so neglected by most second century Christians that it would be quite difficult if not impossible to reconstruct them from second century writings. In fact it is probably correct to say that Paul's letters meant quite little for the thought of the Church during its first 350 years until their use by Augustine. The psalms also were not widely used in the first two centuries when the early Christians used rather their own songs and hymns. It would be an interesting study to trace the use of each biblical book in the Church's history.

Lightfoot[55] gives five reasons for the relative neglect of Mark in Church history and the preference for Matthew:

1. Matthew was believed to be the work of an apostle whereas Mark was not.

2. Matthew is almost twice the length of Mark which has very little not found in Matthew: in the R.S.V. Mark from 1:1—16:8 has 666 verses of which only about 50 have no parallel in Matthew.

3. Matthew must have proved far superior to Mark for practical purposes, e.g., its symmetry and the admirable arrangement of the material made it easy to memorize.

4. Lightfoot's personal belief is that "the Person and portrait of

the Lord, as offered for our reverent contemplation and worship in Matthew, is likely to be more intelligible and attractive to Catholic churchmen, when we recall their devotion to law and order and precise definition, than the Person and the portrait, deeply human it is true, but also profoundly mysterious and baffling, in the pages of Mark."

5. The prevailing view in the early centuries is expressed in Augustine's opinion that Mark was the abbreviator and follower of Matthew.

This period up to the eighteenth century has been almost completely ignored by modern Scripture scholars who use in their commentaries modern critical, historical methods to jump over a large and important section of biblical interpretation. It has also become very obvious in recent studies that these scholars have ignored to a large extent the way that the early Christians and the Jewish tradition interpreted the Old Testament. However, in the current dissatisfaction with the modern approach and in the increasing pastoral emphasis of commentaries one can perhaps see the beginning of a much needed re-evaluation of and a cautious interest in older biblical commentaries. Such commentaries are often accused of flights of fancy, of lack of adequate scientific controls and "eisegesis" ("reading into") instead of "exegesis" ("reading out of"). However, a brief history such as the present shows that such accusations can just as easily be leveled against many modern scholars who are not lacking in outrageous theories and whose scientific method is anything but scientific at times. There is an arbitrary quality about every kind of exegesis for the simple fact that one cannot prove everything, not to mention one's personal position. These older commentaries had their essential priorities (i.e., pastoral) right and were concerned to present a wholeness in their commentaries to unify theological, moral and spiritual reflections, all based on the same text unlike modern commentaries which tend to separate the one from the other and in particular to divide theology from the Bible. In brief these commentators believed that a biblical text should be interpreted on four levels: first, the literal dealing with what happened; second, the allegorical or hidden theological meaning; third, the anagogical or heavenly or eschatological meaning; and fourth, the moral or what we would call the relevant to my life meaning. In particular the allegorical level was used to discover the mystery of Christ in each part of Scripture, e.g., a reference to wood recalls his cross.

A celebrated distich by Augustine of Dacia (d. 1282) which was widely circulated as late as the sixteenth century sums up the fourfold medieval hermeneutic which emerged in the fourth century with the Donatist Tyconius and the monk John Cassian.

> Littera gesta docet, quid credas allegoria,
> Moralis quid agas, quo tendas anagogia.

It has been loosely translated:

> The letter shows what God and our fathers did;
> The allegory shows us where our faith is hid;
> The moral meaning gives us rules of daily life;
> The anagogy shows us where we end our strife.

A careful commentator like Thomas Aquinas[56] would insist that the literal meaning was the basic meaning for the spiritual interpretations, i.e., the moral, allegorical and eschatological interpretations.

> Nothing necessary to faith is contained under the spiritual sense that is not elsewhere put forward by Scripture in its literal sense.

Thomas appealed for support to Augustine:[57]

> I do not censure those who have succeeded in carrying out a spiritual meaning from each and every event in the narrative, always provided that they have maintained its original basis of historical truth.

Although Thomas did not specialize in biblical scholarship he is said to have made a new approach both possible and desirable and to have stated the most actual of problems.[58]

A persuasive plea for the spiritual interpretation as practiced in the Middle Ages has been made by H. de Lubac.[59] This is a very useful corrective to the attitude described so well by C. S. Lewis:[60]

> "Why—damn it—it's *medieval*," I exclaimed; for I still had all the chronological snobbery of my period and used the names of earlier periods as terms of abuse.

Today we are more aware of the continuity between the Middle Ages and the Renaissance and the Reformation and as a result are far more hesitant to indulge in cultural high-handedness of any kind. According to de Lubac the spiritual interpretation enables the student to bridge the Old and New Testament, to see them as one revelation, to find Christian morals taught in both and to close the gap between the New Testament and the last things.

This period was dominated by certain factors in the approach to the Bible[61] that would be changed but not always for the better with the resurgence of learning in the eleventh and twelfth centuries which gave rise to the newly founded universities of Paris and Oxford with their "schoolmen," the scholastics. This was followed in the fifteenth and sixteenth centuries by the Renaissance and the Reformation with their move toward "historical consciousness" and their interest in recovering the original, pure Christianity of the New Testament despite the difficulties in exegesis caused by their polemical approach and emphasis on private judgment and interpretation.

A more radical change would come about with the emphasis on the scientific method from the nineteenth century to the present.[62] This scientific method and such modern developments as the archaeological and critical historical approaches enabled scholars at least to attempt to reconstruct the original historical period and to bypass later developments. But it is still important if not essential to ask what a particular book or even verse meant to the believing community throughout the centuries since it was first written.

The dominant approach of the medieval period—and, it may be said, of many Christians long after—can be summarized in four points:

1. There was a pastoral preoccupation with the spiritual and theological meaning rather than the literal meaning so that the true meaning of the text was often obscured. Problems of text, history, etc., were not important. A general lack of adequate knowledge of the original biblical languages and historical investigation made scientific exegesis almost impossible. Patrick Henry in his survey of *New Directions in New Testament Study* (p 59), remarking that most of the biblical interpreters of the ancient and medieval church were bishops and monks, not professors, makes the interesting comment:

> It might turn out that the "strangeness" of the interpretations of many centuries ago is a result not only of their different philosophical assumptions but also of their being directed to a community of all sorts and conditions of persons, and not simply to students and professors.

2. There was an absence of rigorous, scientific and historic questioning and problem posing, since the Bible was rather a norm for the spiritual life than a source for theological thinking. The Fa-

thers showed little concern for the meaning of a book as an organic whole and made little effort to give a synthesis of the teaching of one gospel as distinct from another. In fact until the nineteenth century most commentaries on the gospels can be said to have presupposed some kind of harmonization so that if Matthew was expounded there would seem to be no need to comment on Mark.

3. There was an excessive respect for the authority of tradition. The exegete was especially interested in handing on the interpretation of the Fathers and not as concerned with new ideas and methods as modern scholars. R. M. Grant[63] comments in a significant sentence which contrasts sharply with the modern desire for the new that "there is little in medieval interpretation that is strikingly novel." The coming of the Enlightenment (1650–1800) with its emphasis on reason instead of authority and revelation, with its ideal of mathematical precision and empiricism, with its method the testing and verification of the physical sciences, would change the scholars' approach radically.

4. The absence of dialectic and conflict among the biblical exegetes produced an unhealthy uniformity based on the unanimous acceptance of tradition. This approach to the Bible would of course gradually be shattered by the rediscovery of the ancient classics during the Renaissance, by the Reformation and by the radical criticisms of the gospels from such scholars as Reimarus and Strauss. Even biblical translations would become instruments for polemics— e.g., the notes, comments and innuendos in John Wycliffe's English translation (1382–1384)—so that eventually most notes were in time banned from English Protestant Bibles. Thus it is rare that one would find in medieval exegesis a critical and independent approach like the following comment from the Franciscan, Nicolas of Lyra (d. 1340) who was a master of Hebrew, Jewish and Arabic literature and who in his commentary on both the Old and New Testaments repudiated arbitrary mystical senses in favor of the literal and historical.

> The writings of the Fathers are not of such great authority that no one is allowed to think in a contrary sense in those matters which have not been determined by Sacred Scripture itself.

No wonder it was said of Lyra's influence on the reformers:

> Si Lyra non lyrasset, Lutherus non saltasset (If Lyra had not played on his lyre, Luther would not have danced).

Since in this section we are generally content to list the main commentaries in the hope of further studies by other scholars, two brief examples at the beginning will be useful to give an indication of the common type of fourfold exegesis which was typical. Thus a standard fourfold understanding of Jerusalem is found throughout the Middle Ages as late as the writings of Luther and Melanchthon. Historically, Jerusalem signified the city of the Jews; allegorically, it signified the Church of Christ, the new spiritual center of God's people. Anagogically it pointed to that heavenly city which is the mother of us all, and morally it indicates the human soul. It is curious to note that symbolic exegesis (e.g., Galilee) has become popular among several modern interpreters of Mark's gospel. Another example is the common interpretations of water in Scripture which can have the literal sense of water, the allegorical sense of baptism, the anagogical sense of the water of life in the heavenly Jerusalem, and the moral sense of the purity of life.

c. 650

Cummeanus (?): This is one of the few complete commentaries on Mark from the patristic age or after, and has been described as a commentary of

> high quality, sophisticated exegesis with allegorical, historical and moral interpretations.[64]

The writer of the commentary begins by describing the commentator's task in Matthew's words:

> Every scribe who is learned in the kingdom of heaven is like a householder who brings from his treasure new and old.

But he, in his poverty, is rather like the poor widow, throwing in her two small coins, to his listeners who are avidly listening like the Syrophoenician woman. He notes that his predecessors have bypassed Mark because he almost tells the same tales as Matthew, just as birds flying parallel almost touch their wings. Yet he carefully examines the canons or lists of parallel readings and finds that Mark alone has eighteen capitula out of 235, and these in particular he decides to explain, noting as he proceeds in his commentary what is proper to Mark. Thus he seems to be the first commentator to emphasize the uniqueness of Mark. He is well aware of the problems of Mark's structure. He notes that Mark

> did not follow the order of history but the order of the mysteries [i.e., arranging the words of the gospel "in semetipso, non in se-metipsis"].

His commentary is carefully ordered, e.g., he numbers the miracles as he goes along. An interesting reflection is his remark that the gospels are woven together from four qualities—precepts, commands, testimonies, and examples. In precepts justice "consists," in commands charity, in testimonies faith, in examples perfection. An illustration of a precept is Jesus' command to the disciples not to go in the way of the Gentiles, i.e., to turn aside from evil. An illustration of a command is the new command to love one another, i.e., to do good and fulfill charity. Testimonies are found in the mouth of two or three witnesses, e.g., John bears witness about me but I have a greater witness than John—the Father himself. Examples in truth are those which imitate Jesus who said: "Learn of me because I am meek, etc."

c. 650–700

Pseudo-Jerome. Frequently spurious commentaries were circulated under the names of the Fathers to increase their authority. This commentary which is part of a successive commentary on each of the four gospels with a common introduction is also attributed to Walafrid Strabo. On Mark it is quite brief and selective, as the following example shows:

> "Dismissing the crowd of Jews, he departs into the ship," i.e., into the Church from the people (gentibus). Other boats were with him, i.e., different Churches of heretics. "Through a squall of wind" indicates persecutions against the faithful. "The waves were breaking into the boat so that it was being filled" indicates the persecution of Antichrist, so cruel that many come close to denying; the beloved of God persevere in faith. Christ asleep in the storm indicates the testing of the faithful in persecution. "They wake him up," i.e., they invoke him in their persecution to come to their assistance. "A great calm took place," i.e., after the persecution of Antichrist and after the resurrection.

673–735

Bede was the most competent exegete in the early medieval period. His aim was primarily to present clearly the opinions of the great Latin Fathers, especially Augustine, Jerome, Ambrose and Gregory. Thus following closely St. Augustine's comments on John's gospel, Bede reflects on Mark's ending (16:20):

> As the evangelist Mark begins his gospel late, so he continues later in his account of events. For he speaks neither of the nativity of the Lord, nor of his infancy, nor of that of his precursor, but begins from the beginning of the preaching of the gospel, which was made by John, and continues his narrative till that time in which the apostles have sown the same word of the gospel through the whole earth.

Typical of this pastoral type of commentary is his quotation from Gregory the Great on the relevance of the Baptist for the gospel heralds of every generation.

> Whoever preaches right faith and good works prepares nothing other than a road for the Lord to come into the hearers' hearts so that this gracious power might penetrate and the light of truth illumine them. Thus may he make straight paths for God, while he forms pure thoughts in the soul by the word of good preaching.[65]

The importance of Bede's commentary is seen from the reflection on Mark's style by the thirteenth century Franciscan, Salimbene:

> Of Mark it is likewise plain that he followed in the footsteps of Matthew, for he repeats what Matthew has already said without verbal adornment, for he had a rustic style and coarse country grammar. But, because he was brief, he is highly praised by the saints and most of all by Bede, who expounded him.[66]

c. 850

Sedulius Scotus: An explanation of the Monarchian Prologue to Mark's Gospel. (Migne, P. L. 103:279–286)

Eleventh–Fifteenth Centuries

During this period the *Glossa Ordinaria,* the great medieval compilation of biblical annotation, was made. Each book of the Bible is introduced with the prologue or prologues of Jerome and other prefatory matter. The text is glossed in the margin and between the lines. This tremendous work was printed many times from the fifteenth to the eighteenth centuries in six volumes and was included by Migne in his great collection (P. L. 114. 179ff). Lectures on Scripture frequently took the form of "glossing the Gloss." Thus the "Gloss" with the Bible became the standard textbook for students from about the time of Anselm of Laon (d. 1117).

c. 1077

Theophylact of Ochryda, Bulgaria (d.c. 1108). He was a Byzantine exegete who commented lucidly on the whole New Testament except the Apocalypse and owed much to the earlier Greek commentaries, especially his model Chrysostom. He closely followed the text in his "Hermeneia on Mark's Gospel" and was especially concerned with practical morality. The following is his commentary on Mark 16:17ff:

> "And these signs shall follow them that believe . . . they shall take up serpents. . . ." That is, they will destroy serpents, those seen by the mind; according to the words of Luke: I have given you power to tread upon serpents and scorpions (Lk 10:19) spiritually interpreted. It can also be understood of real serpents as happened to Paul who was unhurt by the viper. "And if they shall drink any deadly thing": Many such happenings are read in history, and that many of them, protected by the sign of Christ, remained unharmed by poisons they had drunk. . . . We must keep this before our mind even now: that the word is confirmed by works, as in the times of the Apostles works confirmed their words "by signs that followed." May it be, O Christ, that our words which speak of your glory, shall be confirmed by signs and deeds that we may at last be made perfect, with you cooperating in all our words and works, for to you is the glory both of the words and the works. Amen.

According to Theophylact Mark was written at Rome ten years after the assumption of Christ by Mark the disciple of Peter, the cousin of Barnabas and the companion of Paul. (Migne, P. G. 123–491ff)

c. 1115

Euthymius Zigabenus, a Byzantine theologian and a monk at Constantinople. His "Hermeneia" on the four gospels used Patristic sources, especially Chrysostom. It is remarkable for his emphasis on the literal sense of the Bible in an age when the allegorical method of exegesis predominated. For Euthymius

> the second gospel is in close agreement with the first, except where the first is fuller.

Thus he scarcely considers Mark as deserving of a separate commentary. His notes on Mark are generally mere cross-references to those on Matthew. However, where Mark differs from Matthew he occasionally has useful comments.

c. 1125

Bruno Astensis, Abbot of Monte Cassino, had a brief exposition on Mark. He considers that Mark does not need much study because there are very few sections which are not in Matthew. (P. L. 165. 314–331)

+1135

Rupert of Deutz (Tuitiensis) near Cologne produced a commentary on the four gospels. See Migne, P. L. Clxvii. Rupert was a defender of the allegorical interpretation of the Bible against the dialectic methods introduced under the influence of Anselm of Laon and William of Champeaux.

1148–1150

Peter the Lombard produced his famous *Sentences,* the standard textbook on theology during the Middle Ages which marked the gradual separation of theology from the Bible, the result in no small measure of its lucid arrangement and comprehensiveness. It was the first major effort at a biblical theology and was commented upon by all the great theologians until eventually it was replaced as a textbook by the Summa of Thomas Aquinas. Containing a wealth of quotations from the Latin and Greek Fathers, especially Augustine, Hilary and John of Damascus, it is arranged in four parts: (1) The

Trinity, (2) The Creation and the Son, (3) The Incarnation and the Virtues, (4) The Seven Sacraments and the Four Last Things. Such treatises which collected together Scripture texts on similar subjects would contribute to the rise of speculative theology and its separation from the Bible until the re-emphasis on the Bible at the Reformation and its restoration to the center of theology at Vatican II.

+1171

Dionysius bar Salibi: Among the Syriac commentaries on the gospels by Dionysius, the monophysite bishop of Amida, is a catena treatment of Mark's gospel. Like many other commentaries on the four gospels, when it comes to Mark it skips over those parts already expounded in the treatment of Matthew. A Latin version of this commentary is given in the *Corpus Script. Christ. Orient.* Vol. 114.

+1228

Stephen Langton, professor at Paris and later Archbishop of Canterbury, is generally credited with the introduction of the modern division and enumeration of the Bible into chapters. Langton also produced a gloss of the gospels and was famous for his emendations. Robert Etienne (Stephanus), the Paris printer, seems to have been the first to number the verses of the New Testament in his edition of the Greek New Testament in 1551. He had produced the first critical apparatus in his edition of 1550. Generally it is agreed that the chapter and verse divisions of the Bible, although useful for reference purposes, are critically valueless.

1262–1268

St. Thomas Aquinas produced his *Catena Aurea* which was a stringing together of selected passages from fifty-four Greek and Latin Fathers and ecclesiastical writers. His work showed very good knowledge of the Greek Fathers and contained much of his theology and spirituality. Aquinas sees the parable of the sower as a threefold image of the perfection of the spiritual life. The seed which produces thirtyfold represents the normal or average achievement. Sixtyfold refers to the person who has gone beyond the average and attained a further degree. The hundredfold symbolizes the one who has grown so far in the spiritual life that he has experienced a foretaste of the ultimate salvation.

An interesting example is his quotation from St. Gregory the Great's *Explanations and Reflections on the Ascension* on Mark 16:18:

> "They shall lay their hands upon the sick and they shall recover": Is it that we do not believe because we do not now perform these wonders? But these were needed for the beginning of the Church; so that the faith of those who believed might become strong it had to be nourished by wonders, because just as when we plant a vineyard we must water it till we see it flourishing in the soil, and when the vines have begun to take root we no longer water them.
>
> There are certain things about these signs and wonders which we should carefully consider. Each day the Church does spiritually that which she then did corporeally by the hands of the Apostles. For when her priests giving the grace of exorcism lay hands on those who believe, and forbid the unclean spirits to dwell in their souls, what is it they do but "cast out devils"? And the faithful, who have put aside the speech of the world and speak of holy things, are speaking "with new tongues." While they who by their pious encouragement draw evil out of the hearts of others "take up serpents." And when they hear evil counsels, and yet are not drawn to evil doing, "they drink a deadly thing and it shall not hurt them." And they who as often as they see their neighbor grow lax in doing good strengthen him by the example of their own good works "lay their hands upon the sick" that they may recover. And the more spiritual are these wonders the greater are they; and the greater they are the more, by means of them, not bodies but souls are restored to life.

1272–1275

Albert the Great, *Commentary on the Gospels* His aim was similar to that of his pupil St. Thomas, namely to put the literal first without neglecting the allegorical when it can be deduced from the literal. For Albert the literal truth is not an easy preliminary but the difficult goal of exegesis. Thus he dismisses as a distraction the moralizing of the story of Peter's denial, i.e., Peter signifying the sinner, and the servants and bystanders signifying the three stages of sin— temptation, consent, and misdoing.

1311

The Council of Vienne ordered the cultivation of Hebrew studies for exegesis and the setting up of chairs endowed from local ecclesiastical revenues for the study of Greek and Oriental languages in the leading studia of Latin Christendom. By the fifteenth century the use of Greek in biblical studies became rather common.

1402–1471

Dionysius the Carthusian. He commented on the four gospels as part of a series of very extensive and popular commentaries on the whole Bible but has little claim to originality.

1450

The first printing of the Bible (Latin) by Gutenberg in Mainz. The invention of printing and the resultant growth of great publishing houses, new editions of the classics and an international book trade led, not surprisingly, to an intellectual ferment, the battle of the books as it is called, with the Bible as the most influential book.

c. 1455–1536

Jacobus Faber Stapulensis. An early French humanist whose writings include the first printed text of the Ignatian Epistles in Latin and a translation of the New Testament into French (1523) and an introductory commentary on the four gospels. Faber's commentaries were placed on the list of prohibited books by the Council of Trent. Faber, with a series of asterisks and obelisks, added to the bottom of the text a series of brief notes to emend and illustrate the text in the light of the Greek.

1516

Erasmus produced the first of his successive editions of the Greek New Testament. He also supplied a new Latin translation with notes explaining a number of his Latin renderings. This text, although based on six or seven rather late medieval manuscripts, and filled with printing errors, became the basis of most of the scientific exegesis of the entire Reformation period and such popular translations as the King James. Erasmus had also published in 1501 Lorenzo Valla's philological annotations on the Latin New Testament and in 1517 his own Latin paraphrases of the gospels which were designed for the common people and were translated into several European languages. Valla, for example, criticized those who thought that theology was not subservient to the rules of grammar, the exact philological exegesis of the sacred text and the usage of both the spoken and written language. Erasmus, in a famous passage, advocated the translation of the Bible.

> Should that they might be translated into all the languages of all Christian people, that they might be read and known not merely by the Scotch and the Irish but by the Turks and Saracens. I wish that the husbandman might sing parts of them at the plough; that the weaver may warble them at his shuttle; that the traveler may with their narratives beguile the weariness of the way.[67]

An example of Erasmus' paraphrases is his comment on the raising of Jairus' daughter:

> Such as are in a deep sleep cannot many times be awakened, although men call them oftentimes with a loud voice, and pinch them never so much: and when they be called up yet do they not by and by awake, but being half awake and drowsy, gape, stretch their arms, nod their heads, that many times the chin striketh the breast: and if a man call not still upon them, they fall asleep again. But this dead maiden arose forthwith and walked at the voice of Jesus.

1517

Martin Luther: For Luther the actual writing down of the gospels was an unfortunate if necessary concession to human weakness because both Christ and his apostles had only spoken and had written nothing. Only when the gospels were turned back into the spoken word of the sermon were they what they were intended to be.[68] Luther observed that the gospels followed no order in recording the acts and miracles of Jesus but did not consider it a matter of much importance. His approach when confronted with such a difficulty in the Bible which he could not solve was wisely to leave it alone. His theory of the inspiration of Scripture did not allow him to proceed to a critical analysis of such problems.

After 1517, when Luther made his definitive break with the Catholic Church,

> he ceased to make use of allegorization, and insisted on the necessity of "one simple solid sense" for the arming of theologians against Satan.[69]

While recognizing the existence of allegories in the Bible he thought that only those intended by the sacred authors were to be recognized and that the historical understanding of the author and his times was essential for an interpretation. Luther felt that

> experience is necessary for the understanding of the Word. It is not merely to be repeated or known but to be lived and felt.

However, as Grant points out, this led to a subjective interpretation as also did Luther's belief that there could be unanimity in the theory that Romans and Galatians, the fourth gospel and 1 Peter contained the kernel of Christology.[70] Luther's protest against allegorization, which had reigned since the time of Origen, was not even sustained subsequently by Lutherans but persisted even into the twentieth century in varying forms.

Luther devoted much consideration to his German language which "teemed with a Shakespearean or Miltonic richness" and to the problems of translation:

> Sometimes for three or four weeks we have sought and asked for a single word and sometimes we have not found it even then.[71]

1527–1528

During these years Cajetan published his commentary on the gospels. Insisting that the Latin Vulgate was insufficient for biblical studies, he used the Greek text of Erasmus and had strong doubts about the authenticity of Mark 16:9–20. He sought the assistance of scholarly philologists and his commentaries on the Bible are said to contain "much enlightened criticism of an unexpectedly 'modern' kind."[72]

1537

A. Osiander (1498–1552) published the very influential Greek and Latin Gospel Harmony, indicating his methodology in his lengthy title:

> The gospel story is combined according to the four evangelists, in such a way that no word of any one of them is omitted, no foreign word added, the order of none of them disturbed, and nothing is displaced, in which, however, the whole is marked by letters and

signs which permit one to see at a first glance the points peculiar
to each evangelist, those which he has in common with the others,
and with which of them.

Due to his theory of verbal inspiration Osiander concluded that if a
saying or activity of Jesus was described two or three times in a different order or form, then it must have taken place two or three different times, e.g., there were three different raisings of Jairus'
daughter, the temple was cleansed on three different occasions.

1543

The publication by the Polish cleric Copernicus of his treatise
De Revolutionibus Orbium Coelestium introduced the age of science
and the disintegration of the biblico-Graeco-medieval world view. In
the years after Copernicus' death the experimental method would be
developed, a method by which questions of fact would be settled by
experiment and not by authority.

1546

At the Council of Trent the longer ending of Mark was discussed when the Vulgate was declared sacred and canonical in all its
parts. The ending of Mark was used as an example of a "part."

1552

Theodore Bibliander: *Index Verborum in Marcum* (Basle 1552).
This Latin index is given according to the Greek Alphabet.

1553

Martin Bucer, *Reflections on the Four Gospels,* published by Ro-
bertus Stephanus. Only two and a half pages of brief notes are given
to Mark. He comments that Mark has only one part omitted by Matthew and that it is included in Luke.

1555

J. Calvin, *Commentary on a Harmony of the Evangelists Matthew, Mark, Luke.*[73] Calvin, it is interesting to note, could see no evidence for what he described as Jerome's remark that Mark was an

"Epitome" or an abridgement of Matthew.[74] Calvin, who, instead of writing separate commentaries, commented on a harmony of the first three, was typical of many in that he saw the fourth gospel as the key to the understanding of the other three gospels. Yet Calvin differed with Osiander's methodology (1537) and denied that the sequence of teachings and events in each gospel was historical. Rather the evangelists disregarded the order of time and were content to present in a summary fashion the main events of Jesus' life.

Calvin noted the problem of the relation between repentance and forgiveness in 1:4, insisting that repentance like the kingdom was a gift of God.

> Repentance is not placed first, as some ignorantly suppose, as if it were the ground of the forgiveness of sins, or as if it induced God to begin to be gracious to us; but men are commended to repent, that they may receive the reconciliation which is offered to them.

Further Calvin considered both Jerome and Victor of Antioch incorrect in saying that John's baptism differed from that of Christ in that John's baptism was only symbolic and preparatory. For Calvin both in John's baptism and in Christian baptism it is only through the preached word that the sign produces its effect (Vol 1, pp 179f).

Calvin sees the parable of the seed growing silently (4:26–29) as parallel to the parables of the sower and the mustard seed. Jesus is particularly referring to ministers of the word and advising them to be diligent and enthusiastic even though no fruit appears immediately.

> Therefore he tells them to be like farmers who sow seed in the hope of harvesting it and are not worried and anxious but go to bed and get up—in other words, they get on with their daily work and are refreshed by a good night's sleep—until at last in its own time the corn is ripe. Therefore although the seed of the Word lies choked for a while, Christ bids all godly teachers to be of good cheer and not to let distrust diminish their zeal.

In his exposition of the wicked vinedressers, Calvin departs from a strictly literal interpretation. Its twofold aim is

> to reproach the priests for their base and criminal ingratitude and to remove the offense which was coming in the approaching death of Christ.

Although God planted a vineyard and thus appointed pastors for his Church, this does not mean that he gave up his rights but rather that he expects the pastors to cultivate and to deliver the proceeds annually. The winepress and the tower symbolize the

> aids that were added to strengthen the faith of the people in the teaching of the Law such as sacrifices and other rites. God, like a provident and careful head of the house, spares no effort to arm his Church with every means of defense.

Calvin sees this parable as strengthening a Christian's faith in two aspects. First God warns us of wicked men's efforts to obstruct Christ's kingdom and therefore we should not be troubled by them. Secondly, it is a testimony to the victory of the kingdom and should make us not only mild and flexible in disposition but strong and courageous in the face of evil because a dreadful end awaits those who do evil.

An interesting remark is his comment on the "for many" of the words of the institution (Mk 12:24; Mt 26:28):

> By the word many he means not a part of the world only, but the whole human race.

Luke, he suggests, has replaced "for many" with "for you" (Lk 22:20) to remind the reader to appropriate personally what Jesus has provided for all:

> Let us not only remember in general that the world has been redeemed by the blood of Christ, but let each one of us consider for himself that his own sins have been expiated thereby.

1562

Johannes Hoffmeister: Commentary on Mark and Luke. Hoffmeister, a contemporary Augustinian with Luther, was one of his strongest opponents. His commentaries were published in Louvain. He begins with a detailed index of topics in Mark and Luke and then gives a ninety-six page exposition of the literal meaning of the gospel. Hoffmeister quickly summarizes the popular traditions about Mark but does not describe him as an abbreviator of Matthew. Rather he sees Mark as a real author and quotes from the concluding words of John's gospel to illustrate the number of books which could be written and also that Mark's aim was to give sufficient material to help his audience believe in Jesus as the Son of God. His method is to explain the gospel using the rest of the Bible. Thus he explains the seed growing of itself through 1 Cor 3:6. As he gives his relevant exposition he compares Mark especially with the other synoptics, noting, for example, that the miracle of the gradual healing of the blind man (8:22–26) is not found in Matthew or Luke. His exposition is generally his own composition and not a chain of quotations from the Fathers. There is little emphasis on allegorical interpretation.

1566

Sixtus of Siena, a converted Jew, is said to have begun the science of introduction to the Bible with his Bibliotheca Sancta in eight volumes which was frequently reprinted. This included an historical and alphabetical index, alphabetic list of interpreters, a study in hermeneutics, exegesis and apology.

1570

There were 139 Homilies on the Gospel of Mark by Rudolph Walter (1518–1586) published at Tiguri.

1583

An exposition of the Gospel According to Mark and Luke translated from the Latin original of Augustine Marlorat (1506–1562) and published by Thomas Marsh, London.

1594

Lambert Danaeus, *Questions and Scholia on the Gospel of Mark.* These seventy-five questions deal with such problems as Mark's opening quotation from the prophets, the problem of the apparitions in Jerusalem or Galilee, and the lack of miracles in the Church of the day.

1595

A logical analysis of the Gospel According to Mark with notes and doctrinal observations by John Piscatora (1546–1625), London.

1596–1598

Maldonatus, a Spanish Jesuit exegete, published commentaries on the four gospels which "are held in deservedly high repute" and were considered among the best ever written. He had a distrust of allegorizing and in his treatment of the parables concentrated on the central point and message.

1600

Hutter's Nuremberg Polyglot New Testament: Elias Hutter seems to have been the first to publish a complete New Testament in Hebrew. His Polyglot was remarkable in that it contained Mark's gospel in twelve languages: Syriac, Hebrew, Greek, Latin, German, Bohemian, Italian, Spanish, French, English, Danish, and Polish.

1606

Franciscus Lucas from Bruges. His commentary on the four gospels was highly praised for his diligence, accuracy, penetrating judgment and study of both Protestant and ancient commentators. Lucas also published a series of notes to explain the different readings both Greek and Latin found in the gospel tradition.

1613

Francis Junius, *An Analytic Exposition of the Gospel According to Mark* (Geneva).

1623

The Franciscan historian, Luke Wadding, published posthumously the commentary on Mark by Angelo de Paz, a friar renowned for his learning. Angelo commented extensively on the synoptics, beginning each section with a brief literal exposition followed by a moral commentary, including many quotations from the Fathers.

1639 (a)

Cornelius Jansenius Yprensis (1596–1638). His commentaries on each volume of the Tetrateuch, as he called the four gospels, were published after his death. They are marked by a concern for literal exegesis and an extensive knowledge of the Fathers.

1639 (b)

Cornelius à Lapide, a Belgian exegete well versed in Greek and Hebrew. His works have had an enduring popularity especially among preachers until modern times due

> to their clarity, deep spirituality and allegorical and mystical exegesis buttressed by a wide erudition, which enables the author to draw extensively on the Fathers and medieval theologians.[76]

There are many interesting reflections to be found in Lapide's introduction in which he reflects on different aspects of the tradition about Mark, giving one of the earliest of the modern critical introductions to a gospel. The name Mark in Hebrew, according to Pagninus, means smoothed, polished, cleansed from rust, deriving from *marak,* to clean or polish (Jer 46:4), but it may also signify "high in commandment" as Isidore interprets it or also *mar cos,* the Lord of the chalice, i.e., of suffering and martyrdom. In Latin Marcus may mean one who is born in the month of March or, as Isidore says, "a strong hammer" moving people to repentance and a Christian life. Romans, it seems, gave it to firstborn sons (such as Cicero: 1 P 5:13).

Lapide thinks this Mark was a different person from the John Mark who was Barnabas' nephew and Paul's companion. Augustine called Mark the abbreviator of Matthew

> not because he made a compendium of his gospel, as some say, but because he often relates more briefly, as he had received them from St. Peter, the things which Matthew records at greater length. I said "often" for occasionally Mark relates events in the life of Christ more fully than Matthew does as is plain from the account of Peter's denial. Some things also he unfolds with greater clarity than Matthew. Mark is fuller in narrative than Matthew but has less of Christ's doctrine. Mark was therefore a true evangelist.

Mark wrote in A.D. 45 in the third year of the reign of Claudius, as Eusebius says, shortly before he went to Alexandria. There his disciples, the first religious, were called Essaei (Essenes), that is, holy and pious because of the excellence of their lives.

Lapide questions the opinion of many that Mark wrote in Latin, not Greek, quoting the poem of St. Gregory Nazianzen in which he assigned the evangelists to different languages and nations.

> Matthew the wonders of Christ for Hebrews did write;
> For Westerns (Ausonibus) Mark, the learned Luke for Greeks;
> For all John, penetrating the heavenly matters with his vision.

Scholars such as Genebrard, Barradi, Possevin, Peter Natalis, and Pagnini suggested a compromise that Mark wrote both in Greek and Latin. But for Lapide the opinion of Jerome and Augustine that Mark originally wrote in Greek is more probable. Similarly Paul wrote to the Romans in Greek. However, immediately afterward either Mark himself or some other translator produced a Latin version. As Bellarmine perceived in his Ecclesiastical Writers on Mark, a collation of the Greek and Latin texts shows that the Latin versions of both Matthew and Mark were translated from the Greek. This was proved by Franciscus Lucas (1606) with many examples. Lapide adds that the Latin translator Grecized in such verses as 2:2; 4:10; 7:17, 18, 20.

He notes that Mark's whole emphasis is on narrative. Since Mark is not interested in the order in which things were done but, as Jerome pointed out, in their truth, he narrates events which happened later before some which were prior to them in order of time and vice versa.

1650–1880

The Cambridge History of the Bible (p 533) remarks that from 1650–1880 there was no biblical commentator of note. In addition to those we have listed we can also add John Sylveira, a Carmelite exegete, who died in 1687, and Bernard Lamy of the Oratory (1640–1715). Sylveira in five volumes expounded the text of the gospels with many questions giving the opinions of many scholars. Lamy gave a brief and lucid commentary (1687), beginning like Jansenius from a harmony of the gospels. He believed that the Baptist was twice imprisoned, once by the Sanhedrin in Jerusalem and again by Herod in Galilee. He believed that Jesus did not eat the paschal lamb during the Last Supper and that he was crucified on the day of the Pasch. He defended the identity of Magdalene with the sister of Lazarus and with the sinful woman.

However, it was the eighteenth century German rationalist scholars, beginning with J. D.Michaelis (1717–1791), who formulated the right questions and by their substantial investigations into the evidence and their attempt to approach this study without presupposition laid the basis for the modern scientific approach to the gospels. Since Mark and Luke had no claim to be apostles and therefore no guarantee of inspiration, Michaelis judged them on a lesser level of inspiration than Matthew and John. The typical rationalist approach was to emphasize Jesus' moral teaching and to consider the gospel miracles as due to the common superstitious beliefs of ancient peoples. It also suggested that Christianity had borrowed such ideas as the divinity of Christ and the virgin birth.

1661

George Petter, London: "A learned, pious and practical commentary upon the Gospel According to St. Mark; wherein the sacred text is logically analyzed; the meaning of the Holy Spirit clearly and soundly opened; doctrines naturally raised, strongly confirmed, vindicated from exceptions, and excellent inferences deduced from them; all seeming differences in the history between this and the other evangelists fairly reconciled: many important cases of conscience, judiciously, succinctly and perspicuously solved."

+1662

David Pareus: Adversaria in S. Marcum.

1663

John Lightfoot, *Evangelium S. Marci, Horae Hebraicae et Talmudicae* (Cambridge, 1663).

1689

Richard Simon, *Critical History of the Text of the New Testament.* Simon is regarded as the scholar who really established the science of New Testament introduction with his three critical studies of the text, the translation and the interpretation of the New Testament. He pointed out that the superscriptions of the gospels with their indications of authorship do not come from the evangelists. He carefully examined the tradition and the available Mss on the ending of Mark. He suggested that Mark may have published both a Roman and an Egyptian edition of his gospel. In 1750 J. D. Michaelis, building on Simon's work, produced the first truly historical and critical introduction to the New Testament, using such auxiliary sciences as philosophy, geography and archaeology.

1703

Alexander Natalis (Noel), 1639–1724: The Dominican Alexander published a literal and moral commentary on one hundred and sixty gospels for Sundays and feast days and on the epistles of the New Testament, a work which has often been re-edited in different forms.

1707

Moral reflections on the Gospel of St. Mark to make reading of it more profitable and the meditating on it more easy. Translated into English from the French of Pasquier Quesnel (1634–1719).

1707–1716

Augustine Calmet: His commentary on all the books of the New Testament is rather a compilation and "lacks critical judgment"[77a] and originality, but is a work of great erudition.

1716

George Friedrich Herpel: Mark's Gospel illustrated with critical, grammatical and historical notes. Argentorati.

1737

Lorenz Reinhard: Philological and Exegetical Observations on Mark's Gospel. Leipzig.

1742

J. A. Bengel, *Gnomon Novi Testamenti* (Tübingen). His critical edition of the Greek New Testament (1734) with its classification of manuscripts marked the beginning of modern scientific textual criticism. His *Gnomon* (Rule of Life) became a classic and was celebrated for its penetrating pithy exegesis giving a word for word explanation of the Greek text, opening up the possibility of independent thinking on the part of the interpreter.[77b]

1751–1752

J. J. Wettstein published his edition of the New Testament on which he had spent some forty years. He insisted in his essay *On the Interpretation of the New Testament* that the first duty of a good interpreter was to establish the text of an ancient writer and then to bring out the meaning of the words.

> If you wish to get a thorough and complete understanding of the books of the New Testament, put yourself in the place of those to whom they were first delivered by the apostles as a legacy. Transfer yourself in thought to that time and that area where they were first read. Endeavor, so far as possible, to acquaint yourself with the customs, practices, habits, opinions, accepted ways of thought, proverbs, symbolic language, and everyday expressions of these men, and with the ways and means by which they attempt to persuade others or to furnish a foundation for faith. Above all, keep in mind when you turn to a passage that you can make no progress by means of any modern system, whether of theology or of logic, or by means of opinions current today.

According to Wettstein we get the meaning of the words and sentences in the first place from other passages by the same author and then from the rest of the sacred writings:

> It is certain that all the writers of the New Testament studied the Greek version of the Old Testament by day and by night and since it is agreed on the basis of the testimony of the ancients and on that of the matter itself that the Gospel of Matthew was avidly read by Mark and the Gospels of Matthew and Mark, together with the letters of Paul, by Luke, who then can doubt that the one can be illuminated by the other? And since the sacred writers invented no new language, but made use of the one they learned from their contemporaries, the same judgment is also required of their writings. By "common usage" I understand the common speech of the apostolic age, but not the usage of the medieval writers, and much less that of the scholastic and modern theologians.[78]

Wettstein not only invented the letters and numbers for manuscripts still in use but he also offered

> a collection of parallel passages from classical and Jewish literature unsurpassed to this day that is intended to make possible an understanding of the New Testament text against the background of its time.[79]

1773

Jacques Elsner (1692–1750) authored *A Critical Philological Commentary on the Gospel of Mark* (Lugdini-Batav.). Elsner's commentary, which concentrates on what is not already found in Matthew, is an interesting specimen to study as he carefully gives the sources for his many opinions as he proceeds. It is therefore a useful summary for Marcan studies at the end of the eighteenth century. He accepts the ancient opinions that Mark was the disciple, companion and interpreter of Peter (1 Pet 5:13) and also the companion of Paul and that he died in Alexandria. But as other scholars have pointed out, Mark the evangelist is to be distinguished from the John Mark mentioned in Acts. He gives the explanation for this popular Roman name as "commandment," the explanation found in Hesychius and in the Glossae.

Elsner agrees with Richard Simon, Renaudot and Calmet against other scholars that Mark was not originally written in Latin but in Greek. Further, a comparison with Matthew's Gospel proves to him the falsity of the Augustinian belief that Mark was an abbreviator of Matthew. Matthew is not so large as to need a compendium, while Mark is not so brief that he can be described as a compendium. Further, as the comparison between Mark and Matthew of Rollius (1753) showed, Mark has many parts in common with Luke which are not found in Matthew.

The common date assigned to Mark which is also found in several codices is the tenth year after the ascension of Christ. But Millius and Fabricius, based on Irenaeus' reference to the "departure" of Peter and Paul from Rome, give the year as 63, while Hardiunus places it before 60. Calmet, who in his Preface gives many opinions, is himself convinced that Mark was produced after Matthew but is not definite as to the time.

Elsner affirms that the final twelve verses of Mark are genuine since they are found in the best witnesses and translations. Further, Mark's gospel could not conclude with "they were afraid for," since a further conclusion is obviously demanded. Elsner contradicts the view of Grotius that Mark's style, which was more Hebrew than Greek, was mediocre, quoting Blackwall who in his study of classical writers admired the first chapter of Mark for its variety and pleasing style. Mark's style which imitates the concise and elegant brevity of his master Peter is adapted to his material and reflects also his concern for truth, trustworthiness and candor. Further, he criticizes Richard Simon's view that the gospels are collections of the apostolic preaching without any temporal order. This view was based on Papias who Eusebius had testified was worthy of the least credibility.

In his line by line commentary proper, Elsner's procedure is first to print in Greek the gospel verse and then to criticize the various explanations given by the scholars. He skips those verses found and treated in his Matthaean commentary. Interestingly he rejects the view of Clericus that 1:1 ("beginning . . .") should be considered as an inscription of the whole book like the opening of Hosea. Rather, this verse is the beginning of the book. In his second verse Elsner reads "as is written in the prophets" while discussing at length the various opinions about the reading "in the prophet Isaiah" given by other scholars.

3
Mark the First Gospel: Reimarus and the Nineteenth Century Liberals

1774–1778

A revolutionary change may be said to have begun in gospel studies in these years when G. E. Lessing posthumously published *Fragments by an Unknown Author,* one of which was entitled *The Aim of Jesus and His Disciples.* These seven fragments were the *Apology on Behalf of the Rational Worshippers of God* by the deist, H. S. Reimarus (1694–1768), who had circulated his manuscript of over four thousand pages among his friends during his lifetime. Rational criticism and the belief that liberty, equality, fraternity, social reform and education would produce the enlightened man was in vogue as is evident from Kant's challenge in his *Critique of Pure Reason* (1781) to religious faith to appear before the court of critical reason. Advocates of

> religion, on the strength of its sanctity, and law, on the strength of its majesty, try to withdraw themselves from it; but by so doing they arouse just suspicions, and cannot claim that sincere respect which reason pays to those only who have been able to stand its free and open examination.[80]

Rationalism, the search for a religion within the bounds of reason, was certainly in the air, from the Frenchman Voltaire and the German Christian Wolff to the English deists, Collins, Chubb and Woolstan. These rationalized the miracles of Jesus by explaining the raising of the dead as if from a lethargic sleep and the appearances of the risen Jesus as phantoms seen by dreamers and visionaries if not pure inventions. Jesus was seen as a prophet and the founder of a higher form of natural religion, theories which can be traced back to the sixteenth century Socinus and Serventus who had both denied the divinity of Jesus.

Thus the common assertion is not surprising that the eighteenth century discovered in the gospels a rational Jesus in contrast to the Jesus of feeling of Schleiermacher and the Romantics, the liberal Jesus of the nineteenth century and the crisis or eschatological Jesus produced against the war and revolutionary background of the twentieth century.

Reimarus who published in 1754 a book called *The Principal Truths of Natural Religion* was typical of many critics who were in fact quite uncritical in regard to their own negative assumptions about the supernatural, the mysterious, miracles and mysteries. Schweitzer is eloquent on the hate, scorn and superiority to contemporary opinion which motivated Reimarus' reconstruction of the process through which the gospels came into existence. The inconsistencies in the different resurrection accounts, for Reimarus, implied falsification. The resurrection was a fraud perpetrated by the disciples who were disappointed in Jesus' death and who stole his body, having waited some fifty days so that there could be no examining of the body. They utilized for their purpose a view found in some Jewish traditions that the Messiah would come first in suffering and misery and a second time in power and glory. The disciples were motivated in their inventions by their discovery that the wandering life of an apostle would provide them with abundant friends, food and clothing.

Reimarus can be considered the father of modern gospel criticism and even of its most recent emphasis—redaction criticism. He, for all his faults, recognized that a gospel writer had other than purely biographical concerns and had a creative attitude toward the gospel tradition. Reimarus is usually put first in the list of the many scholars who would seek to discover "the real historical Jesus."[81] He believed that the evangelists did not describe Jesus as he really lived and taught, as a Jew among Jews for whom such words as Son and Spirit had no metaphysical connotations. They described a later view of Jesus when doctrines had been developed and copyists introduced such statements as the command to baptize in the name of the Trinity (Mt 28:16ff). Jesus' purpose was to establish the political kingdom of the Messiah, to free the Jewish people from political oppression and make them instead the rulers of the world.

1774

J. J. Griesbach, who had made an important contribution to the classification of gospel manuscripts, published *A Synopsis of the Gospels Matthew, Mark and Luke* "together with those pericopes of John which can be compared with the other evangelists" as a text book for lecturers. He confessed to a "heresy," namely the belief that little real profit can be gained from a harmonizing of the gospels, since

> none of the evangelists anywhere exactly follows the temporal sequence

and there is not sufficient evidence to deduce

> who deviates from the chronological order and at what point he does so.

Thus with Griesbach the differences between the gospels began to be critically observed and the way was paved for the tremendous development of the following century and the rediscovery of Mark in particular.

Griesbach in his further writings (1789-1790) opposed the traditional Augustinian hypothesis (Matthew-Mark-Luke-John) that Mark used Matthew and that Luke used both. Matthew was written first and Luke not Mark came second. When Mark wrote he had in front of his eyes not only Matthew but Luke as well, and he excerpted from them whatever he intended to preserve of Jesus' deeds, words and destiny. Griesbach concluded that

> whoever assumes that Mark wrote as an inspired author must think of him as having been very meagerly informed.[82]

Luke's direct dependence on Matthew explained the passages which they had in common.

Mark, he concluded, simply wanted to write a smaller book and confine himself to the kerygmatic activities of Jesus. He therefore omitted several of the longer sermons of Jesus and also whatever did not pertain to the public teaching of Jesus, e.g., Mt 1—2; Lk 1—2. Thus Griesbach is typical of many after him who would attempt to penetrate the psychology of the evangelist's motivation. For example he concluded that Mark followed Matthew up to 4:21 and then passed over to Luke, since the Sermon on the Mount followed at that point in Matthew. This long sermon

> seemed to him too verbose, and besides, it comprises things which specially pertained only to those persons who heard Christ speaking on the mountain (p 371).

However, he recognized that although Mark is the shorter work nevertheless he is often more detailed than the other two synoptics (p 368). These details were added to illustrate matters which were either useful or necessary for a better understanding of his narrative (e.g., 7:3, 4, 5; 11:13; 12:42). Other details were added to the stories found in Mt/Lk to please his readers. Often Mark "expressed by paraphrase" and "expounds more plainly" what he had received in a briefer form. In an acute remark aimed at Koppe (1782) Griesbach insisted:

> It depends entirely on the intention of the author whether it is possible to add to, or to subtract from, what others have written before him (p 396).

An important point concerning Griesbach's view of Mark's aim which is often forgotten is that it was

> neither to copy out their books nor to summarize them, but with their guidance to compose a new narrative adapted to his readers (p 402).

This statement is in tension with his earlier remark that Mark compiled his whole work, apart from twenty-four verses which he added on his own account, from Matthew and Luke. Thus he recognized as Mark's own composition the two detailed episodes of the healing of the deaf-mute (7:32–37) and the blind man (8:22–26) which are not given in the other synoptics.

What Griesbach did was to separate John's gospel from the other three and to print the latter together in three parallel columns. He coined the word synopsis which is not the English word meaning a summary but a convenient printing of the gospel in parallel columns. Thus he made possible for the first time a truly historical investigation and an accurate examination of the agreements and differences of what henceforth were called the synoptics. Griesbach's synopsis should however be seen as a development of the famous Eusebian Canons which are still found in many critical texts of the New Testament and which were developed by Eusebius to indicate the parallel passages in the gospels and were widely printed in the texts of the Middle Ages. According to Bernard Orchard, Griesbach expounded his synoptic theory in pamphlets in 1783/4 and 1789/90. However, in all probalitity he borrowed his hypothesis from the work of the Englishman H. Owen who had invented it some twenty years earlier and in 1764 published his *Observations on the Four Gospels.*[83]

For Owen a comparison showed that Mark was simply an abridged compilation of Matthew and Luke:

> He copies largely from both: and takes either the one or the other perpetually for his guide. The order indeed is his own and is very close and well connected (p 50).

Particularly because of Griesbach's high reputation this hypothesis was accepted and used by most of the leading biblical scholars and theologians of the first half of the nineteenth century. It was the basis of the gospel commentaries and introductions of Paulus (1800), De Wette (1826) and Fritzsche (1830) which were considered by D. F. Strauss (1835) as the best basis for a critical study of the life of Jesus. Strauss considered that Griesbach had solved the synoptic problem and concluded that since Mark was a compilation of the other two synoptics Mark had no source of his own and could not be based on Peter's oral account.

1778

G. E. Lessing, who had published Reimarus, himself tried to explain the problem of the contradictions within the synoptic gospels, especially in his essay *New Hypothesis Concerning the Evangelists Regarded as Merely Human Historians.* Lessing was the first to treat the relationship between the gospels as a purely literary problem without the presupposition of inspiration. On Mark he wrote:

> It is still more obvious that Mark, who is commonly held to be only an abbreviation of Matthew, appears to be so only because he drew upon the same Hebrew document of Matthew which everyone interpreted as well as he could.[84]

Unlike Reimarus, who treated all the gospels as equal in value, Lessing had recourse to source criticism. His hypothesis of a lost Aramaic Gospel of the Nazarenes of which each evangelist used a different Greek translation, if accepted, would of course deny the trustworthiness of the canonical gospels of which he surprisingly considered John as more authentic than the synoptics. But his opinion that the true gospel lay somewhere behind the canonical gospels was a very influential idea until recent times when the value of four differing portraits has been emphasized.

1782

J. B. Koppe took issue with the popular Augustinian theory in a dissertation entitled *Marcus non epitomator Matthaei* and recalled Papias' statements that Peter's testimony was found in Mark. For Koppe Mark could not be an "epitomator" (abbreviator) since in fact he was "a locupletator" (expander). Therefore Koppe concluded (p 9):

> It is probable that the shortest gospel was chronologically earlier and that the longer ones, in which the evangelists supplied and amplified matters that had been either omitted or else related too concisely, were composed at a later date.

He also noted that Luke's preference of Mark's order to that of Matthew would be difficult to explain if Matthew were the first and the authoritative gospel.[85]

1787

It is commonly recognized that the inaugural lecture of Johann Philip Gabler at the University of Altdorf marked a key turning point in the history of biblical studies. His lecture which was concerned with method bore the title "On the Proper Distinction Between Biblical and Dogmatic Theology and the Limits To Be Drawn for Each." A clear distinction, he argued, would help overcome the points of contention and the fatal discords of the various sects which were due to ascribing to the biblical writers "individual frivolous opinions." He concluded that biblical theology was historical in nature and that its aim was to convey what the sacred writers thought about divine matters. Dogmatic theology, on the other hand, was didactic in nature and taught the rational philosophizing of the particular theologian according to his ability, his historical situation, his sect and other similar factors.

Gabler recognized that there were stages in the development of revelation in the Bible and that not all the biblical writers attest to the same form of religion. Inspiration does not destroy completely a man's native intelligence and his natural ways of knowing things. One must carefully ask, collect and classify what each, e.g., Jesus, Paul, Peter, John, James, thought about the things of God. Such questions must be asked as: What meaning did a particular word have for the writer in question? Does he speak his own words or transmit those of others? Then a careful comparison of the ideas of all the sacred writers among themselves must be made. A distinction should be seen between what in the New Testament is said in accommodation to the ideas or the needs of the first Christians and what is said in reference to the unchanging ideas of the doctrine of salvation. Thus no one would apply to our times the Mosaic rites which Jesus had invalidated or Paul's advice about women veiling themselves in church. The aim of biblical theology was to single out universal ideas which alone are useful in dogmatic theology.

1794

J. G. Eichorn proposed the famous alternative:

> Either the three gospel writers made use of one another, or they depended upon a common source,

i.e., an inner synoptic or a pre-synoptic solution. Eichorn decided for the second alternative, holding that

> a mutual use of one synoptic by the other two is impossible because none of the gospels consistently offers the better text and context when compared with the others.[86]

He developed Lessing's hypothesis of a lost Hebrew or Aramaic primal gospel in a rather complicated fashion. However, instead of Eichorn's alternative, C. L. Gieseler in 1818 would propose an oral gospel. He tried to explain the divergencies by the wide dissemination of this oral tradition but failed to explain the agreements such as the exact correspondence of whole sentences and often rare expressions and words.

1796

F. A. Wolf, *Prolegomena to Homer*. In this controversial examination of the "bible" of classical literature, Wolf concluded that both the *Iliad* and the *Odyssey* were the final products of an oral process by which poems from different poets originally were handed on by rhapsodists and after being written down were polished by redactors who endeavored to bring them into line with accepted literary taste. This critical approach, to Wolf's own dismay, destroyed his belief in a single Homer. In the same year as Wolf, J. G. Herder, who claimed that he himself was the originator of the "rhapsodist" view of Homer and that Wolf plagiarized his ideas, made the claim, which would anticipate modern form criticism, that

> the first evangelists were, so to speak, rhapsodists who handed on orally independent units of tradition which, since they were passed on in the interests of preaching, had no biographical interest, and that for this reason the words of Jesus had been more faithfully preserved by them than the historical narratives.[87]

Mark, according to Herder, had the fewest literary qualities of the gospels but possessed the lively sound of someone telling a story in common language for public reading. Mark was intended to be read aloud. He omits what is unsuitable for his audience but knits together words and shortens discourses for heart and ear. In contrast, Matthew and Luke do not speak but write.

To this comparison between the oral tradition behind the writings of Homer and the evangelists, it is worth adding a mention of the famous opening essay of Erich Auerbach's *Mimesis* published in 1946. In this study of the presentation of reality in Western literature, Auerbach makes an interesting comparison between the style of the homecoming scene found in the nineteenth book of the Odyssey and the Elohistic narrative of the sacrifice of Isaac described in Genesis. He finds it difficult to imagine two more contrasting styles than these two equally ancient and equally epic texts. In Homer there is very little suspense with every detail of time, place, thoughts and feelings expressed. In sharp contrast, in the Elohist only the decisive points necessary for the purpose of the narrative are externalized while all else is left in obscurity. It is an abrupt narrative where many points call for interpretation and many details such as time and place are undefined. Thoughts and feelings are unexpressed and only suggested by the silences and the fragmentary speeches. The whole is dominated by a profound suspense and directed toward a single goal. That two such diverse styles could be the product of oral tradition is a possibility which seems to have escaped our modern form critics in their reflections on the absence of such detail in the gospel narratives.

1796–1797

J. G. von Herder was the first to insist that any historical harmonization between John and the synoptics was impossible. In fact he attacked all harmonization:

> There are four evangelists, and let each retain his special purpose, complexion, time, and locale.

This was a very modern idea. He regarded all four as independent elaborators of a primal gospel which was oral rather than literary. Mark, the shorter and simpler gospel, like the view of Jesus' life sketched in Acts 1:22, is most primitive and the best reproduction: Matthew, an expanded version; Luke, an attempt to create an actual historical account; John, some forty years later, an "echo of the earlier gospels at a higher pitch."[88] While the synoptics were Palestinian and historical, John was not historical but doctrinal in character.

1800–1802

H. E. G. Paulus wrote a three volume work entitled *A Philological, Critical, and Historical Commentary on the First Three Gospels,* in which the Greek text, after the recognition of variants, punctuations and sections, is made to serve through introductions, indications of content and uninterrupted marginal comments, as the basis for a synoptic and chronological history of primitive Christianity. In 1828 Paulus produced his rationalistic *Life of Jesus as the Basis of a Purely Historical Account of Early Christianity.* For Paulus, Jesus was the outstanding example of serene holiness and human character for the imitation of mankind. He is best known for his rationalistic interpretation of the miracles which he considered to be explanations of ordinary simple people ignorant about the laws of nature and of certain puzzling but in reality natural events. Jesus' healing miracles could be explained in terms of his knowledge of medicine, sedatives, special food and care, and the effect of spiritual power on the central nervous system. The walking on the water can be explained by the sandbar theory whereby Jesus as he walks along the shore in a mist is taken for a ghost by the frightened disciples. The feeding of the five thousand was just the rich sharing their food with the poor. The transfiguration was due to the early morning time when the disciples were not fully awake and they saw Jesus against the background of the rising sun. Those supposedly raised from the dead were really in a coma. A similar theory is applied to Jesus' resurrection:

> Jesus was only in a deathlike trance; the lance thrust, a mere surface wound, had the same effect as the ancient practice of bleeding, which was thought to have healing value; the cool grave and aromatic spices continued the process of resuscitation; the storm and earthquake rolled away the stone and aroused Jesus to full consciousness; Jesus then stripped away his own clothes and put on the gardener's clothes, and was mistaken for the gardener; though sometimes weak from suffering, he then ate with his disciples and for a period of about forty days appeared in both Galilee and Jerusalem; finally on the Mount of Olives as he was speaking to the disciples for the last time (again in the early morning!), a cloud came between them and he disappeared never to return again, an event the disciples came to call the ascension.[89a]

1811

B. Van Willes: *Specimen Hermeneuticum* (Utrecht). This deals with those parts which are narrarated by Mark alone or which are more fully expounded by Mark than by the other evangelists. According to Willes the diversity of the different evangelists contributed greatly to understanding, explaining and illustrating the deeds of Jesus. Because the other three evangelists made a greater contribution than Mark to our knowledge of the life of Jesus, the result was that Mark tended to be ignored and considered of little value by some scholars. However, this opinion was generally due to a superficial reading of Mark. Willes, by a careful comparison of the gospels and an examination of what was proper to Mark, concluded that Mark's contribution was important for a proper understanding of the life of Jesus and that he possessed an excellent source.

1814

Caballero Raimundo Diosdado S.J. (1740–c. 1829). In his *Commentariola Critica . . . de lingua Evangelica* (Roma, 1798) Caballero proved that the language of Jesus and his apostles was Syriac, not Greek, as Diodato insisted in his *De Christo loquente Exercitatio* (Naples, 1767). He also produced in Rome a multilingual version of

Mark in addition to a Marcology which showed his wide biblical knowledge.[89b]

> Tetraglotton D. Marci Evangelium, et Marcologia critica. El Evangelio de S. Marcos escrito en latin, griego, y hebreo, con los tres alfabetos.

1826

C. G. Wilke in an article on the *Labourers in the Vineyard* (Mt 20:1–16) seems to be the first to provide evidence that Matthew used Mark. He later (1838) published a comprehensive investigation of the synoptic problem with the significant title *Der Urevangelist* (The Original Evangelist). He showed that the hypothesis of an oral primal gospel or individual collections of narrative is not an adequate explanation. The presence of almost all of Mark in Matthew and Luke leads to the assumption that his gospel, "the original gospel," is basic to them. His conclusion:

> Mark is the original Evangelist. It is his work which serves as the foundation for that of Matthew and Luke (p 684)

was a real academic sensation among his contemporaries. For while scholars such as Lessing had suggested that the original basic gospel might be a work such as the gospel of the Nazarenes of which Jerome had preserved a fragment, no one had thought that Mark or one of the canonical gospels might be the long sought original. It

> is not a copy of an oral primal gospel but an artistic composition [and] despite the fact that it has assumed the appearance of an historical narrative, its composition is conditioned less by historical than by premeditated general principles.[90]

Together with C. H. Weisse whose fundamental work appeared a few months earlier than Wilke's in the year 1838, Wilke is regarded as the inaugurator of the Marcan hypothesis. Weisse, who developed ideas from Schleiermacher and Lachmann, is called not only the principal founder of the Marcan hypothesis but the originator of the two-source theory. However, apart from the fact that Mark was the source for the other two synoptics, Weisse and Wilke agreed on little else and a sharp controversy broke out between the two scholars.

1830

K. F. A. Fritzsche: *Evangelium Marci* (Leipzig). This is the second volume of his commentary on the four gospels. Some interesting reflections are found in this commentary. Thus he criticizes the interpretation of 6:52 by J. G. Rosenmuellerus (1815) which saw the reference to "the breads" as meaning that the disciples had not understood after the miracle performed with the breads. In 6:3 he prefers the reading "the son of the carpenter and Mary."[91]

1832

F. Schleiermacher in a study *Concerning the Witnesses of Papias for Our First Gospels* suggested that a collection of the sayings of Jesus mentioned by Papias as going back to the apostle Matthew had been incorporated into Matthew's gospel, a suggestion found earlier in H. March (1798) and used later by Weisse in 1838. He also had a theory of "diegeses" or brief accounts which were written down early on and then later put together to produce the synoptics.[92] His conclusion was that a connected biography of Jesus was impossible.

Schleiermacher was one of the most influential of the romantics. He saw the reality of religion as rooted in feeling in contrast to the enlightened rationalists who reduced religion to thought (metaphysics) or action (ethics based on the practical reason according to Kant). Developing the ideas of Plato and Kant, he saw Jesus as the ideal archetype, the model for the self-consciousness that is filled with consciousness of God, the pure expression of the immediate feeling of absolute dependence on God, the one who can draw believers into the power of his consciousness of God and give them a new life in the present.[93]

1835 (a)

D. F. Strauss in *The Life of Jesus Critically Examined* proposed his myth theory based on his philosophical presuppositions while ignoring any serious textual study.[94] Yet it should be said at the outset that Strauss raised most of the important issues which still fascinate gospel researchers. For Strauss:

> Orthodox and rationalists alike proceed from the false assumption that we have always in the gospels testimony, sometimes even that of eye-witness, to fact. [On the contrary] the narrators testify

sometimes, not to outward facts, but to ideas, often most practical and beautiful ideas; constructions which even eye-witnesses had unconsciously put upon facts, imagination concerning them, reflections upon them, reflections such as were natural to the time, and at the authors' level of culture. What we have here is . . . a plastic, naive and, at the same time, often most profound apprehension of truth within the area of religious feeling and poetic truth. It results in narrative, legendary, mythical in nature, illustrative often of spiritual truth in a manner more perfect than any hard, prosaic statement could achieve.[95]

For Strauss John represented the most advanced stage of the mythopoetic development of the gospels and was therefore quite inferior to the other gospels as an historical source. John had in fact substituted Greek metaphysical ideas (e.g., Logos, Sonship) for the Jewish, messianic and eschatological ideas of the synoptics. Thus Strauss was the first to effectively question the common approach of reading the synoptics through Johannine spectacles and to use John as freely as the other three in apologetic arguments and in reconstructing the historical and geographical facts of Jesus' life.

He accepted Jesus as an historical person but saw the gospels and the early preaching as a kind of Christian ideology not based on facts but on ideas, on Old Testament messianic dreams and the use of their vivid imagination. Older scholars such as Heyne, Semler, Eichorn and Gabler had already applied the notion of myth to Hebrew thought and to the infancy narratives in the New Testament. For Eichorn,

myths in both Hebrew and pagan history were not the product of deceit and falsehood, but the way primitiveness spontaneously expressed events and unseen reality in sensuous, visual, and dramatic imagery characteristic of their times. The older the sources, the more they were pervaded with "myths."[96a]

Denis C. Duling gives this example of Strauss' method in his treatment of Jesus' baptism:

Strauss noted that the orthodox interpreters said (thesis) that Jesus was conscious of being Messiah already but that he refrained from assuming his Messianic prerogatives until he was acclaimed publicly. However, the rationalists pointed (antithesis) to the problems in the text such as the opening of the heavens, the descent of the dove, and the voice of God. Was there originally a flash of lightning, a clap of thunder and, at the same time, a dove hovering overhead? After noting the divergence of the various interpretations, Strauss pointed (synthesis) to God's speaking in Isaiah 42:1 ("Here is my servant whom I uphold, my chosen one in whom my soul delights"), which Matthew 12:17ff says was applied to Jesus the Messiah. On the basis of the Old Testament it was believed that God would speak to the Messiah this way. Strauss also pointed to Psalm 2:7 ("Thou art my son: today I have begotten thee") which was considered messianic by Jewish interpreters. The two Old Testament texts were combined in the Gospel of Hebrews (apocryphal) and Luke's version of the baptism (Luke 3:1ff). This explains the origin of the voice in the account: the popular mind believed it would happen that way and so portrayed it. Similarly, the dove as the image of the spirit was based on the view that the spirit would come in messianic times (Joel 3:1; Is 11:1ff), and that the spirit was presented in concrete images in the Old Testament (for example, a fire) and spoken of as "hovering" like a bird (Gn 1:2). In the East, the dove was considered a sacred bird, was given special significance in the Noah-flood story, and was esteemed in Jewish writings. It would therefore have been natural to associate the dove with baptism by water and the Spirit, which comes from the heavens. For it to come, the heavens, of course, had to be opened. These items were therefore not factual (that is, historical) but "mythical." Was the baptism itself historical or mythical? Interestingly, Strauss believed that it was probably historical, for it would have provided a reason for Jesus' messianic project.[96b]

By modern standards Strauss' understanding of myth was inadequate and too narrow. He confined myth to the darkness which he thought preceded the dawn of the historic age and failed to see myth as a meaningful form of communication and an almost essential part of human life in every age.[97] Strauss overcame the difficulty that the traditional dates did not allow time for myth to develop by dating the gospels in the middle of the second century. Nevertheless Strauss' demythologized Jesus as put together from scattered statements in his long book is quite substantial.[98] He

appears as a disciple of John who pursued his mission first in Galilee, who came to regard himself as the Messiah, called disciples to himself on this understanding, went to Jerusalem intending the recognition of his messiahship, had premonitions there of his violent death, predicted his return as the apocalyptic figure of the Son of Man and had his colorful career ended by a Roman execution.

Strauss' rationalism provoked a storm of protest. Later in France the romantic J. E. Renan's *Life of Jesus Christ* (1863), which removed the miraculous and the supernatural, i.e., the legendary, from Jesus' life, provoked a similar reaction. Renan's popular work described a wise Galilean prophet, a simple, gentle, handsome, charming person at home among the pastoral delights of Galilee but a stranger to Jerusalem and its walls of resistance which he could not penetrate. Jesus, according to Renan, like the ancients, felt the divine within himself and taught a kingdom of the poor with a moral but not a polemical aim. His religion was a simple one free of priests and external observance,

> resting entirely on the feelings of the heart, on the imitation of God, on the direct relation of the conscience with the heavenly Father

and on human brotherhood.[99] But a change came over Jesus in

> the strange, arid, scholastic, priest-infested capital of Jerusalem so that Jesus felt that no compromise with them was possible and as Renan put it "Jesus was no longer a Jew."[100]

It is against this background that the tremendous nineteenth century emphasis on Mark as the earliest life of Jesus and the key to the synoptic problem must be seen.

1835 (b)

In the same year (1835) as Strauss' *Life of Jesus* K. Lachmann, who applied to the New Testament the same criteria which he used in editing the classics and endeavored to reconstruct the New Testament text of the fourth century from early Greek manuscripts, showed that the agreement of the three synoptics in the order of the narrative exists only when Matthew and Luke agree with Mark's order and that when they do not follow Mark's order they do not agree with each other. But Lachmann's argument from order did not lead him to conclude as many[101] have thought that Mark was a source for Matthew and Luke. Although Lachmann's article did lead eventually to the *Two Document Hypothesis* he himself concluded that all three gospels were derived from an original gospel which Mark followed more closely than the other evangelists who followed him. Thus he claimed that Mark was the source closest to the original tradition and therefore of primary importance in any investigation of Christian origins.

1838

C. H. Weisse, a philosopher, saw Strauss' work as something to be welcomed and beneficial to true Christian knowledge and saw himself challenged to attempt the "reconstruction of the picture of Christ." Weisse fully shared Strauss' negative views about John's gospel and in particular the impossibility that the historic Jesus could have preached the doctrine of the Johannine Christ.

> It is not so much a picture of Christ that John sets forth, as a conception of Christ; his Christ does not speak in his own Person, but of his own Person.[102]

He saw Mark as the oldest of the synoptics and that the gospels of both Matthew and Luke combined Mark or the proto-gospel which underlay Mark with "a collection of Jesus' sayings that goes back to the apostle Matthew." He saw the many doublets in Matthew and the less frequent doublets in Luke as proof of this.

Like Lachmann he did not think that Matthew and Luke actually used Mark but rather a common document which Mark reproduced more simply and fully. Thus he made a fundamental contribution to the "two-source hypothesis." For Weisse, Mark, in his Greek style, is the most Hebraizing of the evangelists and is distinguished from them by "a fresh naturalness and an unpretentious spontaneity." Matthew is, with few exceptions, an epitomizer of the sections in common with Mark, smoothing his roughness, purging his idiomatic expressions and substituting more varied constructions for Mark's "and." He insisted that Mark's long recognized vivid details (e.g., the green grass in 5:39) were not the kind an author would add if he were touching up Matthew but were the kind a Matthew and a Luke would omit in expanding Mark as they needed the space for other purposes. Thus Weisse can be said to have initiated the pattern of Marcan priority and objective historicity.[103] But Weisse did not accept all of Mark as reliably historical. Like many after him he tended to exclude those parts of the gospel which did not suit his presuppositions about the spiritual nature of Jesus' message and his psychological interpretation of Jesus' person. Contrary to Strauss he excluded Jesus' expectation of the imminent end as unworthy of "a spirit of such stature," and he reduced the judgment Jesus preached to an inward subjective experience. He described the "flash of the higher consciousness" which Jesus had at his baptism as undergoing a long period of fermentation until it was finally suppressed.[104]

1841

Richard C. Trench wrote *Notes on the Parables of Our Lord,* an encyclopedic work which was a mine of learning from the Fathers and became the standard work in English on the parables for many years. Trench distinguished the parable from the fable, the myth, the proverb and the allegory. The distinction, for example, between a parable and an allegory is in form rather than essence. An allegory compares one thing with another by transferring the properties and qualities and relations from one to the other whereas in a parable the two are kept separate and distinct and placed side by side. Trench concentrates on Matthew and Luke's parables, noting that John has only allegories while Mark's parables have no distinctive features. Matthew's are statelier and more theocratic, more parables of judgment and deal with the mysteries of God's kingdom. Luke's tenderer parables are more ethical with the concept of mercy more pronounced.

1847

F. C. Baur (1792–1860), the teacher of Strauss and the founder of the Tübingen school, published his study on the gospels. Baur is famous more for the importance of the questions he raised than for the solutions he proposed. Most important, he saw that the New Testament was the product of the history and differing situations of the early Church as differing writers and communities struggled to understand and interpret the relevance of Jesus. Thus he is often described as the father of historical theology. He criticized Schleiermacher's view of the ideal Christ as not adequately rooted in history. He clearly saw, however, that scholars like Reimarus in interpreting historical texts were to a large extent revealing the prejudices of their own philosophical presuppositions. He himself of course fell into the same trap as he, in Procrustean fashion, tried to apply a Hegelian philosophy of history to the New Testament period. He maintained that Jesus realized in himself the highest point of the development of the human spirit as he tried to steer a middle course between the Scylla of supernaturalism (i.e., a religion prepackaged with mysteries from heaven and recommended by miracles on earth) and the Charybdis of Rationalism.[105]

For Hegel, progress takes place by a dialectic of thesis, antithesis and synthesis as a movement in human affairs produces by reaction its contrary, leading to an ultimate synthesis. Not only Hegel but also such thinkers as Comte, Darwin and Spencer revolutionized contemporary attitudes to history in the early and middle nineteenth century. For Auguste Comte (1798–1857) all kinds of history passed through three stages. Childhood, the theological stage which explained things by divine powers, was followed by youth, the metaphysical stage which sought the essence of things and explained them by impersonal abstract forces. The third stage, the scientific stage, was the stage in which there was no concern for origins or final causes but it was sufficient to describe things as they are and their mutual cause and effect relationships. Charles Darwin (1809–1882), influenced by Lyell's discovery of the great age of the earth and Malthus' population theory that those with the greatest power for self-preservation survive, not to mention his own discoveries of fossils and varying species of animals and birds, concluded that history had evolved over a large extreme of time by natural selection and that therefore the literal interpretation of Genesis was inaccurate. Herbert Spencer (1820–1903), the philosopher of evolution, argued that all of history and society had evolved from lower to higher and more complex forms according to his theory of the survival of the fittest. Only Hegel retained the notion of the Spirit because, in general, the idea of the providence of God directing history was replaced by ideas of human progress in science, technology and medicine. All this kind of evolutionary thinking would influence the scholars' theories on the development of the gospels from the primitive form found in Mark.

Baur's basic insight developed from an 1831 article, "The Christ Party in the Corinthian Church." His view was that at Corinth the Hellenistic followers of Paul were opposed to the more Jewish followers of Peter and that this division could be traced in other New Testament writings. The epistles of Paul were the earliest Christian documents bringing us into contact with the earliest Christian communities. He only recognized four as authentic, Romans, 1 and 2 Corinthians, and Galatians which he dated in the 50's and 60's. One must begin the reconstruction of the events of the Christian faith with Paul. He saw the early Christian history as a struggle between the narrow Jewish Christianity of Jesus' original disciples, e.g., Peter and John, and the universalism of Paul. Books like Acts and Hebrews as opposed to the Judaizing Apocalypse were attempts at a harmony and by that very fact were post-apostolic in date and perspective. Influenced by his Hegelian approach he sought out the "tendency," as he called it, of each gospel writer and criticized Strauss for his failure to appreciate this aspect. He accepted Griesbach's theory that Matthew was the earliest gospel which Luke used and that Mark was an abridgement of both. Matthew, composed around 130 in connection with the revolt of Bar Cochba, he saw as more historically reliable although having a tendency toward Judaism. Luke (140–180), dependent on Matthew, is clearly Pauline in character and a work of anti-Petrine tendency. Mark is the last of the synoptics, reconciling the Jewish Matthew and the Gentile Luke and showing no opposition between Jew and Gentile. It is a clearly arranged version of the essential facts, generally ignoring repetitions and giving little teaching material. John is clearly distinct from the synoptics and inferior as an historical source. Not written by the apostle, its aim is not the writing of history but to describe the final reconciliation of the Catholic Church, the ideal community of Jew and Gentile (Jn 10:16). This reconciliation was in fact a closing of ranks in the Church in face of the second century threats from the gnostic and Montanist movements. To support his thesis he proposed that works like Acts, Mark, and John were only composed around A.D. 150. His historical synthesis collapsed in face of investigations by scholars like Lightfoot into the Clementine (c. A.D. 95) and Ignatian (c. 110–115) letters which described both Peter and Paul without a trace of rivalry and the discovery of a papyrus fragment (p[52]) of John c. A.D. 130.

For Baur, Jesus' teaching was

> somewhat like that of his Jewish background, but he went beyond that background in an original and radical way. Whereas the kingdom of God for Jews stressed God's rule breaking in from without to reestablish the nation of Israel, Jesus' radical transformation led to a spiritual and inward kingdom for all people. The heart of Jesus' teaching about the kingdom of God was found in the Sermon on the Mount (Mt 5—7), and within that in the Beatitudes (Mt 5:3–10). In this teaching Jesus brought out the great tension human beings felt between the world as it is, full of anxiety, separation, incompleteness, sinfulness, and death, and the world as it might be, full of peace, reconciliation, perfection, salvation, and life with God. This tension, primarily expressed by Jesus in language about time—present and future, this world and the world to come—is for Jesus a qualitative relationship between

God and persons and it is more clearly present in Jesus' parables. The more a person is tied to the cares of the "present" world, the less that person is committed to the future world and vice versa.[106]

Baur, it is interesting to note, observed the three different uses for the title Son of Man in the gospels: the future apocalyptic sayings which reflect Dn 7:13f, the sayings about the Son of Man's human fate or authority on earth, and the passion prediction sayings. But, for Baur, Jesus' own emphasis was not apocalyptic; rather he spoke in the second category to indicate his kingdom mission of reconciliation between God and man on earth.

G. F. Moore, in *Judaism in the First Centuries of the Christian Era* (Harvard, 1927), made the interesting remark that until the nineteenth century historical theories of scholars like Hegel, it was normal to consider Jesus and his followers as essentially part of the Judaism of their time. With the new ideas Jesus was depicted as the antithesis of the whole Jewish religious system which in turn was portrayed in such terms as legalistic, rigid, narrow, stifling and at a low point in its evolution.

1849

Henry Alford had a monumental edition of the Greek New Testament (1849–1861) that was praised for its freshness of treatment and wide learning. Alford accepts the traditional secretary-interpreter connection between Mark and Peter as probably founded on fact. Nevertheless, the idea of any considerable or direct influence of Peter over the writing of the gospel is not borne out by the work itself. None of the synoptics, he insists, could have been "originally written" after the destruction of Jerusalem because then the omission of every allusion to so signal a fulfillment of Jesus' prophecies would be inexplicable.

Alford has no doubt that Mark wrote in Greek, even though two Syriac versions contain a marginal note that Mark preached in Rome in Latin and many Roman Catholic writers defend the hypothesis of a Latin original because of their desire to maintain the authority of the Vulgate. That Mark wrote for Gentiles is seen from his omission of genealogies and Old Testament citations (apart from 1:2f), his interpretation of Hebrew or Aramaic terms (5:41; 7:11, 34), his explanation of Jewish customs (5:41; 7:11, 34), and such remarkable insertions as 11:17 and omissions like Matthew 10:5.

Alford finds the internal evidence against the genuineness of

Mark 16:9–20 as very weighty because no less than seventeen words and expressions occur in it, and some of them several times, which are never found elsewhere in Mark whose adherence to his own peculiar phrases is remarkable.

1850

A. Hilgenfield (*Markusevangelium,* Leipzig) claimed that up to his time the interest of scholars had been concerned almost entirely with the details of Mark. He worked out quite a detailed plan and insisted that one should examine the whole movement and outline of Mark.

1851

Bruno Bauer in his *Criticism of the Synoptic Gospels' History* reached the ultimate conclusion of historical skepticism. Since he considered Strauss' myth too vague, he eventually concluded that there never was an historical Jesus or Paul. Bauer had little difficulty in showing that John's gospel was not a biography but rather an artistic creation. Expecting to find greater historical reliability in the synoptics, he began to defend Mark's priority and the view that Matthew and Luke were based on Mark. But he was compelled to conclude that Mark also was a literary creation written by an artist who described the experience of his community in the form of the life of Jesus. Thus Mark was not only not a biography but it did not even contain accurate memories of Jesus. He assigned the "original gospel" to the reign of Hadrian (117–138) and Paul's epistles to that of Marcus Aurelius (161–180). For Strauss, the gospel story was the product of the community's imagination. But Bauer for a time thought that there must have been some powerful person behind the community's experience. However, at the end of his life he denied the existence of this person and suggested that Christianity was a hybrid born from a union of traditions about the Jewish Philo of Alexandria and the Roman Stoic, Seneca.

Bauer, in his *Christianity Exposed* (1843), had made a devastating critique of all religion and saw a humanistic self-consciousness as the new form of thought. Not surprisingly, his writings which influenced Marx and Engels became standard reading for Marxists and communists. Seldom in human history has religion come so severely under fire. Feuerbach (1804–1872) explained religion as the projection of man's needs, wishes and desires, "the dream of the human mind." Karl Marx (1813–1833) divided history into five main periods: (1) primitive communism, (2) the slave system of ancient Greece and Rome, (3) the feudal system of medieval Europe, (4) the modern capitalist system with its industrial technology and religion the tool of the bourgeoisie used as an opiate to keep the people happy in their oppressed condition without ownership, (5) communism, the classless society, the system of the future. Influenced by Hegel and Feuerbach, Marx saw history as economically determined with the control of property as the key. History was the story of man's freedom, the story of the material (economic) conflicts for the control of economic production.

C. F. Dapuis had affirmed that Jesus never existed, and Bauer's idea was not new, for as early as 1791 Volney had proposed that Jesus was no more than the sun god. Arthur Drews (*The Christ Myth,* Chicago, 1911) proposed that the historical Jesus was a creation of the Church based on a historicizing of Old Testament texts. He noted the close similarity between Psalm 22 and the gospel account of Jesus' crucifixion and death, and he concluded that the gospel account was derived from the psalm. Other writers, such as Paul-Louis Couchoud in 1923 in *Jesus God Become Man* and Prosper Alfaric in *The Most Ancient Life of Jesus: The Gospel According to Mark,* would make similar theories run counter to ancient historical evidence drawn even from writers hostile to Christianity. Again the obviously Jewish atmosphere of the gospels makes a creation by a Hellenized Church impossible. In addition to modern Soviet propagandists can be mentioned Marc Stephane, *The Passion of Christ,*[107] and Georges Ory, *The Christ and Jesus.*[108] There is also the fantastic thesis of John Allegro, *The Sacred Mushroom and the Cross,*[109a] which seems aimed at the modern drug generation and which by some unusual etymologies proposes that Christianity is a revival of an ancient Mesopotamian cult based on the ecstasy produced by eating a sacred mushroom.

While one could bring forward even the extra-biblical witnesses such as Pliny, Suetonius, and Tacitus, not to mention the Jewish historian Josephus and the Talmudic literature, the refutation of such theories on Jesus' existence can be summed up in Bultmann's blunt statement:

> The doubt as to whether Jesus really existed is unfounded and not worth refutation. No sane person can doubt that Jesus stands as founder behind the historical movement whose first distinct stage is represented by the oldest Palestinian community.[109b]

A similar skeptical approach could deny the existence of a Buddha, an Augustus or a Charlemagne. In fact the historian R. Whateley (1787–1863), who was actually a contemporary of Napoleon, applied the same method which such authors applied to Christ to conclude that even Napoleon did not exist.

1860

B. F. Westcott wrote *Introduction to the Study of the Gospels,* a work many times reprinted, whose first edition according to Stephen Neill and Norman Perrin can be dated as early as 1851. Westcott, reacting to Strauss whose theory he considered "subversive of all faith in history," stated the Marcan hypothesis which saw Mark as both the earliest gospel and as a reliable historical source. This second point was a conclusion from the first point and was strengthened by the observation of the realistic character of Mark. Westcott and other scholars defended the popular tradition-hypothesis of J. L. Giesler (1818) which presupposed the existence of an original oral tradition handed on from the apostles to early missionaries. It attained a written form in the gospels but contained a lot more than was actually written down in the gospels, since each evangelist only selected what he needed for his own particular purpose. Thus Westcott described Mark as "conspicuous for its vivid simplicity" and as "the most direct representative of the first evangelic tradition, the common foundation on which the others were reared" (p 213). He saw Mark as "essentially a transcript from life" in substance, style and treatment. This "vivid and simple record, stamped with the most distinct impress of independence and originality" (p 369), reflected the course of Jesus' life in the clearest outline and even without the evidence of the other gospels was sufficient to refute Strauss.

In *The New Testament in the Original Greek* (1881–1882) Westcott together with his colleague F. J. A. Hort made a fundamental contribution to the study of the Greek text of the New Testament. In this they attempted to penetrate behind the fourth century uncial manuscripts to an earlier text taking into consideration not only internal and external evidence for each reading and manuscript but also the genealogical relationships of the manuscripts. With their four types of text they brought to a climax the investigations of many scholars such as J. A. Bengel who in 1725 initiated textual classification. Their principles would bear fruit in such English translations as the R.S.V. Modern discoveries and insights, however, have led to a modification of their classification.

1863

H. J. Holtzmann: Hitherto in general one can say that scholars had worked largely by insight or intuition. Now the basic verification of the hypothesis of Lachmann and Weisse, which convinced most scholars of the late nineteenth century, was provided by Holtzmann's painstaking study of the synoptic gospels. This is often said to mark a turning point in the history of synoptic studies.

Hitherto only a few scholars had accepted the source theory of C. H. Weisse, and it was in danger of sinking into oblivion. But Holtzmann rescued Weisse's theory and praised his work as providing the first evidence that the life of Jesus could be portrayed in accordance with the highest demands of historical scholarship. He considered that Weisse had not only rediscovered the Marcan hypothesis but had given it for the first time a scholarly basis. However Holtzmann's own widespread influence as a lecturer and scholar among his contemporaries and students played a large part in the widespread acceptance of the two-source theory. Thus his most famous pupil, Albert Schweitzer, concluded that he had brought the Marcan hypothesis so near to being a certainty that it could no longer be considered as a mere hypothesis. For Holtzmann himself the two-source theory offered the most probable solution to the synoptic problem.

Holtzmann developed the systematic research on the linguistic nature of the gospels begun for the first time by G. Gersdorf in 1816. Holtzmann repeated two important sayings of Gersdorf whose valuable contribution Griesbach had already recognized. The first statement was to the effect that it is the small details which enable a student to differentiate more precisely the evangelists. Secondly, Holtzmann agreed that an exact philological examination and a careful study of the nature of language were essential for a proper study of the synoptic relationships.

By observing the primitive character of its style and diction Holtzmann showed the priority of Mark, what was later called the Marcan hypothesis, and the dependence of the other two synoptics on Mark, e.g., softening the roughness and violence of his Passion narrative. He also indicated that behind Matthew and Luke where they agree there lay a written document consisting mainly of discourses. The famous Q symbol had not yet been invented.

These theories became classic and had a widespread influence in the second part of the nineteenth century. His apparent proof that Mark was the original apostolic gospel and that it was mainly an objective historical account of the historical Jesus convinced many and was a strong bulwark against the skepticism of the times, especially that of Strauss who accepted the Griesbach hypothesis. For Strauss concluded that since Mark was the last of the synoptics his detailed expansions were evidence of mythological development, since such would increase with the writer's distance from the actual events. Holtzmann provided a reliable framework for a succession of lives of Jesus. He also attempted to prove but later discarded the idea that behind Mark there lay a longer document A which Mark shortened by deleting its discourses.

About three years before his death Holtzmann wrote in a treatise on the Marcan-controversy that no one who has really read the simultaneously published works of Paul Wernle, *Die Synoptische Frage* and J. Hawkins, *Horae Synopticae* could doubt any more that Mark was the common root and stock of the synoptic gospels. Paul Wernle (1899), called "the consummator of the two-source theory," saw no compelling reason to indicate a shorter or longer "original" Mark distinct from Mark as we have it. Wernle introduced a new method by beginning his study not from a theory such as the two-source theory but from the more concrete and objective point of Luke's prologue which is the only clear statement of an evangelist of his relationship to his predecessors. In Luke's prologue three solid facts were evident to Wernle. First it was clear that Luke was not the earliest gospel but that he had many predecessors. Second, these predecessors had used the common oral tradition and were not themselves eyewitnesses. Third, Luke's intention was to surpass these predecessors both in completeness and in chronological accuracy. The key question then was whether Mark or Matthew or both were to be included among the many predecessors. Wernle, who noted how Luke above all changed Mark's vocabulary, concluded that Luke had treated Mark as a source. He has absorbed nearly all of Mark with twelve exceptions (3:20–30; 4:26–34; 6:17–19; 6:45—8:25; 9:11–13; 9:41—10:12; 10:35–45; 11:11, 12–15a, 19–27a; 12:28–34; 14:3–9; 15:1). These he had omitted generally because of his dislike of duplication or because they lacked significance for his readers but rarely because of dogmatic reasons. On the contrary, if Mark has used Luke, Wernle could discover no adequate reasons for his considerable omissions of material although he believed that Mark's sole aim was to give a brief sketch of Jesus' life in order to prove his divinity. Similarly he found it easier to explain Matthew's mere eight omissions from Mark than Mark's omission of more than thirty longer and shorter parts of Matthew. However, he honestly admitted the danger of the proverbial "seek and you shall find." He was all too familiar with the sophistries and pedantic "Procrustean" solutions offered by contemporaries when one disdains to take simple things, simply insisting that not everything can be explained, that some things are simply coincidence and that one cannot always expect to recognize the author's motives.

In brief, Wernle saw both Luke and Matthew as essentially revisions of Mark and as commentators with the intention of improving it. Matthew was in particular motivated by a scribe's understanding of the Old Testament and by a more exalted faith. For Wernle Mark alone has a clear understandable structure. It was essentially "the Petrine Gospel," the most valuable source for Peter's theology, clearly giving the impression of its origin from an eyewitness report. The leading position of Peter in Mark's gospel had already been emphasised by Wilke and Weisse and was a leading argument in their hypothesis of the Marcan priority. An interesting point about Mark which Wernle also noticed was the gradual progress from the sermon before the people to the teaching of the small group of disciples.

But for Holtzmann himself more important was the picture of the historical Jesus and the psychological development of his messianic consciousness which he drew from Mark. For he considered that only Mark provides a continuous, unified and natural portrayal of the actual historical development. Only Mark shows steady progress toward the final unfolding of the messianic banner. He saw two periods in Jesus' ministry. One was a period of success beginning with the messianic consciousness which came to Jesus at his baptism and was followed by the progressive revelation of his messianic dignity which reached a climax at Caesarea Philippi and led to a rethinking of Jesus' strategy. There he revealed that he was a spiritual Messiah who would suffer and die to establish his earthly kingdom characterized by brotherly love and ethical concern but a kingdom which could be described as neither Davidic, i.e., opposed to Rome, nor dominated by an apocalyptic vision.

The second period, in which Jesus marched to meet his tragic end in Jerusalem, was a period of "failure" with the new idea of a Suffering Messiah. For Holtzmann as for Weisse, the kingdom was not so much an inbreaking intervention based on God's direct and personal action. It was rather an inner and spiritual change within the hearts of men, a kingdom of reason and good will. He denied completely any expectation on Jesus' part of a second coming or of a visible manifestation of God's coming.

1864–1900

T. Colani, in a study of the messianic beliefs of Jesus' time, proposed that the author of Mark used a Jewish "little apocalypse" as a source for Mark 13, an opinion which influenced many subsequent scholars.

Quite a number of commentaries on Mark were published in the second half of the nineteenth century. These include Patrizi (1862), Klostermann (1867), Bisping (1868), Schegg (1870), Weisse (1872), MacEvilly (1877), Cook in the Speaker's Commentary (1878), Plumpton (1879), Schanz (1881), Fillion (1883), Liagre (1889), Holtzmann (1892), Pobzl (1893), Knabenbauer (1894), Tiegenthal (1894), Gould (1896), Bruce (1897), Swete (1898), Coulemans (1899), Menzies (1901), Hort (1902), Gutjahr (1904), and Rose (1904).

1888

Adolf Jülicher wrote *Die Gleichnisreden Jesu,* a study of the parables which has never been translated into English and like many great books is often known only from summaries in other books. It has been rightly described as responsible for one of the deepest scars left by biblical criticism on the body of Christian tradition. The reason for this, as Evans points out,[110] is not

> its governing principle that a genuine parable has a single discoverable point (a principle that has had to be modified at times though it has on the whole weathered well); and still less by its Aristotelian-type logic which was manifestly not a key to the thinking behind the parables; but rather by its opening up a vista of a Christian tradition that was marked from the first by two forms of statement, the doctrinal and the parabolic, distinct in form and distinct perhaps also in origin, and so raising the question of how they belonged together if the one was no longer to be simply subsumed in the other. Exploration of the subject since Jülicher has shown how complex it is at every stage and how difficult it is to be precise at any point.

Jülicher in brief rejected allegorization and insisted that the essence of the parable was similitude and that its purpose was to make one central point, a general moral truth. Four years after the publication of Jülicher's study the Norwegian scholar, Christian A. Bugge (*Die Haupt-Parabeln*), paid tribute to his achievement and his stimulus to other scholars. Bugge accepted the idea that the main parables lead to one conclusion and deal with one idea. But he challenged Jülicher's exclusion of allegorization and found his methodology too closely based on Aristotelian and Greek views of simile and metaphor while ignoring the Jewish background and rabbinic roots. The Jewish expression "mashal" includes both allegory and parable as well as mixed forms, and the Old Testament has allegories in Ez 31:6; 17:22; Dn 4:12. Bugge saw no reason why in the parable of the mustard seed (4:30–32), which illustrates a great truth about the kingdom, the birds do not represent the nations. Contrary to Jülicher's view of the parables as clear, Bugge found four reasons why Jesus used "secret parables" as in 4:1ff and thus spoke obscurely:

1. Jesus did not want to reveal his unusual idea of messiahship and the kingdom.

2. The crowds were obtuse and lacking in insight.

3. Jesus needed to consider his disciples.

4. It was unnecessary for him to reveal so much because of the slow development of his messianic ideas.

Similarly in 1904 P. Fiebig reacted to Jülicher's lack of familiarity with rabbinic literature and developed in more detail his belief that Jesus' method was similar to that of the rabbis but that Jesus' parables were clearly of a superior quality. Thus while the kingdom is the object of most of Jesus' parables Fiebig could not find a single parable in Jewish literature concerned with the kingdom. He agreed with Jülicher that Jesus' parables were no mere imitation of tradition but that they originated with a single creative individual.

A good example of Jülicher's work is his treatment of Mark's parable of the seed growing of itself (Mk 4:26–29). The salient point is the regularly progressive growth of the kingdom of heaven "independently of man's good or bad will" (2.543ff). Unlike earlier writers such as Victor of Antioch he does not consider further the details of God's relations with his kingdom. However to achieve his interpretation Jülicher has to eliminate the final verse 29 about the sickle and the harvest as a later addition due to "Mark's hypochondria," echoing Strauss' criticism of Mark's "somewhat hypochondriac way of looking at things." Strauss had regarded this parable "as a thing without head or tail." Other nineteenth century scholars also had seen Mark's interpretation as attempting to provide consolation for the delay of the expected parousia. Strauss also saw this parable as a Marcan recast in a biased form of Matthew's parable of the weeds (Mt 13:24–30). Calmet had seen it as a brief resume of Matthew while Weiss and others also saw it as a simplified version yet "a self-

contained product without seams or tacks." Jülicher, while considering the dispute as to its genuineness an unlawful audacity, nevertheless distinguished between Mark's older source found in vv 25–28
and v 29 which Mark added. But in general he considered the interpretations and explanations of the parables by the evangelists to be
"nonsense" or "well meant but more or less complete blunders." In
particular Jülicher and many others until recent times rejected the authenticity of Mk 4:12 and considered it the product of later Christian
belief which was strongly influenced by Rom 9–11.

1892

Martin Kähler, in *The So-called Historical Jesus and the Historic Biblical Christ,* had the excellent goal to make the biblical text
"speak to its hearers as though the author, able to employ our idiom,
were speaking to us today."[111] He saw in a statement beloved by the
Form-Critics that as

> in every drop in the dewy meadows, the sun's light is mirrored
> and reflected, so in each little episode the entire person of our
> Lord encounters us.[112]

He made a (too radical) attack on the validity of historical study of
the Bible and the lives of Jesus of his time which he considered as
little more than the results of the imagination of their writers.

> The historical Jesus portrayed by modern authors conceals from
> us the living Christ. The Jesus of the "life of Jesus" school is only
> a modern variety of the fruits of the inventive genius of men no
> better than the ill-found dogmatic Christ of Byzantine Christol-
> ogy; both stand equally distant from the real Christ. . . . The New
> Testament accounts are not concerned to afford a view of how Je-
> sus developed; they let him proclaim and manifest himself, but
> not give information, let alone involuntary information, about
> himself. . . . Consequently, they provide absolutely no grounds for
> any deduction concerning the nature and form of his earlier devel-
> opment.[113]

Thus he insisted that the gospels are not historical in the sense that
their aim was not to provide

> sources for a life of Jesus which a historian can accept as reliable
> and adequate. I repeat: we have no sources for a biography of Je-

sus of Nazareth which measure up to the standards of contemporary science. . . . He could be taken as a product of the Church's
fantasy around the year A.D. 100. Furthermore, these sources
cannot be traced with certainty to eyewitnesses. In addition to
this, they tell us only about the shortest and last period of his life.
And finally, these sources appear in two basic forms (the Gospel
of John and the synoptics) whose variations must—in view of the
proximity of the alleged or probable time of origin of these
forms—awaken serious doubts about the faithfulness of the recol-
lections.[114]

He distinguished "historic" from "historical" in the sense that "historic" aims not to provide particular data but to describe the impact
Jesus had on the people of his time. The historical Jesus is the attempted reconstruction of the Jesus of history which varies from
scholar to scholar. The

> historic Christ is the figure who originated and passed on his per-
> manent influence, the person whom history has remembered, the
> divine Son of God whom Christians believe redeemed them. He is
> God revealed, the Christ of the *whole* New Testament including
> the "portrait" of Christ in the gospels and his words, for what he
> said of himself was in perfect harmony with who he was and what
> he did. He is also the Christ of the creeds and the Church, and
> most of all he is, said Kahler, the Christ who is preached as he has
> been preached from the very beginning..[115]

The Gospels, and in particular it seems he referred to Mark, are, to
quote his famous phrase, "passion narratives with extended introductions" written by believers and containing the early Christian
proclamation and intended to awaken the faith of the readers in
Christ as Savior. They are exclusively religious documents of which
every detail was preserved for the sake of its religious significance.
Almost all scholars today would agree with Kähler that the passion
and death of Jesus are at the very center of Mark's theology.
Kähler's influence was only felt later, particularly in the school of
Rudolph Bultmann and also Karl Barth and Paul Tillich. He maintained that while little could be known with certainty about Jesus,
this was not important, since it was the biblical Christ, the Christ of
faith, not the historical Jesus which was important. A clear line led
from this kind of thinking to Bultmann's famous sentence:

> Faith, being personal decision, cannot be dependent upon an his-
> torian's labours.

Kähler's achievement was

> to place a large question mark against the current doctrine that
> the Gospels record plain, uninterested history, capable of verifica-
> tion by the methods of historical science and revelatory of the se-
> cret of Jesus' person to the impartial investigator.[116]

Like Bultmann's Lutheran idea of faith, his divorce of faith
from its historical content is extreme. The problem is not with the
historical method but with its use and with the pre-conceptions of
those who use it. Jesus is alive today to the believers, but it is Jesus of
Nazareth who is alive, the Jesus in whom faith rests and whose real
historical life and teaching is the basis of the Christian's faith and
life. In simple terms one does not have to be a scholar to be a good
Christian, for

> how can Jesus Christ be the authentic object of the faith of all
> Christians if the questions what and who he really was can be es-
> tablished only by ingenious investigation and if it is solely the
> scholarship of our time which proves itself equal to this task?[117]

1897

A. A. Bruce, in *The Synoptic Gospels* (The Expositor's Greek
Testament), is typical of the view that Mark is the simplest of the
gospels with no conscious didactic aim but whose purpose "seems to
be mainly just to tell what he knows about Jesus" (p 32f). According
to Bruce, whoever "desires to see the Jesus of history" should read
Mark who presents the character and the person of Jesus in an unre-
served manner, taking the facts as they are "when one might be
tempted not to state them at all, or to exhibit them in a subdued
light." While Mark writes from the viewpoint of loving, vivid recollection, Luke writes from the viewpoint of reverential faith.

Bruce who published a critical study of the parables in 1882 is
considered to be the first to have attempted to deal with the parables
according to the approach of the new higher criticism. Jülicher
praised his extensive knowledge of works in German, English, Greek
and Latin, his breaking with the allegorical method and his adoption
of the linguistic approach to the parables. He saw the importance of
methodology and attempted to classify the parables according to a
given principle, the real and important resemblances which they
manifested, instead of considering them one by one as they occurred

in the gospels beginning with Matthew and then proceeding to Mark and Luke.

Bruce divides Jesus' teaching ministry and parables into three aspects, a classification for which he claimed to have found an increasing consensus of opinion:

1. Jesus the master or rabbi teaching his disciples—the theocratic or didactic parables containing a general truth about the nature of the kingdom, e.g., the seed growing secretly (4:26–29).

2. Jesus the evangelist and healer preaching the kingdom of the poor among the common people, emphasizing grace, mercy, love—the wedding guests (2:19f), which is an apology for the joy of the kingdom's children.

3. Jesus the prophet, not so much in the predictive sense as that Jesus proclaimed God's moral government over the world, especially Israel, and the doom of the impenitent, e.g., Lk 12:42f; Mt 24:45f.

4
Mark the Theologian:
Wrede and the Twentieth Century

1901 (a)

W. Wrede (pronounced Vrāda). According to H. C. Kee[118] the major issues concerning Mark's intention and meaning, which still concern recent scholars who see these issues within the context of the primitive Church, were posed by scholars at the beginning of the twentieth century.

> The centrality for Mark of Jesus' announcement of the imminent end of the age and of the cosmic conflict that would culminate in the kingdom of God was discerned against the background of Jewish apocalypticism by Johann Weiss in 1892. It was a constitutive element in Wilhelm Wrede's study of the Messianic secret in Mark; its potency in the message and activity of Jesus furnished Albert Schweitzer with his clue for understanding the historical Jesus. Of continuing significance for more recent interpreters of Mark has been Wrede's conviction that the theme of eschatological secrecy in Mark was to be traced to the evangelist, rather than to Jesus. Thus the ground was already laid by the turn of the century for a view of Mark as interpreter rather than as archivist or neutral reporter.

The man who really convinced many that Mark was no unadorned presentation of the facts of the historical Jesus, uninfluenced by the dogmatic and apologetic ideas of the evangelist, was Wilhelm Wrede (1859–1906) who published *The Messianic Secret in the Gospels,* which dealt a serious blow to the optimism of the liberals' quest for the historical Jesus.[119] He saw the story of the New Testament studies in the eighteenth and nineteenth centuries as the constant struggle of historical research to escape from dogmatic convictions and pre-judgments. For Wrede who was influenced by the "history of religions" school, Paul was the perverter or second founder of Christianity who introduced an already existing myth of a heavenly redeemer and thus did not base his theology on the actual teaching of Jesus himself.

> The picture of Christ did not originate in an impression of the personality of Jesus. This view it has often been asserted, but never proved. . . . There remains only one explanation: Paul already believed in such a heavenly being, in a divine Christ, before he believed in Jesus. . . . Unless we deny both figures any historicity, it follows that to call Paul "a disciple of Jesus" is quite inappropriate if this is meant to describe his historical relationship to Jesus.[120]

For Wrede the "messianic secret" was portrayed differently in each gospel and therefore each must be interpreted separately. Matthew, he noted, has toned down the idea, especially the ignorance of the disciples. Luke has reinterpreted their misunderstanding in terms of the traditional Jewish nationalistic understanding of the Messiah. Even John has a different tradition of the "secret."

Wrede disagreed with the view of such as Schweitzer who saw a turning point in Jesus' life in Mark at Caesarea Philippi. Such a turning point could not have occurred because some of the disciples evidently knew of Jesus' messianic power from the early days of his career. There is a hint of the coming passion as early as 2:19f, and from 2:10, 28 it is evident that Jesus knew that he himself was the Son of Man also from his early ministry. Therefore Wrede concluded that the psychological and historical portrayal of the lives of Jesus had in fact been read into Mark's text.

> Present-day study of the gospels starts from the assumption that Mark had more or less clearly before his eyes, though not without gaps, the real circumstances of Jesus' life. It presupposes that Mark thinks in terms of the life of Jesus, bases the various features of his story on the real circumstances of this life, on Jesus' real thoughts and feelings and that he links the events which he describes in a historical and psychological sense. . . . This view and method must be recognized to be false in principle. It must be plainly stated that Mark no longer has any real picture of the historical life of Jesus.[121]

Wrede concluded that Mark had elaborated the community material about Jesus. He found the starting point for his theory in Mark 9:9 where Jesus tells the disciples after the transfiguration

> not to tell anyone what they had seen, before the Son of Man had risen from the dead.

Wrede was apparently impressed by Adolph Jülicher's (1888) views on the parables in which he distinguished between the simple original parables proposed by Jesus and the meaning imposed by the Church. He concluded that Mark's interpretation of the parables was not historical and that Mark 4:11 should be translated "to those outside everything happens in riddles."[122] "The mystery of the kingdom" (4:11) is that Jesus is the Messiah, the Son of God, a mystery which only the disciples know and which must be concealed until the resurrection when its disclosure follows. The resurrection is the key to Wrede's view and is the beginning of Jesus' messiahship.

In brief, Wrede insisted that the Christ of dogma had been superimposed on the historical Jesus and that Mark's gospel was a theological work similar to what Strauss and Weiss found in John. He saw the messianic secret and in particular the commands to silence which are often historically implausible (1:34, 44; 3:12; 5:43; 7:36; 8:26, 30; 9:9) as a kind of literary device constructed by Mark to explain the lack of faith in Jesus' messiahship while he was alive. How could Jairus and his wife have kept the cure of their daughter secret when her death had already been publicly announced (5:43)? He sees no progression in the understanding of the disciples who are just as imperceptive about Jesus at the end as at the beginning. It was the post-resurrection appearances which supplied the basis for the disciples' confession of Jesus as Messiah. Thus, under the umbrella of the messianic secret theme, Wrede included three rather different items: Mark's parable theory; Jesus enjoining silence on the demons, the disciples and also the crowds after the miracles; the misunderstanding of the disciples and the transfiguration scene.

Probably Wrede's main contribution to gospel study was his conviction which he worked out in great detail that a gospel is a theological rather than an historical work and that an evangelist is rather interested in a theological Jesus than in giving an historical presentation of the facts. In this Wrede radically questioned the "assured results" of his day and anticipated the basic approach of the redaction critics. Like the other gospels,

> Mark also was quite distant from the actual life of Jesus and is governed by dogmatically developed points of view. If one examines Mark through a magnifying glass, then one finds a writing of the same kind as the gospel of John (p 145).

Wrede failed to distinguish consistently between Mark's tradition and his redaction. Later Bultmann would show that Mark had worked the messianic secret into his materials.

1901 (b)

Albert Schweitzer: *The Secret of the Messiahship and the Passion: A Sketch of the Life of Jesus* (1901) and *The Quest for the Historical Jesus* (German title *From Reimarus to Wrede,* 1906).[123] These polemical writings of Schweitzer marked the end of the liberal quest for the historical Jesus. According to Nineham[124] Schweitzer's work was a recall to the essential core of truth in Reimarus' position. Reimarus had provided the essential answer to the problem of Jesus but the preoccupation of the nineteenth century had led to its being ignored and finally repudiated in Wrede's work. Schweitzer concluded from his review of more than a hundred years of rationalistic, mythical and liberal interpretations of Jesus that they were unsuccessful.

For Schweitzer there is no historical undertaking which is more personal than an attempt to write a life of Jesus. To quote a popular phrase, "By their Lives of Jesus you shall know them," i.e., their assumptions and presuppositions and what has been well described as the claim to prove historically what one has accepted theologically. He saw clearly how each age and scholar tries to confine Jesus to his own Procrustean vision. "Hate as well as love," said Schweitzer in a famous line, "can write a life of Jesus." Thus he observed that some of the most important contributions were made by those who intensely disliked "the supernatural nimbus" with which the traditional picture surrounded the figure of Jesus.

Schweitzer, whose floor was covered with about two hundred and fifty books as he carried out his quest significantly from books in German style, constantly complained that these scholars knew more about the historical Jesus than do the gospels themselves. Today of course we see that a serious difficulty lay in the meager historical and cultural information which prevented these scholars from adequately situating Jesus in the cultural context of his time.

Schweitzer showed that the division of Jesus' life into two contrasting epochs—a successful Galilean period followed by a period of disillusion and defeat—was historically untenable. But he accepted as basically valid Mark's structure in which Jesus claimed to be the Messiah yet insisted on silence for those who discovered his secret. The heart of the secret was a combination of an apocalyptic eschatology (Daniel 7) and an "interim ethics" such as is found in the Suffering Servant of Isaiah (52:13—53:12). He disagreed with Wrede's view of Mark's creation of the messianic secret. Rather it was Jesus himself for prudential reasons who tried to conceal his secret.

It is often forgotten that Schweitzer's first published work was a study of contemporary interpretations of the Lord's Supper and that his studies on the life of Jesus developed from his concern with interpreting the Lord's Supper. In fact his study of Mk 14:22–25 is the most detailed exegesis which he published. There he developed Schleiermacher's observation that neither Matthew nor Mark has the command "Do this in memory of me" and his suggestion that the repetition of the Lord's Supper was not instituted by Jesus but was a development of the disciples. For Schweitzer Mark's account, which is historically prior to the others, is the authentic account which Matthew, Paul and Luke developed. He notes that Mark has no command "Eat it" after the words over the bread and that only after the cup was drunk comes the statement "This is my blood of the covenant" which is followed by v 25, "I shall not drink again. . . ." Obviously, Schweitzer concluded, Jesus expected that his death would inaugurate the kingdom and that they would experience an imminent reunion at the eschatological meal in his new kingdom.

Schweitzer believed that the parables in Mark 4 were not intended to be interpreted and understood. Rather they teach the fact that in the affairs of the kingdom there is a mystery or a secret like that which can be observed in nature. The evolutionary interpretation of these parables, however attractive, takes away their character of secrets and the idea which is foremost in them, i.e., the apparent absence of causation.

Schweitzer in particular criticized the common understanding of the kingdom of God which was and still is prevalent wherever man looks to the gospels for confirmation of his own particular values and for encouragement in his own selective ethical endeavor. As a modern scholar put it:

> Men think of it as an ideal state of brotherhood, charity and good will, and we are urged to establish, or to build it. There is no need to defend such an ideal; and it is fortunate that we can add that

few men have done more than Albert Schweitzer to plant brotherhood, charity and good will in our world. For he, more than anyone else, has made it unmistakably clear that this is not what the
kingdom of God means in the gospels. The background of the
phrase is the apocalyptic of the first-century Judaism. Men felt
that they could no longer look, as the Old Testament prophets
had done, for a manifestation of God's will in ordinary historical
circumstances; things were now too bad for that. For some reason
of his own, inscrutable to men, God had permitted the reins of
power to be taken out of his hands, and they were now held by the
devil, whose sovereignty over mankind was attended by evil of every kind—sin, oppression, physical suffering, and death. The only
hope was that God, the rightful ruler of mankind, would assert
his own royal power—his kingdom—defeating and driving out
the devil and putting an end to his works. This was not man's
task, but God's; and there is preserved in the Qaddish, an ancient
prayer, similar to "Thy kingdom come" which Jesus taught his
disciples. . . .[125]

For Schweitzer, Jesus not only preached the kingdom but acted
it out in his life. He believed that his ministry would be the ending of
history and the coming of the kingdom of which the contemporary
apocalyptic writers dreamed, a kingdom of which he would be the
leader. When he saw that his message was not being accepted he decided to go to Jerusalem to force the hand of God. Schweitzer was
very impressed by Matthew 10 and 11 and their predictions which he
considered highly unlikely to have been created by the early Church
and placed on Jesus' lips if he had not actually pronounced them. Jesus had tried to hasten the end-time, the final catastrophe, by sending out his twelve disciples in twos to bring down upon themselves
the final woes (Mt 10:16–34). He did not expect to see them back in
this age (Mt 10:23). But when this failed he saw that he must go to
Jerusalem.

Peter, however, discovered Jesus' messianic identity during Jesus' ecstatic trance at the transfiguration. It was revealed to the others at Caesarea Philippi. Schweitzer conveniently transposed the two
events. They kept it secret as Jesus had commanded them until Judas
betrayed Jesus' secret to the Jewish leaders who had Jesus immediately killed as a dangerous pretender.

In Jerusalem Jesus revealed himself as the Messiah before the
high priest but ended in disaster and died in despair. He had shared
with his contemporaries the expectation of a speedy end to the
world, and when this did not happen he concluded that he himself

must suffer to save his people from the tribulations expected to pre-
cede the last days.

For Schweitzer, the historical Jesus is to a large extent irrelevant inasmuch as he was completely at the mercy of the ideas of his
time and had no freedom of thought:

> We must be prepared to find that the historical knowledge of the
> personality and life of Jesus will not be a help, but perhaps even
> an offense to religion.

But his heroic spirit, which Schweitzer admires, which

> goes forth from him, and in the spirits of men strives for a new
> influence and rule, is that which overcomes the world.[126]

Jesus' ethic was only intended as a provisional code, an "interim ethics" before the expected kingdom.

Schweitzer rightly insisted that the liberals' spiritual view of Jesus' kingdom was the creation of a relevant Jesus "like ourselves."
Jesus can only be understood against the historical background of his
time as part of a world view which expected a speedy end of the
world.

> Jesus of Nazareth will not suffer himself to be modernized as an
> historical figure. He refuses to be detached from his own time.
> The historical Jesus will be to our time a stranger and an enig-
> ma.[127]

He also pointed out that we do not have sufficient materials in the
gospels for a modern biography. The quest for the historical Jesus,
for what he did and meant and what actually happened to him, is as
old as the early Church itself. It was only with the nineteenth century critics that the adequacy of the materials available was questioned. He attacked the psychologizing interpretations of his
predecessors and insisted that when Mark is examined in sections
there is no obvious psychological connection between the sections
but rather in almost every case a positive break and that a gospel is
not a free-flowing narrative. Further he accused them of the prejudice that, underlying every gospel story however miraculous, there is
always an actual if not miraculous event.

However, Schweitzer fell into the sin he condemned so roundly
and filled in the gaps with his own psychological and chronological
interpretation of Jesus which he imposed on "the chaotic confusion

of the narratives" as he described them. He restored what he called "thoroughgoing eschatology" to the interpretation of Jesus' thinking. However, scarcely any scholar accepted Schweitzer's radical interpretation. It was indeed an unusual interpretation of the expression "eschatology" which normally means the last things, i.e., death, resurrection, judgment and eternal life. The term "eschatology" seems to have been first used in 1804 by G. Bretschneider. "Apocalyptic" would probably have been a more suitable word to describe "the sudden intervention of God in the affairs of the world to put all things right and to bring history to an end."[128] The choice according to Schweitzer had to be made between the thoroughgoing skepticism implied by Wrede in his challenge to the common belief that Mark was a historical view of Jesus and the thoroughgoing eschatology to which J. Weiss had pointed in a study published in 1892. Weiss argued that according to Jesus the kingdom would be established by a cataclysmic act of God only when the people's guilt which blocked its coming was removed by Jesus' "ransom for the many" (Mt 10:45). Schweitzer developed such ideas and concluded that Jesus' apocalyptic vision was the motivating force for all his thinking, teaching and activity. He recognized that such rationalists as Reimarus, Paulus, Strauss and Baldensperger were close to his own thinking.

Schweitzer oversimplified the problem of the gospels in his frequently posed dilemma according to which the earliest gospels must be accepted "en bloc" or must be considered as dogmatic treaties dressed up in a historical form. Typical of his simplifications was his summary of the three basic problems of nineteenth century research (p 238):

> The first was laid down by Strauss: either purely historical or purely supernatural. The second had been worked out by the Tübingen school and Holtzmann: either synoptic or Johannine. Now came the third: either eschatological or non-eschatological.

He separated both Matthew and Mark from the other two gospels and dated their origin to Palestine about A.D. 70. He believed that both Matthew and Mark were based on a common source which now one, now the other, more accurately reproduces. He also suggested that this common source as well as Matthew's special material goes back to eyewitnesses of Jesus' ministry who have a

> clear conception of the order of events and give a reliable report of the speeches of Jesus.[129]

In brief, for Schweitzer we need to de-eschatologize the gospel of Jesus in contrast to Bultmann's view that we need to demythologize the gospel. Schweitzer, reflecting on the two great commandments of love (Mk 12:28–34), was able in his genius to sum up his philosophy in the phrase "reverence for life" by which he attempted to live life without killing any living thing, even a mosquito.[130] Despite all the talk of Schweitzer, Weiss, Barth and Bultmann about the eschatological character of Christianity, it was only with the publication in 1967 of Jürgen Moltmann's *Theology of Hope: On the Ground and the Implications of a Christian Eschatology* that the futuristic expectations of the earliest Christians began to be taken seriously in twentieth century theology and seen as relevant to the modern world so filled with oppression, deprivation and inhumanity and not as a mere inoffensive part of the gospels.

1903 (a)

J. Wellhausen in *The Gospel of Mark* (1903) and *Introduction to the First Three Gospels* (1905) by hints rather than definite conclusions gave expression for the first time to

> many of what came to be the characteristic emphases of twentieth century synoptic scholarship![131]

Wellhausen is better known for his classic presentation of the sources of the Pentateuch and his development of the hypothesis that the biblical books were arranged anachronistically whereas the writing of the Law was historically to be placed after the prophets. This study obviously influenced his views on the gospels. Norman Perrin[132] gives three points from Wellhausen's discussion of Mark which the form-critics would develop into major axioms:

1. The original source for the material in the Gospel is oral tradition in which that material circulated in small units.

2. This material has been brought together and redacted in various ways and at various stages in the community, only one of which is that of the evangelists.

3. Such material gives us information about the beliefs and circumstances of the early Church as well as about the ministry of Jesus.

To quote Wellhausen himself:

> The intimate source of the Gospels is oral tradition, but this con-
> tains only scattered material. The units, more or less extensive,
> circulate in it separately. Their combination into a whole is al-
> ways the work of an author and, as a rule, the work of a writer
> with literary ambitions. . . . The Passion story need not be exclud-
> ed from the judgment that the Gospel as a whole lacks the distinc-
> tive marks of a history. Our curiosity remains unsatisfied.
> Nothing has motivations indicated or is explained by preliminary
> observations. The pragmatic nexus is missing as is the back-
> ground. Of chronology there is not a trace. Nowhere is there a
> fixed datum. To be sure, there is a geographical orientation, and
> as a rule the situation is specified, although often on indefinite
> terms—a house, a mountain, some solitary place. But the topo-
> graphical connection of the event, the itinerary, leaves almost as
> much to be desired as the chronological; seldom if at all is there
> any indication of a transition in a change of scene. The separate
> units are often presented in lively fashion, without irrelevant or
> merely rhetorical means, but they usually stand side by side like
> anecdotes "rari nantes in gurgite vasto" ("solitary swimmers in a
> vast whirlpool"). They are inadequate as material for a life of Je-
> sus. . . . Mark does not write "de vita et moribus Jesu" ("about
> the life and conduct of Jesus"). He has no intention of making Je-
> sus' person manifest, or even intelligible. For him it has been ab-
> sorbed in Jesus' divine vocation. He wishes to demonstrate that
> Jesus is the Christ.
>   Jesus speaks of himself most explicitly in the parable of the
> sower (Mk 4:3ff). . . . He reflects, just as any other teacher would,
> on the uncertain success of the words he had directed quite gener-
> ally to everyone. And this shows that he regards teaching, about
> the way of God, of course, as his actual vocation.[133]

For Wellhausen, Jesus saw himself only as a teacher and accepted the title of Messiah from his disciples as an accommodation to
popular Jewish belief. The transfiguration was an appearance of the
Risen Christ. Wellhausen rejected the views of "consistent eschatology," and for him Jesus never speculated on his return as Messiah. He
further argued that Mark, writing in the decade subsequent to the
destruction of Jerusalem, deliberately ended his gospel with the cryp-
tic "they were afraid" (Mk 16:8) and that Mark in the condition in
which we have it was known by the other synoptics. He divided
Mark into an introduction (1:1–13) and three sections: region of Ca-

pernaum (ch 1–5); withdrawal from Galilee and approach to Jerusalem (ch 6–10); Jerusalem (ch 11–16), a geographic structure.

1903 (b)

In the same year as Wellhausen, J. Weiss, a teacher of Bultmann, published a study of *Mark: The Oldest Gospel* which developed his earlier study on *Preaching of Jesus on the Kingdom* (1892). Weiss and others had discovered the historical importance of such Jewish apocalyptic writings as Enoch, the Apocalypse of Baruch and II Esdras. This discovery, which influenced Schweitzer so profoundly, led to the understanding of the kingdom of God almost exclusively as an imminent supernatural act by which God terminated human history and transformed the world into God's kingdom. He criticized the view of the mustard seed, the leaven, and the sower parables as teaching that the kingdom was a gradual process of development in the world. Rather these are not parables of growth but of contrast between the small, insignificant and scarcely visible cause and first effects and the overpowering final effects and result. The parable of the seed growing secretly (4:26–29) is an answer to the burning discontentment regarding the coming of the kingdom and the natural desire to do something to hasten its coming. It teaches that man cannot realize the kingdom through his own efforts, but it will come in God's time and one must wait patiently. Jesus, he believed, originally told the parable of the sower as an allegory but Mark incorrectly reproduced its meaning.

For Weiss, Jesus was no contemporary Protestant moral preacher but an eschatological herald who did not inaugurate the kingdom but preached a kingdom that was wholly future and transcendental, to be inaugurated when he, after being killed, would return as judge as the Son of Man according to Daniel.

Like his father Bernhard John Weiss who is often described as the "perfector" of the two-source theory because of his scholarly position and reputation, Johannes Weiss suggested that, in addition to Peter's reminiscences, Mark also used an apostolic source containing sayings and narratives. In contrast to Weisse he insisted that the hypothetical source which Wernle designated Q also contained not only narratives but even a part of the passion narrative, the story of anointing which anticipates Jesus' burial. He honestly admitted that there are too many obscure points in the synoptic relationships which were not clearly explained by applying the Marcan hypothesis. Some of Matthew's pericopes could not be seen as merely adapta-

6 5 4 9 6

tions of the Marcan text. Thus he could not accept that in the story of the paralytic Matthew left out the impressive and popular detail of the stretcher-bearers climbing the roof merely to save paper or for lack of interest in details. He noted that in many places Matthew and Luke agree against Mark in contradiction with the Marcan hypothesis. Both father and son Weiss recognized independently and simultaneously that in many cases Mark's version is secondary to the other synoptics in both sayings and narratives.

For Johannes Peter's reminiscences from the early days in Galilee up to the passion, which Mark incorporated with minor changes, were a coherent account of real historical value. He is doubtful of the identity of Mark with the John Mark of Acts 12:12, 25 and 15:37 because of the deficiency of the Jerusalem tradition in Mark and the vague information in the early Church about Mark.

In brief, for Weiss,

> The significance of the oldest gospel for the Church's history lies before all things in this, that it has fashioned once for all, with vivid touches serving as a model for all who came after, a picture of Jesus on earth which has impressed itself indissolubly on the imagination of the community. In it one can recognize what significance for the Christian mission the "historical" Jesus possessed. Mission preaching, as we have seen, could not dispense with a certain amount of information, touching the life of Jesus. . . . The Gospel of Mark, then, teaches us that the need of a living, concrete picture was far greater than has generally been supposed. Fresh converts desired a fuller knowledge touching Jesus, of whom they were told that he is the Son of God: the communities needed for worship and individual piety a living presentation of him who had died for their sakes. Besides there was, no doubt, already arising a certain historical interest: in particular, as the eyewitnesses of Jesus' life were dying out, the necessity became clear of maintaining what they had given as tradition. The oldest gospel, therefore, is only to be understood and rightly estimated if it is read on the one hand as expressing the conceptions and convictions of the evangelist, and on the other as a collection of older traditions which in part grew out of quite other conceptions.[134a]

1906

F. C. Burkitt in *The Gospel History and Its Transmission* (pp 42ff) asked for the first time the question how to explain the agreements of Matthew and Luke against Mark. Many of these, he thought, could be explained due to grammatical and stylistic variants (e.g., Mt 7:16 and Lk 6:44) or else scribal and editorial corrections. The precedence of Mark and the existence of Q were for him "assured" results of synoptic scholarship. He also thought, against many scholars, that Q contained a passion account (pp 103ff).

Mark he considered to be

> an historical document, a document really in touch with the facts [from which] we may learn who Jesus Christ was and what part he played on earth in human history [and which can be used] if we want to begin at the beginning and reconstruct the portrait of Christ.[134b]

One man, he insisted can be the subject of many adequate portraits. Mark he considered to be

> the only one of the gospels, canonical or uncanonical, which does give an intelligible account of the process by which Jesus Christ broke with the Synagogue, that is, the official embodiment of Jewish religion, or rather the process by which the Synagogue broke with Jesus Christ and forced him to withdraw from their system (p 79).

In *The Earliest Sources for the Life of Jesus* (1922, p 97), he described Matthew as

> "a fresh edition of Mark, revised, rearranged and enriched with new material" [while Luke is] a new historical work made by combining parts of Mark with parts of other documents.

Two apt quotations from Burkitt are worth recording here. The first comes from a review of Harnack[135] which incisively notes:

> We see clearly enough that we could not have reconstructed the Gospel according to St. Mark out of the other two Synoptic gospels, although between them nearly all Mark has been incorporated by Matthew and Luke. How futile, therefore, it is to attempt to reconstruct those other literary sources which seem to have been used by Matthew and Luke, but have not been independently preserved.

The second quotation describes the astonishing effect which the new look at Mark had as he was no longer considered the tame abbreviator of Matthew in Augustinian terms or "the sane and well-poised mind of the plain mechanic of Nazareth" as B. W. Bacon described him. Burkitt comments:

> Till our eyes become accustomed to the atmosphere it is difficult to recognize the conventional Savior, with the gentle unindividualized face, in the stormy and mysterious personage portrayed by the second Gospel.[136]

1907

A. Loisy published *The Synoptic Gospels* (1907) and *The Gospel According to Mark* (1912). He saw the source of Mark as

> a humble collection of notes which originally recorded the essential facts of the Galilean mission and the messianic venture concentrated on Jerusalem, with its culmination at Golgotha.[137]

He thought that the anonymous writer of Mark was trying to cover up the political activity of Jesus and that therefore he removed the chronological and topographical order from his source, leaving a certain confusion in chapters 1–10 which are not governed by any strict principle of history or logic but by mere analogy. For Loisy, Jesus was unconscious of his divinity and the Christ of faith was due to the early Church which is a barrier to the Jesus of history.

Like A. Schweitzer, Loisy reacted strongly against the views of A. von Harnack,[138] the great Protestant liberal thinker who was conscious of the alienation of the great mass of the people of his time from the Church and the gospel while the work of theologians was all too often buried in scholarly learning and books. Harnack's key problem was his question: Is the Church with its hierarchical institution, its ministry and sacraments, its dogma and liturgy, its Virgin and supernatural Christ, its saints and angels and relics, the legitimate evolutionary outgrowth of the primitive gospel of Jesus, or is it, in the final analysis, a distortion of that primitive gospel?

For Harnack, the gospel was the great declaration of the spiritual liberation of mankind which was suffering a threefold threat from the state, the indifference of the masses and the timidity of superficial Christians in his day. The essence of the gospel contained three items: first, the present kingdom which enters the soul through Jesus' healing and forgiving; second, belief in the fatherhood of God and the infinite value of the human soul rather than the nation (Mk 8:36; Mt 10:30); third, the higher righteousness and the commandment of love (Mt 5:27ff) as exemplified in the Beatitudes, the Good Samaritan parable and the golden rule.

Harnack was particularly critical of the influence of Greek religion and civilization:

> It was to destroy this sort of religion that Jesus Christ suffered himself to be nailed to the cross, and now we find it re-established under his name and authority (p 238).

Harnack accepted the priority of Mark and believed that a clear outline of Jesus' teaching was given in the gospels even though they were insufficient for an adequate biography of Jesus. He incisively noticed the difference between Jesus' teaching and the teaching of the different groups in Judaism. He noticed that Jesus neither emphasized the Jewish nation nor taught strict observance to the Mosaic law. Jesus taught a God of mercy and love unlike the old capricious God of fear and judgment. Jesus did not separate himself from the world like the Essenes. Yet he had no relation to the Greek philosophical teaching. He emphasized joy in contrast to the Baptist's stress on judgment. He was a teacher, yet not educated like the rabbis were. Jesus was no political or social reformer but emphasized "poor in spirit" and that the poor would be always "with you" (Mk 14:7).

Harnack was unfortunately often misunderstood because although he had written:

> What belongs to the Gospel, as Jesus preached it, is not the Son but the Father alone.

Yet he had also gone on to add:

> Jesus belongs to his gospel not as part of it, but as its embodiment. He is its personal realization and its power. And such he will always be felt to be.[139]

However, this addition was generally ignored in more popular interpretations of Harnack, and his version of Christianity tended to become a vague system of ethical teaching. For Loisy and Schweitzer the essence of the gospel was not this vague ethics but rather a great hope, although without doubt a deceptive hope which was the key element of Jesus' consciousness. The key text for Loisy was Matthew 4:17:

> Repent for the kingdom of heaven is at hand.

Unlike Harnack who saw a contrast between the proclamation of Jesus and John, Loisy saw a similarity, with both viewing everything in relation to the end of the world. The essence of Christianity for Loisy is not the kernel which historians attempt to reconstruct but rather its constant principles which were there from the beginning and in particular in the faith of the Church as it expanded under the guidance of the Spirit. Thus:

> In the Gospels there remains but an echo, necessarily weakened and a little confused, of the words of Jesus, the general impression he produced upon hearers well-disposed toward him with some of the more striking of his sentences, as they were understood, and interpreted; and finally there remains the movement which he initiated.[140a]

He argued that although Christ did not found the institutional Church or the sacraments, yet they were the natural evolution of the gospel and not a distortion of it.

Like J. Weiss and many others, Loisy thought that Mark was influenced by Paul whose main ideas he borrowed. He dated Mark in Rome A.D. 75–80 like Goguel, Branscomb and Bacon.

1909

B. W. Bacon in *Beginnings of the Gospel Story* remarked on the extraordinary agreement of his results with those of Loisy. He concluded that Mark was a Paulinist and that there was a large redactional element in his gospel. His theory was not unlike that of G. Volkmar (1857) which suggested that Mark was a narrative in the form of an allegory to present the distinctive elements of Paul's teaching, e.g., his emphasis on the cross and the necessity of the disciples dying for Christ's sake. Scholars such as Taylor and Werner have criticized this Pauline hypothesis. They concluded that while Paul and Mark share the early tradition, nevertheless the distinctively Pauline ideas[140b] are not found in Mark or are differently presented. Taylor calls "the suggestion of a recast of the primitive Gospel in terms of Paulinism" a wild and unsubstantiated hypothesis (p 129).

In 1919 in an essay *Is Mark a Roman Gospel?* Bacon examined the ancient testimony and concluded that

> as regards ancient testimony of the provenance of our oldest gospel it is certainly true that "all roads lead to Rome"

and that Papias was the fountainhead of the tradition particularly in the second, third and fourth centuries. Bacon asks how a work so undistinguished as Mark could have circulated so widely in the early Church and have authority when it was in competition with such as Matthew, Luke and John. The only plausible explanation is that it derived from an important Church where it was written by one of its members. Yet he insisted that the evidence of tradition or of dissemination was not sufficient unless supported by internal evidence. He argued that Mark was one of Paul's "the strong" (Rom 14) and that he was anti-Jewish. He noted that Mark

> never introduces the apostle to the circumcision for any individual part without making him the target for severe reproof and condemnation.

In his *Gospel of Mark* (1925) Bacon concluded that although Mark does not seem to have known Paul's epistles, yet "Mark shows a direct, but not a literary dependence" on Paul's teaching. He maintained that a prophecy first made in A.D. 40 due to Caligula's threat to profane the temple and frustrated by Caligula's death was reinterpreted due to the changed circumstances under Claudius in Thessalonians as "a word of the Lord" (2 Th 1:12). This prophecy Mark used in his Little Apocalypse (Mk 13). Bacon would date Mark after the destruction of the temple. Although Titus celebrated his triumph in 71, the fortress of Masada was not conquered until April 73. During this time of woes the Son of Man must have been expected. In the year 75 two Cynic philosophers in Rome denounced Titus for living with Bernice the sister of Agrippa II, and as a result one was flogged and the other beheaded.[141a] Bacon, noting the parallel with John the Baptist, suggested that this well-known scandal led Mark to include his account of the Baptist's death. Bacon also explained the "mutilation" of Mark's final chapter as a result of rivalry between upholders of a Galilean (Matthew) and a Jerusalem (Luke) tradition of christophanies.

The composition of Mark was a process more than "the simple casting into a written form of a single narrative, the unified product of a simple mind. . . ." The Gospel was not written *aus einem Guss,* but has strata of successive periods, seams and faultings, overlappings and duplications, like the other compositions of its type. It has a *past,* whose record, difficult though it may be to decipher, often perplexing to the most patient scrutiny, is written in the phenomena of its structure, and will reveal something of the history of the work to him who patiently analyzes and compares.[141b]

1910

M. J. Lagrange published his commentary on Mark which has been described as

an epoch-making event in the history of Catholic New Testament exegesis: the first truly scientific commentary on a gospel.[142]

Lagrange began with a translation from the original Greek text which he had established by a careful and thorough textual criticism. While biblical scholars were notoriously parochial and tied to their own religious tradition and country (e.g., Germany), Lagrange had a truly catholic approach and faced objectively the modern problems of the times which were discussed outside the Catholic Church scholarship. While he saw Mark as completely dependent on Peter who was an eyewitness to the whole public ministry of Jesus, yet he stressed Mark's dignity as an author. He divided Mark into four sections: introduction (1:1–13), the gospel of the kingdom (1:14—8:26), the preparation of the future gospel (8:27—13:37), and the "great act" (14—16). In the last three sections he detected

a progression in the relations of Jesus with his friends and his enemies, in changing geographical settings

but he concluded that this

does not make it possible to speak of subdivisions corresponding to specific themes.[143]

This commentary ran into many editions and is particularly interesting for its emphasis on the Semitic element in Mark. On Mark's awk-

ward expressions and characteristics which unexpectedly appear
(e.g., 1:28, 32, 38, 45; 2:5, 10; 5:42) and which he carefully analyzed,
Lagrange concluded:

> The details that he introduces into his narrative do not resemble
> the finishing touches given to complete a picture but are more like
> the recollection of real facts. These memories add nothing to the
> moral or apologetic lesson, they do not make the miracle more re-
> markable, they do not exalt Jesus' personality; they are in the ac-
> count because they once happened (p lxxv).

Lagrange carefully studied the synoptic problem and concluded that
Mark depended on Peter's preaching and that Greek Matthew depended both on Aramaic Matthew and Mark.

1911

W. Erbt. According to James Robinson:

> The new tack in the interpretation of Mark rejected so completely
> the accepted canons of Marcan interpretation that the way stood
> open for a series of unlikely hypotheses whose primary strength
> lay in the fact that they did not historicize Mark.[144]

Erbt interpreted Mark in terms of astral mythology. Andrew Drews
(1921) suggested that Mark was the product of mythology, that Old
Babylonian traditions together with astrological speculations had
been taken over by Jewish gnostics to construct the concept of a dying and rising Messiah. Herman Raschke (1924) concluded that
Mark was the Gospel created by Marcion. It was dominated by docetic and gnostic views and the stories were allegories of proper
names. Robinson concludes that Martin Werner's study on the influence of Pauline theology on Mark in 1923

> closed the door through which the anti-historical Marcan inter-
> pretation was moving into gnosticism, docetism and mysticism.[145]

Thus G. Volkmar, in opposition to the Tübingen school, had proposed that Mark was an allegorical presentation in narrative form of
Paul's teaching. Werner showed that the Paulinisms of Mark assumed by Volkmar's study in 1857 were widespread in early Christianity while Paul's specific doctrines were absent. 1 Corinthians 15:3
shows that the view of Jesus' death as redemptive was already pres-

ent in the Christian community. Also Paul's characteristic term "Kyrios" ("Lord") is missing in Mark as well as his emphasis on the humiliation of the Son of God.

1913

Wilhelm Bousset, in his influential work *Kyrios Christos: The History of Christology from the Beginnings of Christianity to Irenaeus,* summarized many of the developments of the "history of religions" school and anticipated several of the developments of the form critics, especially in his chapter on the faith of the community and his picture of Jesus of Nazareth in the first three gospels. For Bousset:

> Mark and the "logia" are not the creators of the gospel tradition. Behind them lies perhaps a generation of oral tradition. And it was this tradition, not a literary personality, that stamped its character on the gospel framework. Above all, it is still abundantly clear that the individual, closed pericope and the individual logion (or the individual parable), as the oral tradition is accustomed to transmit them, constitute its germ cells. . . .
>
> The passion story . . . possessed from the beginning—this is a fact that is still insufficiently grasped—a different character than the other sections of Mark's gospel. In it the narrators were not content with a few disconnected recollections and separate accounts. As far as we can look back over the process of transmission, the passion story seems to have provided a connected report—one perhaps already given literary form at a very early date . . . (pp 172, 220).

He made detailed investigations into the connection between the contemporary Hellenistic religions and later Judaism and the development of early Christianity through its struggle with second century gnosticism as far as Irenaeus. Irenaeus, who quotes every book in the New Testament except Philemon, is described as the first of the great Catholic theologians. For Bousset, who like the form critics put little emphasis on the role of the evangelists, the Jesus of the gospels is a symbol created to meet the needs of the early Christians. He rejects the idea of an explicit or even implicit Christology in the teaching, understanding or self-consciousness of Jesus. Bousset began what many scholars would follow: the discussion of Christology through titles and the recognition of the variety within early Christianity. He could accept that one or other of the Son of Man passages could have been spoken by Jesus but on the whole saw in the Son of

Man sayings the theology of the primitive community. He distinguished two phases of the earliest Christianity: the primitive Palestinian community as seen in the earliest strata of the synoptics, and the Gentile community before Paul.[146]

While apocalyptic Jewish Christianity created the Son of Man Christology, on the other hand the cultic Kyrios Christology was created by Hellenistic Christianity whose title "Lord" ("Kyrios") had clear parallels and therefore a source in the gods of the mystery religions. Thus Bousset originated the classic view that the thoroughly Jewish Palestinian church worshiped the man Jesus who had been exalted to God's right hand as the heavenly Son of Man who was to return to earth in glory. It was only when Christianity took root in the Hellenistic world in Syrian Antioch (Acts 11:20ff) that Jesus was worshiped as Lord like the Hellenistic gods, as a present heavenly divine being.

> An age which by no means lived solely on the simply ethical and simply religious, but on all sorts of more or less fantastic eschatological expectations, on faith in miracle and prophecy, on an imminent, unprecedented, special intervention of God in the course of nature and of history, on all sorts of means of salvation and messiahs, on devils and demons and the early triumph of God and his people over these inimical powers—such an age needed this very picture of Jesus as the first disciples of Jesus created it, and accepted the Eternal in it in the colorful wrappings of temporal clothing. This drama of the creation of a picture of Jesus drawn by faith will unfold for us once again from the standpoint of a purer and higher, a more universal and more generally valid faith; indeed it actually repeats itself infinitely often throughout the entire course of Christian history (p 117f).

Bousset saw a development from Jesus and his simple ethical teaching to Palestinian Christianity to Hellenistic Christianity to Paul. This was followed by John and then gnosticism which further mythologized the Christ myth of Paul and the early Christian writing down to Irenaeus which developed a highly organized and institutionalized Christianity. His most fruitful insight was his recognition of the importance of worship in the early Church since he saw the early Christian groups as primarily worshiping communities where they especially realized their own nature.

1915

C. W. Votaw published two essays, *The Gospels and Contemporary Biographies,* which have been reprinted as a Facet Book in 1970. Votaw saw that the answer to the question "Is a gospel a biography?" depended on one's meaning of the word "biography." Obviously the gospels assume so much and omit so much about Jesus' person, life, psychological development, background, culture and environment that one could not describe them as an historical biography. But Votaw suggested that a gospel was a biography in the popular (not literary) sense of the term of making the reader acquainted with a historical person

> by giving some account of his deeds and words, sketchily chosen and arranged, even when the motive of the writer is practical and hortatory rather than historical (p 49).

The contemporary examples which he chose were Arrian's biography of Epictetus (c. A.D. 125–150), Philostratus' biography of Appollonius of Tyana (c. A.D. 217) and the better known accounts of Socrates by Xenophon (c. 380 B.C.) and Plato who both wrote about him about a generation after his death. However, the Socrates of Xenophon's more practical *Memorabilia* is not identical with Plato's Socrates. Both wrote a history which is "dramatized, idealized and pragmatized." Plato especially in his later writings seems to make use of Socrates as a device with which to expound his further understanding of the Socratic method and insight. These latter had a purpose similar to the gospel:

> to restore the reputation of a great and good man who had been publicly executed and defamed by the state, to re-establish his influence as a supreme teacher in respect to right living and thinking, and to render available to all the message of truth and duty which each had made it his life-work to promulgate.

In all these works the aim is to

> eulogize and idealize their heroes . . . select their best sayings and interpret them for practical use . . . give the memorabilia in an atmosphere of appreciation . . . commend the message to the faith and practice of all (p 55).

The similarities to a gospel are obvious but the difference should not be forgotten. No evangelist believed that Jesus' memory would be forgotten or that he was not a present dynamic reality in the community.[147] Votaw was writing before the era of form-criticism. He insisted that the gospels should not be seen as historical but as "propagandist" writings which were not principally designed to describe "Jesus as a man of history."

> The evangelists selected, revised and arranged their memorabilia in accordance with the idea of what would serve the particular needs of mission.

Their aim was not to make men see Jesus

> in the literal garb of a Galilean prophet, but in the transfigured raiment of the Son of God redeeming the world.

In 1965 C. F. Evans, *The New Testament Gospels,* posed an interesting question as to how a second century A.D. librarian from Alexandria in Egypt would have classified Mark's gospel in his library. He would have available such categories as Lives of Famous Men, Acts and Memoirs, but a gospel would not have fitted any, due to the amount of information omitted and presupposed, the tragic end of Jesus and the fact that it was aimed at a Christian audience.

A similar thesis to Votaw has been propounded recently by C. H. Talbert in *What Is a Gospel?: The Genre of the Canonical Gospels,*[148] claiming that the gospels are biographies though not in the modern sense. He is reacting against the common understanding, the "critical consensus" fostered by R. Bultmann, of the gospels as a unique kind of literature created by presenting in a narrative form the early preaching. He argues to a similarity with the Greek-Roman biographies and circumvents the problem of their second and third century dates by pointing out that many writings contemporary to the gospels were lost or exist only in fragments. He begins by criticizing Bultmann's three features which differentiate the gospels, i.e., that they are mythical, cultic and world negating. He grants that Bultmann's criteria are pivotal in deciding the genre of the gospel and its relation to biography. He notes however that many of the Hellenistic lives were based on the myth of men who became immortals at the end of their lives. The fact that such models were followed does not preclude the idea that the evangelists made creative deviations from them. Talbert claims that

> the average Mediterranean man-in-the-street would assume that Jesus was being portrayed as an immortal in both Luke-Acts and Matthew while Mark would be understood as the account of a divine man who became an immortal at the end of his career as is proved by his empty tomb.

He gives a new classification of Greek-Roman biographies of philosophers into which he fits the gospels:

A the biographies which provide a pattern to follow;
B the biographies which try to dispel a false image of the teacher and provide a true model to follow;
C the biographies which aim at discrediting a teacher;
D the biographies which indicate where the true tradition of a school is to be found;
E the biographies which validate a teacher's doctrine or provide the key to it.

Mark he places in type B as a biography written to defend the Church's Savior against misunderstanding and to point a true image for the disciple to follow. John is also type B. Luke-Acts is basically type D with some features of B. Matthew is essentially type E with some features of B.

Recently M. Hengel in *Acts and the History of Earliest Christianity* has again questioned the commonplace that we can no longer write a biography of Jesus. He points out that apart from Cicero and Caesar there are very few figures in the ancient world about whom this would be possible. Ancient biography was quite different from modern scientific biography. It ranged from a loose collection of anecdotes and sayings (e.g., Lucian's Demonax or Diogenes Laertius' Lives and Opinions of Famous Philosophers) to romance like popular books such as the Life of Aesop. Aesop, the slave, in his wisdom put to shame his master, the philosopher, Xanthus and many other kings and wise men but is finally lured to his death by the inhabitants of Delphi because of his courage and wisdom. The aim was quite different. It did not give a detailed character analysis or portray the psychological development or changes in personality of a person against a carefully ordered chronological background. From the beginning the hero appeared

> as a rounded personality, and the deeds and events of his youth
> illuminated his destiny (p 8).

Neither the hero nor his character changed but only the world around him.

Hengel thinks that more attention should be given to Justin Martyr's description of the synoptic gospels as "reminiscences" ("apomnemoneumata"), a description he uses some fifteen times, quite possibly alluding to Xenophon's "reminiscences" of Socrates which he also certainly knew. For Justin the gospels were really biographical "reminiscences" of Jesus written down by the apostles or their pupils. The Latin equivalent "commentarii" appears in Tertullian who described the evangelists as commentators. Similar words expressing the idea of "remembrance" are found in Papias, Irenaeus, Clement and Polycarp, and therefore the idea "can least of all be banished from the Jesus tradition" (p 28). But for Hengel the model for the gospels is not the so-called "aretalogical romance," a form of romantic biography with markedly miraculous traits, e.g., Philo's Life of Moses. The model is to be found in the historical parts of the Old Testament and Judaism, e.g., the biographies of the patriarchs in Genesis and the life of Moses found in Exodus and Deuteronomy. What distinguishes the gospels is their concentration on Jesus as Messiah and Son of God and the absolute and final claim to revelation which they contain.

5
The Form Critics

1919 (a)

After the First World War which interrupted academic study in Germany and had a profound effect on the confidence in progress of European liberal theology, three scholars working independently of one another, K. L. Schmidt (1891–1956). M. Dibelius (1891–1956), and R. Bultmann (1884–1976), produced the first works of the modern movement known as form-criticism or, to give a more precise translation of the German expression, form-history. The two-source theory had explained the interdependence of the synoptics in terms of Mark and Q but these were a rather developed stage of the Jesus tradition from its beginning in the life of Jesus.

Form-criticism, building upon the Old Testament studies, especially those of Hermann Gunkel,[149] postulated an intervening period of oral transmission as it attempted to penetrate the period behind such extensive literary sources as Mark and Q. It was evident that Mark's gospel in its written form had incorporated older material. Its indications of time and place are frequently quite vague and sayings of Jesus are often juxtaposed because of key words in common. Thus on examination, the whole seemed like a mosaic built up of many pieces after a period of oral tradition. During the oral period the tradition took on various literary forms each with its own history and successive life settings (Sitz im Leben) in the life of the early Church as the sayings and descriptions of Jesus' deeds were adapted and applied to the interests and needs of the local community, its preaching and liturgy, its pastoral instructions and missionary needs. Thus the form-critics tended to see the gospels as rather reflective products of the early communities projected back into the life of Jesus than factual accounts of his life. In particular the form-critics concentrated on the individual pericope, paying little interest to a gospel as a literary whole. As Robert C. Tannehill put it:

> Preoccupation with the pre-Gospel units of tradition and with the modification of those units obscured the fact that Mark is a continuous narrative presenting a meaningful development to a climax and that each narrative should be understood in light of its relation to the story as a whole.

Tannehill, an advocate of the new "literary" approaches to the Bible, suggests that when Mark is read as a unitary narrative with the aid of perspectives from literary studies, the message and art of Mark stand out with new clarity.[150]

1919 (b)

K. L. Schmidt published the first work of the movement, with the significant title in German which translates as *The Framework of the Historical Jesus* (1919). He recognized the work of the evangelist himself not only in the arrangement, the insertion of such insignificant connecting words as "immediately," "again" and such vague time and place indications as "in the old days" or "and passing along by the Sea of Galilee," but especially in the short generalizing summaries which lack the concreteness and particularity of the pericope and relate nothing which belongs to one point in space and time.

He examined these connecting links and bridge passages (e.g., Mk 1:14f, 21f; 2:13) and concluded that they were inventions of the evangelist and not based on historical, chronological or geographical facts. Therefore they provide no certain basis for the tracing of a developing sequence in Jesus' life. Schmidt saw that apart from chapters 14—16 the narrative sections of Mark consist of separate anecdotes or small groups of two or three (1:21-23; 2:1—3:6; 4:35—5:43; 6:30-56; 9:2—29). The section 3:7—6:13, he suggested, was dominated by the idea of the hardening of Israel's heart. Therefore, with the one exception of the passion narrative,

> there is no life of Jesus in the sense of a developing biography, no chronological sketch of Jesus' history, but only individual stories which are put into a framework

to quote the closing sentence of his work. A good example is seen in the controversy-stories which the evangelist has connected on a topical basis in 2:1ff. The framework is due to the evangelist's theology, and thus his gospel reflects rather his Church situation than the life situation of Jesus. However, although Schmidt claimed that Mark's order was exclusively topical he failed on his own admission to discover Mark's precise topical basis in the case of every pericope, e.g., the relevance of the discussion on divorce (10:2–12) in the general section of 8:27—10:45 to which he gave the topical rubric, *The Thought of the Approaching Passion.*

Years earlier the well-known Strauss had a similar idea when he compared the stories of Jesus in the gospels to a handful of pearls of which the framework, the connecting string, had been broken. For Schmidt the gospels were "originally non-literary rather than literary documents," "cultic books for ordinary people or even popular cultic books." Like the German Faust literature it did not come from the academic or learned sphere but from popular traditions handed down generation after generation so that

> such a writer of a folk book does not so much have an author's personality as he is a mere collector and hence exponent of a tradition carried on by the folk. . . . A synopsis of the various Faust books makes clear that all their writers were only quite secondarily authors but were in the main collectors, transmitters, and redactors, and that the units brought together by them had already previously attained formal unity.[151]

1919 (c)

In the same year M. Dibelius published his *From Tradition to Gospel* (lit., *The Form-History of the Gospels*), thus giving the movement its name. Of the three great form-critics he was most aware of the limitations of the method. The method is of course in itself neutral as regards the quest of the historical Jesus. Over-emphasis on the creativity of the early community or negative pre-suppositions about miracles and the supernatural would lead some of its practitioners to be very skeptical of our knowledge of the facts about Jesus' life and teaching. For Dibelius, Peter was the ultimate source of many of Mark's stories (e.g., 8:14–21, 27ff; 14:66–72). However, before their arrival in Mark they had gone through a process of community tradition. Thus he believed that the gospels contained a solid core of historical information about Jesus which could be recovered by form-criticism. He insisted that the most skeptical historian must postulate an "x" to explain the complete change in the disciples' behavior from running away to a bold preaching of the gospel. For Dibelius the gospels were popular literature ("Kleinliteratur") and the evangelists were not true authors but rather compilers or handers-on. This position has provoked quite a strong reaction from the more recent redaction-criticism movement.

Following the foundation of his predecessor, J. Weiss at Heidelberg, Dibelius put great emphasis on preaching as the medium of transmission of Jesus' teaching. He saw Mark as a rather conservative redactor whose main aim was to provide materials for a proclamation of the gospel but not in himself interested in making a theological proclamation, as Bultmann would hold. He classified the gospel material into five groups: (a) paradigms (pronouncement stories), e.g., 2:17; (b) "Noveletter," e.g., short stories generally; (c) miracle stories, e.g., Mk 5:1–20; (d) legends (edifying narratives)—a term taken over from the later Christian vocabulary—e.g., Lk 2:41–52; (e) myths, e.g., baptism, temptation, transfiguration, the passion narrative. It must be remembered that such forms rarely exist in a pure state but what we have are mixed types—compare the common division of Shakespeare's plays into Tragedies, Histories, and Comedies. Then he traced the origin of these forms in the community beginning with the office of preaching. To quote his well known statement:

> At the beginning of all Christian activity there stands the sermon: missionary and hortatory, preaching, narrative and parenesis, prophecy, and the interpretation of scripture.

Preaching obviously needed examples and therefore paradigms were born. Anonymous story tellers added details and created the Novellen which are less likely to be historical. He finds no community office for the legends and myths but suggests that they came later and are quite unhistorical.

Dibelius, however, recognized certain controlling motifs at work in Mark's modification of the tradition which he received, in particular his secret epiphany theme. Thus he described the first part of Mark in a famous phrase as "a book of the secret epiphanies of Jesus" (p 230), signifying according to R. P. Martin that Jesus' appearances are

> so tantalizingly brief and so crisply narrated and so half-veiled in details of mystery and movement [that] the revelation of Jesus' person is both half-displayed and half-concealed.[152]

Mark he saw as bringing together

> in his own way passages from the tradition preserved in the
> Churches, i.e., what were essentially paradigms, etc., of Jesus

with the purpose of representing Jesus as the Messiah. But he saw
the gospel writers as compilers rather than authors.

> The literary understanding of the Synoptic Gospels begins with
> recognition of the fact that they are made up of collections of tra-
> ditional material (Sammelgut). Only in the smallest degree are the
> writers of the Gospels authors; they are in the main collectors,
> transmitters, editors. Their activity consists in the handing on,
> grouping and working over the material that has come down to
> them, and their theological apprehension of the material, insofar
> as one can speak of an apprehension at all, finds expression only
> in this secondary and mediated form. Their attitude to their work
> is far less independent than of the author of the Fourth Gospel,
> far less than that of the writer of the Acts of the Apostles.[153]

For Dibelius, the narratives in Mark's first twelve chapters are so
completely self-contained that their position could be interchanged
without affecting the picture of Jesus' activity. This of course is an
exaggeration. Mark has a clear pattern of preparation, controversy,
tragedy and triumph which has been quite carefully arranged.

1921

Rudolf Bultmann (1884–1976) was a prolific and not always
consistent writer who for some fifty years would straddle like a Co-
lossus the world of New Testament studies and Jesus research in particular. In 1921 he published *The History of the Synoptic Tradition* in
which he developed the insights of Schmidt and Dibelius and continued the application of the form-critical method to the synoptics. In
the concluding section of this study Bultmann sketched the special
theological interests of the evangelists including Mark. One should
also mention here his *Jesus* (1926) which has been described as "a
book about Jesus without Jesus," his highly controversial manifesto
The New Testament and Mythology (1941), and the most recent modification of his theories in his published (1960) lecture *The Relationship of the Primitive Christian Gospel of Christ to the Historical
Jesus.*[154] It is of course impossible to summarize Bultmann briefly,
but many scholars testify to his self-criticism, his immense erudition

and scholarship, and his deep pastoral concern to present Christianity in a meaningful way to his war-shocked and often agnostic contemporaries.

Many themes of previous scholars are developed in Bultmann's thinking. These include the concept of myth as the key to interpreting the gospels (Strauss), the emphasis on oral tradition (H. Gunkel), the idea of the creative community (Reimarus, Wrede) and the non-messianic character of Jesus' life (Wrede). From the History of Religion school (Reitzenstein, Bousset), which endeavored to place the pre-suppositions of early Christianity in its contemporary Near Eastern and Graeco-Roman context, came in particular the idea of a redeemer myth in a pre-Christian form of gnosticism. This redeemer myth, which had mainly Iranian roots, had little or nothing to do with Jewish traditions and yet became the central motif in early Christianity. Bultmann added two new elements which formed the unifying core of his thinking. In the first place there was his rather extreme form of radical individualism based on the Lutheran "justification by faith alone." Already in 1919 with his commentary on Romans, the Swiss theologian Karl Barth, against the background of the First World War, had led a revival of reformation theology. Secondly, there was existentialism, an extreme form of radical individualism based on the Lutheran justification "by faith alone," and the existentialism of his Marburg colleague, Martin Heidegger who distinguished between mere being and existence, especially in his famous *Being and Time* (1927). For Bultmann what the New Testament called sin was the equivalent of Heidegger's "inauthentic existence," whereas "authentic existence" was "life in faith" or "life according to the Spirit." However, Bultmann parted company from Heidegger and the self-confidence of the philosophers in his emphasis on the New Testament teaching on the total incapacity of man to release himself from his fallen state and his need of an "act of God."

Bultmann believed that there is "an unchangeable fundamental structure of the human spirit as such." If the New Testament is properly demythologized it will be found to have an abiding message which is just as relevant to man today and his concern with the question of human existence as it was to its original audience. He rejected the idea of pre-suppositionless exegesis, what B. Lonergan has recently described as "the principle of the Empty Head."[155] Bultmann saw clearly that every interpreter comes to a text with his own particular pre-suppositions and questions and that the answers he gets are to some extent determined by his questions. He did not see the thought of Heidegger as the imposition of foreign thought categories on the Bible but saw Heidegger's thought as actually corresponding to the thought categories of the Bible itself. In brief, Bultmann reduced the content of biblical theology to a single idea, namely, the

> act or decision in which man draws his self-understanding and thus his self into conformity with his authentic being as potentially to be.[156]

This led Bultmann to the conclusion, unlike the conclusions of the nineteenth century ethicists, that Jesus was no Greek thinker with unchangeable standards and final and absolute forms.

> This really means that Jesus teaches no ethics at all in the sense of an intelligible theory valid for all men concerning what should be done and left undone. . . . A man cannot control beforehand the possibilities upon which he must act; he cannot in the moment of decision fall back upon principles, upon a general ethical theory which can relieve him of responsibility for the decision; rather, every moment of decision is essentially new. For man does not meet the crisis of decision armed with a definite standard; he stands on no firm base, but rather alone in empty space. This is what shows the requirement of the good to be actually the demand of God— not the demand of something divine in man, but the demand of God who is beyond man.[157]

For Bultmann as he explained in his 1957 Gifford Lectures, *History and Eschatology,* every moment is an eschatological moment. By this he means that the questions and answers of the past encounter one in the present to produce a responsible choice which results in the newness of the future. Thus he believed that the New Testament helped man to understand and thus transform his existence by liberating him from his bondage to the past and therefore helping him to be open to the future. But this existentialist approach which sees the meaning of the New Testament as basically centered on the individual and the authenticity of his existence has been questioned by recent scholars such as those who see community as a basic category. Jesus himself pre-supposes a community, and in this community there can be found a continuity with the activity and teaching of Jesus. There is more to the New Testament than its existential relevance for today. The legitimate aim of history to reconstruct the past cannot be reduced to providing a key to man's self-understanding.

To Bultmann we owe the clear insight which he pushed too far, namely, that the thought world, language forms and cosmology of the early Church are quite different from our own. Whatever subject one considers—from science to morality, astronomy, medicine, psychology, demonology, genetics—our assumptions in particular are quite different. It was according to him a world mythology in which transcendental gods, angels, and devils are frequently involved, unlike our own scientific world of medicine and electricity.[158] In a well-known sentence Bultmann insisted:

> We can no longer look for the return of the Son of Man on the clouds of heaven or hope that the faithful will meet him in the air.[159]

He does not so much deny the supernatural like the liberals as try to reinterpret. The task is one of hermeneutics, to transfer the key message and scandal of the risen Lord of the New Testament into a philosophy modern man can understand (1 Cor 1:18ff). Very few today would agree with his view that modern man has no myths, today especially when the overconfidence in science of previous generations is so seriously shaken.[160] Not only anthropologists but also psychologists and literary critics in recent times have become convinced of the importance and indeed the necessity of myth as a positive method of both forming and interpreting human experience. The popularity of writers like Tolkien, of books like *Watership Down,* and of films like "The Exorcist" and "Star Wars," not to mention astrology, shows the modern fascination with myth.

For Bultmann, by faith modern man who is in a fallen state and a slave to anxiety can gain true liberty and live in the spirit. Faith means the renouncement of our search for security by means of our own strength and the acceptance of God's judgment in Jesus Christ. Bultmann, it is evident, can only be understood against the pessimism about scientific progress and technological development which arose as a result of the First World War. He was influenced by the existentialists who were opposed to the abstract systems of the past. They did not consider this kind of rational thinking to be sensitive to or begin from man's confused existence and his feelings of isolation, meaninglessness and even despair in his broken world. Thus the founder of existentialism, Sören Kierkegaard (1813–1855), considered Hegel's system as comical since it did not relate to man as a person, to his concrete paradoxical "either/or" decisions and to his individual consciousness.

Bultmann's understanding of "faith alone" and his historical skepticism led to his famous statement:

> Faith, being personal decision, cannot be dependent upon a historian's labors.[161]

This statement was in answer to the question "Was Jesus the Messiah?" to which according to Bultmann only an historian could provide an answer, whereas faith meant a personal decision and was to be distinguished from historical judgment. He did accept with such as Kähler that little could be known with historical certainty about Jesus, but this was not of vital importance to Bultmann. In fact, the quest for the historical Jesus was irrelevant. It was not the historical Jesus but the Christ of faith of the Christian preaching who was of vital interest to a Christian and who must be believed in with total conviction, whereas a historian's judgment and position is always qualified. Again today we see that Bultmann's dilemma, history or faith is too clear-cut, too abstract and even a denial of the key principle of the incarnation. He sees faith as independent of historical facts. Yet his "faith" exegesis is an interesting alternative to the more objective, impersonal exegesis of many scholars.

Bultmann, to his credit, began with a careful analysis of the gospel text, and by trying to determine the laws of its evolution he thought that he could discover its primitive form and its origins. These he saw especially in the "debates" within the communities due to apologetic, polemical and dogmatic needs. He divided early Christianity into two main phases, Palestinian and Hellenistic. This original process he thought went on mainly in Palestine where Aramaic or Hebrew was the primary language. The apophthegms come from the Palestinian church as it tried to define itself in opposition to Judaism. But the miracle stories and legends originated in Hellenistic areas. In fact since the gospels are all written in the Greek language they can be seen as products of the Hellenistic church. In brief, he sees Mark's purpose as

> the union of the Hellenistic kergyma about Christ whose essential content is the Christ myth as we know it from Paul (particularly Phil 2:6ff; Rom 3:24) with the tradition of the story about Jesus.[162]

He carefully noted how Matthew and Luke had modified and interpreted Mark and came to the conclusion that it was Mark who had strung together the "pearls" of the oral tradition to form a life of Jesus. This in turn led to his famous radical statement:

> I do indeed think that we can now know almost nothing concerning the life and personality of Jesus, since the early Christian sources show no interest in either, are moreover fragmentary and legendary, and other sources about Jesus do not exist.[163]

In a later work, *The Historical Jesus and the Kerygmatic Christ,*[164] Bultmann gives the following summary:

> Hence with a bit of caution we can say the following concerning Jesus' activity; characteristic for him are exorcisms, the breach of the Sabbath commandment, the abandonment of ritual purifications, polemic against Jewish legalism, fellowship with outcasts such as publicans and harlots, sympathy for women and children; it can also be seen that Jesus was not an ascetic like John the Baptist, but gladly ate and drank a glass of wine. Perhaps we may add that he called the disciples and assembled about himself a small company of followers—men and women.

However, in the same work *Jesus and the Word,* a few pages later Bultmann does remark:

> We know enough of his message to make for ourselves a consistent picture (p 12).

Bultmann sees the gospels as theological documents not concerned with "objective historicity" and giving no account of Jesus' personality or inward development. He would deny the authenticity of Mark 9:18 where Jesus bluntly expresses an emotional reaction to this faithless generation. Modern redaction studies can be said to have developed Bultmann's view of Mark as a theologian writing a gospel rather than a history. Jesus' existence is of course pre-supposed by the kerygma, and Bultmann himself gives a certain outline to Jesus' Galilean career, but he denies that this information has any valid theological value. According to Bultmann's phrase the message of Jesus is a "pre-supposition of the theology of the New Testament" but not a part of that theology. In fact it is conceivable for Bultmann that, as Martin puts it, Jesus

> died in utter bewilderment and abject despair, a frustrated and rejected prophet of God.[165]

Bultmann sought to place Jesus the Jew squarely against the background of Palestinian Judaism and to show how he was both like and yet different from both the eschatological and rabbinic traditions of Judaism. Like Bousset, Bultmann distinguished two kinds of Palestinian eschatological thought. There was the nationalistic and political type with its messianic expectation of the Son of David. Even though Jesus concentrated on the Jewish people he rejected this kind of eschatology and taught that the Jew as Jew had no special claim before God (Lk 10:29–37; 13:28f). Jesus accepted their second kind of eschatology, the apocalyptic type with its hope in the Son of Man. Yet his was a "reduced eschatology" which refused to describe the details of the end and warned against calculation and the watching for signs (Lk 17:20–24).

Jesus also was related to the rabbinical movement, yet different, for the rabbis did not associate with women, children, tax collectors, and prostitutes. His interpretation of the law was different (Mk 7:15). Jesus was no elitist, nor was he an ascetic like the Baptist (Mt 11:19). Jesus in brief was an eschatological prophet challenging his audience to make what Kierkgaard called an "either/or" decision before it was too late, since it was the last hour, to count the cost of following Jesus and thus make one's ultimate decision for or against the kingdom. The God of Jesus was paradoxical. On the one hand he was transcendent and remote, the "wholly other" of Bultmann's colleague, Rudolf Otto. On the other hand he was near, intimate and imminent, the loving Father. In Bultmann's typical combination of opposites, Jesus' kingdom was miraculous and coming from behind, yet it was "at hand," imminent, a future event that had an important influence on the present. The kingdom was already present in Jesus' exorcisms, was anticipated in Jesus' meals with his disciples (Lk 22:15–18), was giving hope to the poor, the hungry, the weeping (Lk 6:20f), and would reach a tremendous climax when the Son of Man would come with the clouds of heaven and resurrection and judgment would follow.

In his analysis of the narrative material, the stories about Jesus, Bultmann is satisfied with three groups (miracle stories, anecdotes and legends which are edifying and unhistorical pericopes, and the passion narrative). But his main interest is with the words of Jesus which, in contrast to Dibelius who has classified them generally as parenesis (exhortations), he distinguishes in six groups: proverbs, prophetic and apocalyptic sayings, community rules, "I-words" or personal proclamations, parables, and apophthegms which Dibelius called paradigms.

Bultmann too quickly jumped from literary to historical criticism and attributed creativity and invention too easily to the early Church, e.g., the word of Jesus used to justify fasting in Mark's church (Mk 2:20), the controversy over the sabbath (Mk 2:27), such actions of Jesus as the forgiveness of sins (2:10) and the institution of the Eucharist (14:22–25). Thus in fact we have no clear idea how Jesus anticipated his death, since statements like Mark 10:45 are prophecies after the event read back into Jesus' life.

Mark in general he sees as more mythical than Matthew or Luke. As Robinson explains his view:

> In distinction from Matthew's Jewish pattern of prophecy and fulfillment, Mark sees Jesus' life in the Hellenistic pattern of an "epiphany of the Son of God" so that one could speak of the history of Jesus only in quotation marks. Emphasizing miraculous events like the baptism and transfiguration, Mark sees in Jesus "the miraculous manifestation of divine dealing in the cloak of earthly occurrence." Yet Mark, by the very fact of giving his presentation "the form of an historical presentation," a "life of Jesus," reflects the early awareness that their revelation comes not in the pictures of ecstatic visionaries, not by some unconfirmable myth but "by an historical figure, Jesus."[166]

The influence of Dibelius is evident here, as also in such a statement denying a real Markan authorship as:

> Mark is not sufficiently master of his material to venture on a systematic construction himself.[167]

Bultmann, it should be noted, anticipated the view of certain recent scholars such as T. J. Weeden (1971) that Mark used the Twelve in his gospel as an indirect target for the critical portrayal of his contemporary Jewish Christians.[168]

1924 (a)

B. H. Streeter, in *The Four Gospels,* accepted the common assumptions of the two-source theory, namely priority of Mark and the existence of Q, and developed the Four Document Hypothesis which has been widely accepted, although modern scholars influenced by form-criticism speak of sources or cycles of oral tradition and not documents. He separated material peculiar to Matthew (M) and Luke (L) and assigned to each of the four a Church community as its place of origin of both the particular gospel and tradition, and also its textual tradition. He theorized that if Rome had a Jesus tradition which Mark wrote c. 65–70, it was also probable that the other important centers of Christianity in the first century also had their traditions, e.g., Antioch (Q c. A.D. 50), Caesarea (L c. 60), Jerusalem (M c. 65)—Luke was completed c. 80 and Matthew c. 85. Streeter's conclusion on the problem of gospel authorship was:

> The burden of proof is on those who would assert the traditional authorship of Matthew and John and on those who would deny it in the case of Mark and Luke.[169]

Streeter noticed the fact that Mark and Q must have overlapped at least in such pericopes as those dealing with John the Baptist, the baptism, the temptation, the Beelzebub controversy, the parable of the mustard seed, and the mission of the disciples. His deduction was that Mark must have both known and used Q.

An interesting example of Streeter's study is the relation between John and Mark. He selected six examples where there are remarkable verbal agreements between them—Mk 2:11f (Jn 5:8f); Mk 6:37 (Jn 6:7); Mk 14:3, 5 (Jn 12: 3, 5); Mk 14:42 (Jn 14:31); Mk 14:54 (Jn 18:18); Mk 15:9 (Jn 18:39). He concluded that the synoptic parallels to John's teaching material are derived more often from Mark than from Matthew or Luke and that the facts "amount to little short of a demonstration that John knew the Gospel of Mark and knew it well" (p 400). More recent theories suggest that during the development of John's tradition there may have been minor cross-influence with the synoptic tradition.

1924 (b)

C. H. Turner, in his commentary on Mark and especially in a series of articles on *Marcan Usage* (J.T.S. 25–29), although developing the previous work of John Hawkins,[170] made a notable and detailed study of the linguistic features of Mark, drawing attention to his use of "immediately" (forty-two times), the impersonal verb, the historic present (one hundred and fifty-one times), the use of parentheses (2:15f; 6:14f; 7:18f, 25f; 13:10, 14; 14:36) and anacoluthon (3:16f; 4:31f; 5:23; 6:8f; 11:32; 12:19, 38–40; 14:49), his free use of diminutives (compare "a little boat" in 3:9 with "a boat" in 4:1; see also 3:9; 5:23, 39, 41; 6:9; 7:25, 27f; 8:7. He concluded that Mark's use of "immediately" was due to his intention to make his narrative lively. Mark's repeated "they" was based on the "we" and "us" of Peter's reminiscences, an autobiographical trait as he described it (1:21; 11:17; 14:32). Turner, who emphasized the unique historical importance of Mark, saw Mark as

> the unique record, objectively stated, of the experience of an eyewitness, an intimate companion of Jesus throughout his ministry.

While Matthew and Luke wrote lives of Christ, Mark records the experience of an eyewitness and companion. Turner was convinced of the accuracy of Papias' testimony. Many other scholars have built on Turner's studies.[171]

Turner proposed two emendations to Mark's text which are worth recalling. In 10:32 as Jesus walks ahead, for "they were amazed" Turner believed against all the manuscripts that the text should read "he was amazed." Again in 15:35f, against all the Greek Mss which read "Behold, he is calling Elijah . . ." he thinks that with one second century Old Latin manuscript and with the change of a single letter the text should read Helion, the sun. How would the Roman soldiers know about Elijah? Rather as the sun's light failed at the crucifixion it was more natural that they would think he was calling on the sun which was worshiped as a god by many soldiers.

It is interesting today to read Turner's confident answer to the questions, "Who was the author of the Gospel?" and "Where and when was it written?"

> To each of these questions we are fortunate to be able to give a definite and decisive answer. It is not a matter of serious debate that the author was Mark, the disciple of Peter, and that he wrote his Gospel in Rome somewhere about the year A.D. 65.

For Turner, Mark "historically is the most important book ever written."

1925 (a)

A. E. J. Rawlinson, in *The Gospel According to St. Mark,* asserted:

> The New Testament, considered broadly, is the literature of a missionary movement [and always] behind the literature stands the preaching (p 11).

Thus the gospels are not neutral books, since record and revelation cannot be separated.

> At no stage or stratum of the Christian tradition about Jesus can the element of purely historical reminiscence be distinguished and separated from the accompanying element of doctrinal interpretation (p 112).

The gospels reflect the historic impression which Jesus made on those who accepted him in faith and make their appeal from faith to faith.

Rawlinson quotes Goguel's three motives for the writing of a gospel: the theological motive as the Church sought the significance of the incarnation in the divine drama of redemption, the human motive as no Christian could fail to want to know more about what Jesus was like in the days of the flesh, and the moral motive in which what Jesus had said and done would have been essential guides for the Church and Christian behavior.[172]

Rawlinson gave a precise dating to Mark between 65–67 because the Jewish war does not appear to have begun and the references in chapter 13 are quite vague and imprecise. Compare the expectations of the personal antichrist (13:14) with Luke 21:20. Also the persecution of the Church, which has already taken place, is interpreted as being only the beginning of the "travail pangs" and the end is not yet (13:8). Mark then, written for the church in Rome soon after Nero's persecution, is not surprisingly "full of the echoes of martyrdom." It is the story of Jesus' progress toward Calvary and would have direct personal relevance for the Roman Christians who saw themselves as called to take up the cross quite literally.

Rawlinson explained the negative comments on Peter in Mark as due to the fact that Peter's memory as a martyr was so revered that no remarks on his earthly behavior could tarnish his name. He divided Mark into three parts—1:1—8:26; 8:27—12:44; 13:1—16:8. He suggested that at different points Mark depended on a Roman edition of Q (1:2, 12f; 3:22–30; 4:21–25; 6:7–13; 8:15, 34—9:1; 9:33–37, a catena of sayings). He thought that in chapter 4 Mark was drawing on an existing collection of parables. He carefully examined the evidence for the ending of Mark and concluded that the original author never completed his work for reasons which are not clear.

His comment on Mark's style is a good summary of what many would accept:

> The writing all through is vulgar (i.e., popular, uncultured), collo-
> quial, unpolished, and is characterized by a singular monotony of
> style. There are hardly any connecting particles (de rigueur in lit-
> erary Greek): the sentence and paragraphs follow one another in
> rapid succession, linked in the majority of cases by a simple "and"
> or by the curiously frequent "and immediately." Stereotyped
> phrases and ideas recur constantly. There is a tendency to redun-
> dancy of expression (e.g., 1:32, "at even, when the sun did set").
> There is a frequent use of parentheses, a tendency to accumulate
> particles. The Greek of Mark is essentially a non-literary Greek,
> full of roughness and semitisms—the kind of Greek which might
> be spoken by the poor classes at Rome (pp xxxif).

1925 (b)

In a detailed series of synoptic studies from 1925–1931 W. Buss-
man argued that Mark was compiled in three stages, G, B and E, and
Q was composed of two sources, R and T. With many other scholars
he also shared the theory that Matthew used an edition of Mark
shorter than our existing Mark. The existence of an earlier Mark
(Urmarkus) can be traced back to the theory of Schleiermacher
(1832), Credner (1836), Holtzmann (1863), Weiss (1903), and
Wendling (1905) but in modern times has little support, so that V.
Taylor in 1950 could pronounce: "Requiescat Urmarkus."[173]

1925 (c)

C. F. Burney, in *The Poetry of Our Lord* (Oxford), developed
the view of E. Norden (*Agnostos Theos,* Leipzig, 1913) that parallelism was the most certain semitism found in the New Testament. Burney discovered that the teaching of Jesus in all the sources was
characterized by one kind in particular, antithetic parallelism which
he found over one hundred times in the synoptics and thirty times in
Mark (e.g., 2:19, 22, 27; 3:28f, 33f; 4:4, 7f, 21, 25, 31f; 6:10f; 7:6, 8,
10, 11f, 15; 8:12, 35; 10:18, 27, 31, 42ff; 11:17; 12:44; 13:11, 20, 31;
14:7, 38, 58). He also noted that there are places in Mark where a
characteristically clear-cut form of antithesis in Jesus' sayings has to
some extent been lost. He concludes that the other synoptics could
not have been drawing upon Mark in these passages but that both
were drawing upon a common source, i.e., Q.

1926

P. L. Couchoud in a French article translated into English in the *Crozer Quarterly* (January 1928) asked, as his title indicated, "Was the Gospel of Mark Written in Latin?" He concluded that Mark was originally written in Latin and that codex k is a badly done fragment of the lost original. However, it seems that all the Latin words which are merely transliterated into Greek in Mark belonged to the current language of the Greek-speaking regions of the day due to contact with the Roman administration, army, coins and techniques. They were not confined to Rome. Further they seem to have been already in Mark's tradition before its final writing. Underlying Latin words and expressions are found in 3:6; 4:21; 5:9, 15; 6:27, 37; 7:4; 12:14, 42; 14:65; 15:15, 19, 39, 44f.

1927

Henry J. Cadbury, in *The Making of Luke-Acts,* a classic among Lucan studies, has a useful chapter on Mark which discusses how familiarity often obscures the nature of Mark while much is taken for granted both from ancient tradition and current usage which is not well founded. Mark's individuality is often blurred by confusion with its parallels in the other synoptics.

Cadbury sees Mark as beginning with the ministry of the Baptist, while the preceding caption, *The Beginning of the Gospel of Jesus Christ (Son of God),* is a headline of "incipit" rather than part of the text. He finds it difficult to understand how Mark's record which is one of conflict and martyrdom, of warning and rejection, could have achieved the name "good news" because there is a seriousness about Jesus' words and cures which makes Mark "an ominous cryptogram" and no idyll.

Apart from the last hours of Jesus' life, the remainder is

> without any reference to day or season or temporal relation of events, except for controversial scenes on the sabbath and for references to morning (twice) or evening (five times) which are usually implicit in the narrative. Once we read "after six days"; once "on the morrow" . . . there are three references to Capernaum.[174]

Thus the material in Mark evidently existed once in detached units with each scene complete in itself undatable by its contents and normally without allusion to place. Mark has a few editorial phrases—

"for they were fishermen", "for it was not the season of figs"—and at more length on the ritual washings of "the Pharisees and all the Jews." Aramaic words are defined in Greek (3:17; 5:41; 7:11, 34; 15:22, 35). The same phrase "ho estin" (i.e., "which is") is used thrice to explain Greek words, yet strangely the explanatory word is really less Hellenic (12:42: 15:16, 42). The Latin words *census, centurio, denarius, legio,* etc., would have been adopted outside Italy in any of the Greek-speaking provinces of the Roman Empire. Mark's other Latin words, *modius, praetorium, quodrans, sextarius, speculator* and perhaps *flagellum,* do not localize Mark in Italy, as they are found widely distributed even in Aramaic and late Hebrew sources.

Cadbury criticizes as contrary to the evidence and to early Christian traditions the common view that:

> Mark was interested in the deeds, not the words of Jesus, because his gospel has less teaching material than has Matthew, Luke, or John, and we are invited to associate him with Paul, whose emphasis on the cosmic meaning of Jesus' career, and especially on his death and resurrection, and whose silence about Jesus' teaching are counted as significant.[175]

The problem is that we do not know the extent or character of Mark's sources since his material is rather miscellaneous and too incomplete. Therefore attempts to discover in Mark subtle threads of development are not probable whether in Jesus' self-consciousness or in his method of work and change of plan, the opposition against him or the recognition of his messiahship. Mark does not plainly reveal his special interests and seems more simple and naive than his predecessors who shaped his material.

For Cadbury, Mark's picture of Jesus was of a teacher. He had access to parables and detached sayings and could quote Jesus at length on controversial or apocalyptic topics. In fact one-third of Mark is sayings rather than narrative. The large space given to the miracles is due to their evidential value. The account of Jesus' death, if it is dissociated from the Jerusalem material,

> with much of which it has in Mark no hint of causal or chronological association, is not so extended as to suggest that Mark made it the central act of a redemptive drama.[176]

Yet Cadbury quotes with approval the judgment of the historian of the early Church, Edward Meyer, that Mark's passion narrative is one of the greatest creations of all prose literature and that it is all the more so because of its quiet objectivity.

On the relationship between the second gospel and Peter, Cadbury suggests that there was a development in the early tradition from Clement of Alexandria who suggested that it was without Peter's sanction, to Peter's approval (Eusebius), to his direct dictation (Jerome).

1930

A. T. Cadoux wrote *The Parables of Jesus* (1930), *The Sources of the Second Gospel* (1935), and *The Theology of Jesus* (1940). He theorized that Mark was a compilation of three previous gospels, first a Palestinian Aramaic gospel A, c. A.D. 40, perhaps written under Peter's authority, then a Gentile gospel C, c. A.D. 50 written for Paul's work among the Gentiles, and, third, a diaspora gospel written in Alexandria by Mark c. A.D. 67. This hypothesis is intended to explain the many inconsequences, discrepancies and repetitions in Mark, e.g., the three descriptions of Judas (14:10, 20, 43), the names of the women at the tomb (15:40, 47), the use of "Joses" in 15:40, 47 and "Joseph" in 15:43, 45, the three versions of opinions about Jesus in 6:14, 16 and 7:28, the two feeding stories in 6:35–44, and the three prophecies of the passion (8:31; 9:31; 10:33f).

Cadoux, followed by C. H. Dodd (1935) and J. Jeremias (1974), can be said to have introduced a new phase in gospel parable criticism, concentrating particularly on the time of Jesus, seeking to recover the particular sociological situation in his ministry and the parables as Jesus narrated them. Cadoux's main contention is that the parables of Jesus of whose occasion we are fairly sure were spoken in attack or defense in the context of Jesus' relationship to the Jews. The parable is a weapon of controversy, not shaped like a poem in undisturbed concentration but improvised in conflict to meet an unexpected situation. Cadoux questioned whether Jesus ever interpreted his parables. It seems that the Church, finding the parables unintelligible added on interpretations, some of which came to be attributed to Jesus.

Dodd and Jeremias, unlike Cadoux, would stress the eschatological dimension. All three agree with A. Jülicher, who inaugurated the modern period of parable interpretation, in rejecting the allegorical interpretation as secondary. They agree with the form-critics that the parables underwent change during the period of oral tradition.

Their basic principle is that when the necessary surgery has been performed on the parables as we find them in the gospels, we will find that they have a challenging point related to the basic message of Jesus which can be reconstructed from the rest of the gospel material. Jeremias claims to have identified ten laws of transformation which help in the recovery of the original meaning of Jesus' parables. The result he finds is that a few simple essential ideas stand out which Jesus was never tired of expressing in constantly changing images. Therefore in turn he suggests that ten groups of parables emerge which offer a comprehensive conception of Jesus' message: Now Is the Day of Salvation, God's Mercy for Sinners, The Great Assurance, In Sight of Disaster, It May Be Too Late, The Challenge of the Hour, Realized Discipleship, The Via Dolorosa and Exaltation of the Son of Man, The Consummation, Parabolic Actions.

An interesting criticism of Jeremias' thesis that originally there was a homogenous pool of simple parables, all ultimately coming from Jesus himself and appearing at random throughout the synoptics, comes from M. D. Goulder in a study, *Characteristics of the Parables in the Several Gospels.*[177] While Jeremias examined the process of the transmission of the parables, Goulder raises the important question of the creativity of the evangelist. He rightly challenges the popular hypothesis that the simplest form of a parable is the most original and the correlative that the most original is the simplest. Goulder concludes that it was improbable that Jesus used all the kinds of parables found in the gospels but that

> Jesus taught the Marcan parables with their village milieu and their eschatological message and also their highish allegory content.

The parables of Matthew and Luke whom he calls midrashists are at least as much by Matthew and Luke as the Johannine parables are by John. However, Goulder, as he admits, fails to examine Mark's own special interests and to question his assumption that Mark reflects Jesus' original use of parables.

Goulder investigated the synoptic parables under differing aspects:

1. In content Mark follows the Old Testament pattern, including mainly nature parables, whereas Matthew's adaptations and new parables are concerned with people—nobles, slaves, farmers and workmen, fathers and sons. Luke prefers people in the towns, builders, robbers, beggars.

2. In scale Mark's world is the village, perhaps Galilean; Matthew's is the world of the grandiose; Luke brings matters back to reality.

3. As to allegory, Goulder sees Mark as midway between Matthew's considerable allegorizations and Luke's conscious deallegorization.

4. As to response, Mark and Matthew put God and his kingdom before men, whereas Luke emphasizes ethical concerns, faithful endurance, care for the poor, and prayer.

In the late 1960's and 1970's a number of scholars would criticize Dodd and Jeremias as too one-tracked in their concentration on the original setting and purpose of the parables while ignoring their existential and literary dimensions, thus curiously returning to some extent to the older allegorical approach. These exponents of the new hermeneutic such as Ernst Fuchs saw in the parables both an implicit Christology and an authentic core of Jesus' historical teaching which formed a continuity with the Christ of faith. They also studied the existential implications of the metaphorical language of the parables, seeing them as language events relevant to man's present situation, confronting him with the necessity of decision and inviting him to participate, to come to authentic existence.[178a]

1931

E. C. Hoskyns, the translator of Barth's *Romans,* makes a blunt attack on the liberal presentation of Jesus "which he saw dominating the whole religious education" in the English schools with his *The Riddle of the New Testament* which he wrote together with his most distinguished student, F. N. Davey. This very influential book which was translated into eighteen languages was chosen by W. G. Kümmel for the end of his history of the *Investigation of the Problems of the New Testament* since the Enlightenment. Kümmel quoted the judgment of the German version that it

> describes the situation of New Testament research after a century
> of historical and critical study in a more complete and impressive
> fashion than any other book.

Hoskyns criticized the liberals who saw Paul as the real creator of Christianity, the one who transformed the simple Jesus of Nazareth story into a complicated system of redemption and salvation. They excluded the supernatural and the divine from Jesus, gave a rational presentation of his miracles and saw him as an admirable teacher and example. Noting the common order of the events of Jesus' life in the synoptics, e.g., a comparison of Mk 10:13–34, Mt. 19: 13–20 and Lk 18:15–34, he concluded:

> such identity of order cries out for some explanation other than that three evangelists wrote three independent narratives (p 76).

Hoskyns examined those points where Matthew and Luke differ from Mark and concluded:

> In the whole process of editing they nowhere heighten Mark's tremendous conception of Jesus. No deifying of a prophet or of a mere preacher of righteousness can be detected. They do not introduce Hellenistic superstition or submerge in the light of later Christian faith the lineaments of Mark's picture of Jesus. They attempt to simplify Mark. He is more difficult to understand than they are . . . (p 104).

Hoskyns saw like the form-critics that the "riddle," the key problem of the New Testament, was the question of the relationship between the early Church and the historical Jesus. The New Testament everywhere, and not just in the synoptics, puts the same question: "What manner of man is this?" It demands of the historian what he cannot give as an historian, a theological answer, just as "the unbeliever is faced by the problem of faith," to quote the concluding words.

But Hoskyns had more confidence than they in the ability of scientific criticism to penetrate to the character of the historical man Jesus which was the real riddle. Jesus saw his life and death as the fulfillment of the Old Testament messianic promise and all the efforts of the New Testament writers geared toward making this fact more intelligible. However, his key dictum that "the evangelists write as historians and not as theologians" (p 147) would be attacked by the later redaction-critics in particular. Hoskyns insisted that neither Matthew, Mark nor Luke was interpreting a mere series of facts or imposing a Christology on an undefined human personality, but that they received their interpretation from their various sources. They are dealing with an historical figure fully conscious of his task to be completed,

> to work out in a single human life complete obedience to the will of God—to the uttermost, that is, to death (p 249f).

Their purpose was to make more intelligible the historical character of Jesus, the ground of their faith, the real riddle of the New Testament.

By a comparison of Mark with the other three blocks of material, that which is common to Matthew and Luke and that which each alone used, Hoskyns thought that it was possible to discover if there was a characteristically Marcan Christology. Thus a main difference lies in the emphatic description in both Matthew and Luke of Jesus as a teacher. In Mark the word "gospel" is rather "obscure" because to Mark Jesus both announces and is himself the good news. He concludes that the remarkable "Son of Man" Christology is not a creation of Mark or the result of his manipulation of the tradition. Rather, all the sources of tradition emphasize two comings, the first in humiliation which Mark emphasized, and the second in glory, both held together by Jesus' application of the title "Son of Man" to himself, a title found in Mark fourteen times.

Hoskyns raised the question of Mark's title and the importance of a Son of God theology for Mark. He saw that the manuscript evidence for the inclusion of Son of God in the title was evenly divided and that the problem must be decided by internal evidence. His answer was that the climax of the gospel is the centurion's verdict, "Truly this man was the Son of God," and that this title therefore was to be included in Mark's opening verse.

> The ultimate revelation of the power of God took place in the complete humiliation of Jesus.

This title is however used guardedly by Mark who stressed that

> a true understanding of his sonship can be reached only through recognition of his humiliation, completed in the crucifixion, and vindicated by his raising from the dead. And it is in this context of humiliation that the analogy of Father and Son is used, in the parable of the wicked husbandmen and in the saying "of that day and that hour knoweth no man . . ." (13:32).

Hoskyns too, it should be noted, reacted against the current enthusiasm based on the discovery of papyri, showing that the New Testament writers wrote in the popular secular Greek of the time. He insisted that it was Semitic Greek.

> There is a strange and awkward element in the langauge which not only affects the meanings of words, not only disturbs the

grammar and syntax, but lurks everywhere in a maze of literary allusions which no ordinary Greek man or woman could conceivably have understood or even detected. The truth is that behind these writings there lies an intractable Hebraic, Aramaic, Palestinian material. . . .No single New Testament author for one moment imagines that he can interpret his material apart from the knowledge of the Jewish sacred Scriptures. The tension between the Jewish heritage and the Greek world vitally affects the language of the New Testament (pp 19f).

1932

C. H. Dodd, author of *The Framework of the Gospel Narrative* [178b] and *The Apostolic Preaching and Its Development* (1936), was concerned with the current critical atomization of the New Testament and was searching for a synthesis. He insisted:[179]

The Church not only remembered and reported facts. It lived them. If we have understood this, we are near to the secret of the gospels.

He found the underlying unity of the New Testament in the early apostolic kerygma which for him was the virtual equivalent of gospel. He

tried to show that we can trace in the Gospel according to Mark a connecting thread running through much of the narrative, which has some similarity to the brief summary of the story of Jesus in Acts 10 and 13.[180]

Mark conceived himself as rendering in his gospel the apostolic preaching. Dodd agrees with Dibelius that no single outline was universal but that some kind of outline formed a regular part of the kerygma everywhere, e.g., Acts 10:37–41 gives the scheme: preaching of John, baptism of Jesus, beginning of the ministry in Galilee, healing and exorcism, change of scene to Jerusalem, crucifixion and resurrection; Acts 13:23–31 gives a fuller account of the preaching of John at the beginning and of the resurrection at the close. It gives a slighter record of the ministry but establishes a journey in company with disciples from Galilee to Jerusalem, ending with the death of Jesus.

Dodd sees the earliest gospel as pre-eminently a gospel of the passion. Not only does the passion occupy a disproportionate part of the whole (one-fifth), but more than half of the gospel, especially from the middle of chapter 8, is dominated by the shadow of the cross. This corresponds to the emphasis of the apostolic preaching in Acts, Paul and Hebrews. Mark is then a commentary on the kerygma, and as in Acts 10 the story of the passion is prefaced (ch 1—8) by an account of Jesus' ministry in Galilee where he went about doing good and healing those oppressed by the devil. However, Dodd insists that if particular pericopes in Mark are dominated by the passion theme, it is not because of Mark's arbitrary selection and interpretation of them. Rather they originally belonged to that particular phase of Jesus' ministry when Jesus summoned his followers to go to Jerusalem with the prospect of suffering and death.

Thus Mark took over three kinds of material from tradition:[181]

1. Isolated independent pericopae, handed down without any connection.

2. Larger complexes, which again may be of various kinds: genuinely continuous narratives; pericopae strung upon an itinerary; pericopae connected by unity of theme.

3. An outline of the whole ministry, designed perhaps as an introduction to the passion story, but serving also as a background of reference for separate stories; fragments of this survive in the framework of the gospel.

In brief, for Dodd,

> in broad outlines the Marcan order does represent a genuine succession of events, within which movement and development can be traced.[182]

In *The Founder of Christianity* (1970), Dodd summarizes as follows his view of Mark's gospel in his reflection on the documents of the New Testament (p 24):

> Our natural starting point will be the Gospel according to Mark, which provides the main basis of the narrative in Matthew and Luke. It is probably to be dated between A.D. 65 and 70, or thereabouts—just about the time when the first generation of Christians was dying off, but when many who remembered the events must still have been alive. Whether Mark was one of these we cannot say; he may have been, but in any case there is little in his book to suggest that he had been a witness of the events he records. An examination of his work suggests that he was less of an author and more of a compiler than the others. That is to say, he appears to have reproduced what came down to him with com-

paratively little attempt to write it up in his own way, unlike
Luke, who composes with an eye to literary effect and with an effort to give some semblance of chronological continuity, and unlike Matthew, who presents his material with a sure pedagogical
touch. In Mark, within a very broad general scheme, there is a
certain freedom and looseness of arrangement, and in his rather
rough and informal style we seem often to overhear the tones of
the living voice telling a story. We are probably near to the "original eyewitnesses and servants of the gospel" to whom Luke refers.
By "servants of the gospel" he means Christian missionaries who
spread the faith in the earliest days. In defining the contents of his
book as "The Gospel of Jesus Christ" rather than "Memoirs of
Jesus" or the like, Mark has made it clear that he conceives himself as continuing, through the medium of writing, the same work
which the missionaries were doing through the living voice. Elsewhere in the New Testament the term "gospel" always means the
Christian message as preached; its now familiar use, as meaning a
book about Jesus, developed later, and Mark was very likely responsible, indirectly, for this development.

1933

F. C. Grant in such books as *The Growth of the Gospels* (1933),
The Earliest Gospel (1943), and his commentary on Mark in *The Interpreter's Bible* (1951) has some interesting observations, although
his personal estimate was that Luke of all the gospels brings us closer
to the Jesus of history. Grant, like the form-critics, saw the gospel
tradition as a social possession, the common property of a witnessing
and worshiping community and not limited to the recollection of a
few individuals. The significance of this is that the community acted
as a safeguard and a guarantee of the basic trustworthiness of the tradition against the fabrication of individuals who might be tempted to
turn a private fallible recollection or even esoteric experience into a
universal truth. The memories of an individual or a few might be
mistaken. But a community even if anonymous is more trustworthy.

Grant noted three practical subsidiary aims of Mark. The first
was to show that the leadership of the Church was put by Jesus'
choice into the hands of the Twelve (3:13–19). Next there was the
problem of Jesus' relatives (3:32–36), as Eusebius also mentions.
Mark shows that there was in Jesus' intention to be no aristocracy of
leadership based on physical relationship to himself (3:20f, 31–35;
12:35–37). Third, there may have been an exaggeration of the place

of John the Baptist. Mark stresses that John was the great forerunner but nothing more (Acts 19:1–7; Jn 1:8, 15, 19–34).

For Grant the Old Testament was seen by the early Christians not just as the proof but also as "determinative and productive" evidence for describing the events of the life of Jesus, in fact a valid source like an eyewitness, e.g., Ps 22:1; 31:5; 69:21.

1934 (a)

R. H. Lightfoot, in *History and Interpretation in the Gospels,* developed form-criticism to such an extent that he is often called the first redaction critic. He had been taught "to regard Mark as almost exclusively historical" (p 57) but on closer examination he saw that there was no such thing as "pure history" but that history and theology are closely intertwined in the gospels. Mark's main purpose, he saw, was not biographical but theological and that "rightly regarded it may be called the book of the (secret) Messiahship of Jesus," a thesis in which he was clearly influenced by Wrede. The opening verses are 1:1–13, not 1:1–8. These, he saw, reveal Mark's theological purposes. He presents John the Baptist with a Christological aim, in such a way as to show who Jesus is.

He concluded this book with the famous words:

> It seems to me then that the form of the earthly no less than the heavenly Christ is for the most part hidden from us. For all the inestimable value of the gospels, they yield us little more than a whisper of his voice; we trace in them but the outskirts of his ways. Only when we see him hereafter in his fullness shall we know him also as he was on earth. And perhaps the more we ponder the matter, the more clearly shall we understand the reason for it, and therefore shall not wish it otherwise. For probably we are at present as little prepared for the one as for the other.

In fact Lightfoot was alluding to the Book of Job, and his quotation should be completed by the words: "The thunder of his power, who can understand?" (Job 26:14). He was making an essential and all too often forgotten point about the essential mystery of Jesus and his life which on earth man, including scholars, is incapable of penetrating fully.

In a later book, *Locality and Doctrine in the Gospels* (1938), Lightfoot moved his center of interpretation from the messianic secret. He developed the geographical orientation of the German scholar, Ernst Lohmeyer (*Galiläa und Jerusalem*, 1936). In this geographical theology the places and place names in the gospels are seen to have theological significance, e.g., for Mark Galilee is the sphere of redemption, of the divine activity, whereas Judaea is the sphere of hate, misunderstanding, opposition and disaster. Lohmeyer proposed that Mark's gospel was written in Galilee where a Church existed from the beginning, a Church with a different Christology and a different form of celebration, the Eucharist. There were in fact two distinct centers of early Christianity in Galilee and in Jerusalem.[183] Galilee stressed the Son of Man while Jerusalem emphasized the Messiah. Galilee celebrated the breaking of the bread and Jerusalem the memorial meal. For Mark Galilee was the place to which the apocalyptic Son of Man would return before the parousia (e.g., 14:28; 16:7). His proposal, though not proved by any means, highlighted the importance of the place in which a gospel was composed and its influence on the theology of the gospel. The problem with this kind of interpretation which has had a limited success in gospel studies is that there is little direct evidence for it and it lends itself easily to the charge of being subjective.

In his final work on Mark, *The Gospel Message of St. Mark* (1950), Lightfoot concerned himself more with the problem of history in Mark. He made many interesting observations: chapters 4 and 13 are parallel teaching sections, chapter 4 teaching that the kingdom will triumph despite hindrances, while chapter 13 has at least five parallel passages with the passion narrative. Chapter 13 ends with the parable of the absent householder who may return at evening, midnight, cockcrow or dawn. Lightfoot suggests that Mark has used these same watches of the night to punctuate his passion story, showing how in each of these critical moments the householder returned to find one or other of his servants asleep or off guard. Thus Jesus enters Jerusalem "in the evening" (14:17), his betrayal at Gethsemane probably takes place at midnight (14:41), Peter's denial takes place at cockcrow (14:72), and Jesus is brought to Pilate in early morning (15:1). He has already given his account of Jesus' ultimate glory in chapter 13 and therefore he can tell the passion story with stark simplicity and without theological comment. For Lightfoot (p 141):

> The passion is the supreme act of the Messiah, and conversely the Messiahship of Jesus is the explanation of the passion.

Jesus is at prayer at three significant points but always at night. He noted that the healing in 8:22–26 forms a bridge which connects the disciples' blindness in the first part of the gospel with the illumination that came to them in the second part, beginning with the turning point, the revelation at Caesarea Philippi. One of the main aims of Mark was to show that despite the great impression which Jesus made, nevertheless he was free from any effort to arouse public notice and gave no basis for a charge of seditious messianic activity. Lightfoot argued that Mark was written in Rome soon after Nero's persecution of the Church in answer at least partly to the problems of suffering, e.g., Why did the Messiah have to suffer? Why did his disciples have to suffer such horrors?

1934 (b)

J. H. Ropes, in *The Synoptic Gospels,* asserted:

> The form of the gospel of Mark is, to be sure, that of narrative, but the important question is not of its form, but of its purpose; and that is theological (p 10).

Therefore theological considerations just as much as biographical information dictate the position of the various incidents in Mark's gospel—e.g.:

> The series of incidents and sayings in the last part of chapter nine ... are not accidental in their place here, mere survivals of the crude context of an earlier source, nor are they due to a biographical motive. They are deliberately brought in by the Evangelist as part of Jesus' instruction regarding the inseparable connection, inevitable both for leader and for followers, of sufferings with the career and the cause of the Messiah. In this situation the dispute as to who is greatest (v 33f) betrays failure to understand; again, for them to reject any friends however uninstructed and slight in their attachment (38ff) is an arrogance that reveals their inadequate comprehension; what is requisite is sacrifice and self-denial and persistence in it (v 43–49), and that repression of jealousy and ill-feeling (v 50) which alone befits men who are entering on a march toward a cross (pp 23f).

Thus Mark, with his "incomparable touch of reality," is in the form of "a dramatic historical sketch," "a kind of theological pamphlet."

He is discussing the theological problem: Why did Jesus the Messiah die a criminal's death on the cross?

1934 (c)

Rudolf Otto in *The Kingdom of God and the Son of Man* argued that the kingdom of God announced by Jesus was not entirely future but that especially in Jesus' parable teaching (Mk ch 4) it had already begun to break in, e.g., the parable of the four soils and the parable of the seed growing secretly. Otto's view of the reality of religion as consisting in the experience of the "Wholly Other," that mysterious, fascinating and awe-inspiring power outside humanity, would become famous. A similar and even more radical viewpoint of the kingdom is found in the teaching of C. H. Dodd, *The Parables of the Kingdom* (1935), with his "realized eschatology." Jesus' opening proclamation according to Dodd was: "The kingdom of God has come." He thus reduced the future dimension of the kingdom almost to a vanishing point and saw Jesus' ministry as *the* crisis of world history. This position was criticized for ignoring the key importance of the paschal events, and in *The Apostolic Preaching* (1936, pp 46f) and *The Interpretation of the Fourth Gospel* (1953, p 447) he saw that the proclamation of the life, death and resurrection was essential to a proclamation of the kingdom. He agreed that the phrase "realized eschatology" was a "not altogether felicitous term," preferring a phrase from E. Haenchen and J. Jeremias which can be translated "an eschatology which is being realized."

Otto was fascinated by the theme of Jesus and the demonic powers. The kingdom was presently breaking through in Jesus, and its power was involved in an unceasing struggle with the demonic powers bringing rest to the weak and heavy laden. Otto emphasized that there was a key difference between Jesus and the Baptist since about Jesus there was the sense of the "bridegroom."

1936

J. M. C. Crum: *St. Mark's Gospel: Two Stages in Its Making,* Mark I is perhaps an account of the gospel told by a man who grew up in close contact with Peter from A.D. 36–60. Mark II is an amplification of Mark I about A.D. 65 reflecting a later Christology, using the language of the Septuagint and drawing on a document closely related to Q.

1937 (a)

H. J. Chapman in *Matthew, Mark, Luke: A Study in the Order and Interpretation of the Synoptic Gospels* revolted against the two-document hypothesis and proposed a sequence, Mt-Mk-Lk which was proposed by J. L. Hug in 1808. In various forms it has been maintained by B. C. Butler, *The Originality of St. Matthew* (1951), Pierson Parker, *The Gospel before Mark* (1953), and L. Vaganay, *The Synoptic Problem* (1954). Chapman argued that Matthew was not the immediate but the ultimate source of Mark—Matthew could have been used by some early teacher such as Peter as a basis for his oral teaching which Mark in turn committed to writing. Luke in turn used Mark as a source. Butler developed this hypothesis and suggested that the link with Peter accounted for Mark's freshness. Vaganay suggested two sources for the synoptics, Q in Greek and an Aramaic source which later became our Greek Matthew.

Interestingly, the most important new argument for the priority of Mark in recent years has been the success of the redaction critics in expounding and clarifying the theologies of both Matthew and Mark by taking them as commentaries on Mark.

One can say that in recent years despite such efforts there has been a rather general acceptance of the two-source theory as a *working hypothesis* in synoptic studies together with a cautious and critical application in practice. There is also a vociferous minority including the French scholar, Leon-Dufour, who think that this hypothesis should be consigned to an honorable grave.

> None of the three synoptics can be taken as a yardstick by which to judge the historical value of the other two, or of St. John. Matthew in particular should not be regarded as the poor relation; this attitude has been too widespread for too long. Instead, all the details of each gospel should be respected and compared, when a man is trying to discover, without prejudice, which account represents the earliest tradition. All of them have something to offer.[184]

Bernard Orchard has recently provided a welcome presentation of an alternative theory,[185] an updated form of the Griesbach hypothesis. All these studies at least demonstrate that there is less rigidity in current attitudes toward the synoptic problem and serve as a timely warning against what has been described as Western writing-desk logic.

1937 (b)

E. J. Goodspeed in his *Introduction to the New Testament* recalls that R. F. Horton wrote a book entitled *The Cartoons of Saint Mark.* Goodspeed describes Mark as a series of pictures boldly and simply drawn:

> A situation is sketched. Jesus appears in the midst of it, or says something, or does something that relieves it. His words flash through the scene like a bright sword.[186]

1939

H. J. Ebeling in *The Messianic Secret and the Message of the Evangelist Mark* gives a history of the criticism of Wrede's theory. Whereas all scholars agree on the fact of the messianic secret, the emphasis in Mark on keeping secret Jesus' messiahship, they differ in their interpretations. Wrede had seen it as an invitation of the early Church to explain the difference between its cult of the risen Lord and its memories of the past. Jesus had foreseen that it would happen. Dibelius similarly saw it as part of the apologetic of the early Church as it tried to explain the humble nature of Jesus' life. Bultmann related the messianic secret to the evangelist's redaction. Ebeling reduced it to a literary device so that there is no secrecy motif in Mark's gospel.

> What Wrede imagined were efforts to conceal Jesus' person (in the commands to silence, the disciples' misunderstanding and the interpretation of parables to the initiated in 4:11–13) are in fact revelations. Mark's intention is not seen in the injunctions to secrecy but in their disobedience to show that the miracles were not able to remain hidden. He tries to heighten the dramatic effect for the readers so that they can congratulate themselves on being among the chosen who see Jesus as "the secret of God made known in Christ" in contrast to the lack of understanding and appreciation of the disciples.[187]

Thus for Ebeling the reader or hearer of Mark's messianic secret is meant to rejoice in the conclusion that he has been found worthy to perceive the secret of Jesus' messianic dignity. Many other writers have traditionally explained the "messianic secret" as Jesus' pedagogy on the one hand to avoid the Jewish "carnal" interpretation of his messiahship and on the other hand to avoid blinding his contemporaries by too open a revelation of his divinity.[188]

1941

C. J. Cadoux. According to V. Taylor writing in 1950 the most important contribution to the study of Mark since 1940 was C. J. Cadoux, *The Historic Mission of Jesus.* He selects in particular the emphasis on the political factors and

> the recognition of a process of development in the mind of Jesus during his ministry.[189]

1942

W. L. Knox: "The Ending of St. Mark's Gospel" (*Harvard Th. Rev.* 35, pp 13–23). Surveying not only the endings of Mark's major literary units but also the conclusions of ancient narratives both Jewish and Gentile, Knox concluded that Mark did not intend to end his gospel at 16:8. The laws of ancient literature required that an author complete his narrative and leave little or nothing to the imagination. To conclude at 16:8 would mean that Mark "by pure accident" "hit on a conclusion which suits the technique of a highly sophisticated type of modern literature." This supposition would in fact "credit him with a degree of originality which would invalidate the whole method of form criticism" (p 23). Knox noted however that the ending to Jonah and the dramatic endings found in John's gospel (13:30; 18:27ff; 19:22) are exceptions to his thesis which has been criticized of late. A careful reading of Mark shows that it is much more characteristic of him than the other evangelists to end a pericope with a brief and somewhat abrupt sentence which gives the view of the audience (6:45–52; 9:30–32; 12:13–17). A study of Mark's narrative technique by Boomshine and Bartholomew (JBL, 1981, pp 213–223) leads to the conclusion that Mark uses the same narrative technique to end other stories in his gospel. But this does not prove that Mark intended to end his gospel with this episode.

1943

Pope Pius XII. His encyclical *Divino afflante Spiritu* has been described as a Magna Carta for biblical progress. The Pope recognized that the time for fear of the modern approach to the Bible was over, and he condemned the over-critical distrust which was prevalent among many church people. Far from giving a grudging approval to the modern approach to the Bible, he positively commands it for Catholic scholars.[190]

1947

C. C. Torrey, who wrote *The Translations Made from the Original Aramaic Gospels* (1912), *The Four Gospels* (1933), *Our Translated Gospels* (1936), issued a challenge on the dating of the gospels which he later contended was never taken up.

> It is perhaps conceivable that one evangelist writing after the year 70 might fail to allude to the destruction of the temple by the Roman armies (every reader of the Hebrew Bible knew that the prophets had definitely predicted that foreign armies would surround the city and destroy it), but that three (or four) should thus fail is quite incredible. On the contrary what is shown is that all four Gospels were written before the year 70. And indeed there is no evidence of any sort that will bear examination tending to show that any of the gospels were written later than the middle of the century. The challenge to scholars to produce such evidence is hereby presented.[191]

Torrey dated Mark to A.D. 39–40 because the words "the abominable and destructive presence standing where it should not be" (13:14) must have been written just before the assassination of Emperor Caligula on January 24, A.D. 41.

Torrey claimed that Mark, Matthew, most of Luke and all of John were translations from an Aramaic original and demonstrated that at least there was a far-reaching Aramaic substratum in our Greek gospels, a conclusion which has been confirmed by more recent studies such as M. Black, *An Aramaic Approach to the Gospels and Acts* (Oxford, 1946). Several German scholars such as Wellhausen, Nestle and Dalman also made contributions toward elucidating the Aramaic substratum of the gospels. Gustaf Dalman toward the end of the nineteenth century had concluded from the undoubted fact that Jesus' words were originally in Aramaic that scholars had the duty to investigate

> in what form the words of Jesus must have been uttered in their original language, and what meaning they had in this form for the Jewish hearers.[192]

Torrey's rather sensational conclusion was based on a careful comparison of the gospels with the standard Greek prose of the Hellenistic period and an exhaustive search for those awkward phrases in the gospels, those syntactic and idiomatic peculiarities which are difficult to explain except in terms of a translation from the Aramaic. He even suggested direct errors in translation and misinterpretations, but these have not generally been accepted as convincing.

1951 (a)

A. Farrer, author of *A Study in St. Mark* (1951) and *St. Matthew and St. Mark* (1954), criticized the form critical vision of a gospel as "a row of impersonal anecdotes strung together by a colorless compiler" as concerned with small patterns while ignoring the pattern of the whole. Instead he praised Lightfoot's approach by which

> we found ourselves in touch with St. Mark, a living Christian mind, and a mind of great power.

He believed that the gospel must first be studied as a whole, for the pattern of the whole comes first.

> The solid grain of the theological interpretation is that it restores to us the unity of the gospel. The gospel is a genuine and profoundly consistent, complex act of thought (pp 7f, 22f).

Farrer saw Mark as a poet and in particular as a typologist and numerologist who elaborated his ingenious work by investing not only his numbers but even his simplest stories with esoteric and symbolic meanings based on Old Testament pre-figurations. He thought that Mark organized his gospel in cycles and numerical schemes, e.g., the presence of thirteen miracles with negative (exorcisms) and positive miracles alternating. The "Little Gospel" (ch 1—6) consists in two double cycles and three healings.

Critics have admired his ingenuity but almost unanimously rejected his conclusions as too complicated even for Mark's first readers. According to James M. Robinson the basic weakness of such works as Farrer's and Lohmeyer's

> is the same methodological error which Wrede detected in the Marcan research of the nineteenth century; the argument is not built upon what Mark clearly and repeatedly has to say, but upon

inferences as to the basis of the Marcan order, a subject upon which Mark is silent.[193]

Robinson sees the basic insight of such eccentric works as that Mark was not an objective historian but wrote from the point of view of Christian faith. However, they understand Christian faith in reaction to nineteenth century historicism as some mystic, cultic religiosity whereas Mark intends to record the history of a historical person. One could add that Christian tradition has always seen the gospels as comparatively sober and realistic presentations in contrast to the rather bizarre world of the Book of Revelation. Actually, Farrer himself changed his theories and finally rejected them almost completely, not only because of criticisms of them as far-fetched but because he saw that they would turn the gospel accounts of the key Christian historical events into works of fiction.

Farrer questioned the validity of Papias' testimony and suggested that he was writing to prove a point and that

> the Papian tradition must be simply given up as someone's ingenious but false construction (p 20).

Commenting in 1964 on the dating of Matthew, Luke and John, Farrer eloquently expressed the fluidity of the dating of New Testament books:

> The datings of all these books are like a line of tipsy revellers walking home arm-in-arm; each is kept in position by the others and none is firmly grounded. The whole series can lurch five years this way or that, and still not collide with a solid obstacle.[194]

Farrer describes the ending of Mark at 16:8 as an example of "St. Mark's poetical magic." He draws an interesting parallel between "the last experiences of Jesus in the body at the hands of the disciples" and "the body of Jesus in the hands of his disciples after his death." In the first pattern Jesus is anointed at supper, makes the gift of his body and promises to go to Galilee, while at the crisis the disciples abandon him and a young man runs away leaving behind a linen cloth. In the second pattern Joseph of Arimathea wraps the body in a linen cloth, the women come to anoint it and a young man in a white robe tells them that Jesus has gone to Galilee. Farrer finds the key in the naming of Joseph of Arimathea, unlike the young man who is not named. The young man recalls Joseph running from Potiphar's wife without his robe (Gn 39:12). Joseph of Arimathea recalls Joseph asking Pharaoh for permission to bury his father Jacob (Gn 50:4). Joseph had been betrayed by his eleven brothers who thought he was dead. When he proclaimed "I am Joseph" they were unable to answer. The words "for they were afraid" are similar to Genesis 45:3, "for they were confounded." They connect Jesus' resurrection with Joseph's recovery from the dead.

1951 (b)

S. G. F. Brandon in *The Fall of Jerusalem and the Christian Church* began a series of studies of Jesus, the early Christians and politics which have been quite controversial but have not gained widespread acceptance. One suspects that he has been influenced by the contemporary discussion on liberation theology, Church and politics. The thesis of Jesus' political involvement can be traced back through Robert Eisler[195] at least as far back as H. S. Reimarus who insisted:

> Jesus must have been well aware that by such a plain announce-
> ment of the kingdom of heaven, he would only awaken the Jews
> to the hope of a worldly Messiah; consequently, this must have
> been his object in so awakening them.[196]

In a 1971 article, "The Date of the Markan Gospel,"[197] he concludes that it is possible to fix the date in the year 71 and to conclude that Mark is a defensive reaction after the conclusion of the Jewish war of independence. This date was the key to the elusive significance of Mark—the only evidence for which according to Brandon is provided by the gospel itself. Its aim was to make life more tolerable for the Christians in Rome and the Roman Empire after A.D. 70, a time when the rebellious Jews were obviously in disfavor. He notes that in Mark there is no statement of hostility to the Romans or their representatives in Palestine but in fact the climax of the story is the Roman centurion's faith (15:39). Mark's silence about the fall of Jerusalem in A.D. 70 is highly significant for Brandon. He sees the whole New Testament from Mark onward as a careful rewriting of history to cover up the fact that Jesus was a noble martyr for freedom and that the early Christians sympathized with the Zealot cause and were identified with the Jewish revolt which ended in disaster. He insists that the supposed flight of the Christians to Pella is a later fabrication not found until Eusebius and Epiphanius. Mark 12:13–17

is a revised account to emphasize that Jesus was innocent of sedition
and the Christian obligation to pay taxes to Caesar. Originally the
tax scene was a refusal to pay taxes to Rome. Further the Barabbas
scene (15:6ff) explains how Jesus was executed by the Romans because of a Jewish plot to destroy him. Jesus, he insists, was a loyal,
patriotic Jew who could not have refused to take sides in the political
struggle of his country. Every pious Jew according to Brandon
would have felt his faith insulted that Yahweh's land was subject to
the Romans, their census and administration. However, Brandon in
a reply to his critics insisted that Jesus accepted the Zealot approach
"with modification."

In *Jesus and the Zealots* (1967) Brandon describes Mark as an
Apologia ad Christianos Romanos. He traces anti-Semitism throughout Mark's gospel, noting

> a consistent denigration of the Jewish leaders and people, and of
> the family of Jesus and the original apostles, which adds up to a
> damning indictment of the Jews for their treatment of Jesus . . .
> the Jewish leaders and people are responsible for his death (p
> 279).

Jesus he sees portrayed

> as essentially independent of his Jewish origin and relationship
> [and] vehemently rebuking his chief apostle's obsession with a na-
> tionalistic conception of his own status and mission.

Brandon, like P. Winter in his study of Jesus' trial (1961), argues
that Mark, in telling the story of Jesus' crucifixion, shifts the blame
from the Romans to the Jews. He emphasizes Mark's concern to
denigrate the family of Jesus (especially James) and the original
apostles (especially Peter), e.g., his remarks on 3:20f, 31–35:

> So categorical a repudiation of the blood-relationship is truly
> amazing when it is recalled what the prestige of blood-relation-
> ship to Jesus meant in the Jerusalem church. As we have seen,
> this was the cause of the sudden emergence of James, the brother
> of Jesus, to leadership of the movement, and, after his death, it
> ensured the election of Symeon, another close relative, as his
> successor. . . .This defamation of the family of Jesus is paralleled
> by a derogatory presentation of his apostles, who formed the es-
> sential nucleus of the Jerusalem Church. . . .Particularly instruc-
> tive is the presentation of Peter, who is depicted as the leading

apostle. . . .It is significant that Mark chose also to include in his relatively short gospel the long detailed account of Peter's denial. . . .It completes a very uncomplimentary picture of the leading apostle, who was possibly associated with the original Jewish Christian phase of Christianity in Rome (pp 275ff).

1952

P. Carrington, in *The Primitive Christian Calendar: A Study in the Making of the Marcan Gospel,* found the principle of Mark's organization of his gospel in the liturgical life of the Church which in turn was based on the lectionaries of the Jewish synagogue whose scheme of readings for festivals he assumed was taken over by the early Church. That the gospel was transmitted through the liturgical life of the early Church seems self-evident. But that the writing of Mark was organized to a pre-supposed liturgical scheme is an assumption. He suggests that Mark originated in Galilee and was modeled on the Jewish calendar. It was composed of seven pericopes (i.e., up to the end of ch 13): 1:1–37 (Autumn); 1:38—3:6 (Winter); 3:7—6:6 (Spring); 6:7–19 plus the passion texts from 13:1—16:8 (Lent and Easter Eve); 6:30—7:37 (the season of Easter); 8:1—9:1 (the season of Pentecost); 9:2—10:45 (Summer); 10:46—12:44 (Feast of Tabernacles). Later, according to Carrington, Mark was adapted for use in Rome and to the Julian calendar. He admits that the passion narrative (13:1ff) does not quite fit into his plan and suggests that it must have been a separate document which was based on an original core (14:3—15:41 or 15:47). He suggested that chapter 13 had a double function as the last lesson of the Christian year and the first in a special cycle, ch 13—16, which was read at Passion time. He finds external mathematical confirmation of his theories in the chapter divisions of the fourth century Codex Vaticanus (B). Vaticanus has sixty-two sections, of which the passion is divided into fourteen, thus giving forty-eight lectionary divisions for the remainder which is also the number of sections in the fifth century Codex Alexandrinus (A). The starting point of Carrington's hypothesis was his discovery that Mark's narrative includes both a Passover and a Pentecost celebration, i.e., the feeding of the four and five thousands which shows how Mark carefully adapted his material to the Jewish calendar. He finds further evidence in the "major triads" of Mark, especially the three-mountain-triad (3:13ff; 6:30f; 9:2f). Actually the second mountain is missing in Mark but is supplied from John 6:3. Carrington suggests

that the success of the form critics in isolating the individual pericope is because they were actually separated units of the Church's
lectionary.

M. D. Goulder in *The Evangelist's Calendar*[198] agrees with Carrington's instinct but finds his book unpersuasive.

> He (like me) took the Marcan cycle to begin at New Year. But
> then, an annual cycle beginning at New Year should end with the
> Resurrection in September; Carrington's scheme ignores almost
> all the landmarks of the Jewish Year, and he swings between reli-
> ance on the B (Vaticanus) and "non-B" divisions without justifi-
> cation (p 243).

Goulder's thesis is that the gospels are in their present order because they provided lessons for the Christian liturgical year with its
climax at Easter. The oldest part of the gospels is by common consent the passion complex. It is easy to imagine the commemoration
of Jesus' passion at Passovertide the year after the crucifixion.

> For the rest of the year, whatever material seemed suited to the
> theme of feast or ferial reading would be used, and would differ
> from church to church. But with time came the practice of receiv-
> ing converts in baptism at Eastertide, and the practice therefore of
> preparing them with a course of instruction from around Dedica-
> tion; and so would grow the regular use, in this period, of material
> on the Christian Way, told in the context of Jesus' journey up to
> Jerusalem to his passion. The gospels grew backward from Pass-
> overtide, backward from the passion. Inevitably, with time, the
> urge was felt to make something of a continuous story of Jesus'
> ministry, extending back from the last journey to its opening with
> John the Baptist. The step was taken by Mark in Rome, in virtue
> of his familiarity with the Petrine traditions. He began at New
> Year, and it is for this reason that his Gospel looks like a passion
> story with an extended introduction. But once this move was
> made, its essential unsatisfactoriness became obvious, for there is
> no sale for six-and-a-half-month lectionaries. Churches wanted a
> cycle that ran around the whole year, and this is exactly what
> Matthew and Luke were designed to supply. Both of them, in
> their different ways, supplied readings for the whole year, from
> Easter round to Easter: Matthew for a more conservative, Jewish-
> Christian church with the accent on the festivals; Luke for a more
> Pauline, Gentile church with the accent on the Saturday Old Tes-
> tament lessons. Mark is thus the middle term in a development of
> fifty years, from a set paschal recitation and a free use for the rest
> of the year in the 30s, to two alternative complete cycles in the

80s. A Marcan beginning at New Year would not only be natural; it would explain a lot (pp 244f).

1952

V. Taylor published his commentary *The Gospel According to Mark* in the same year as Carrington. Already in 1933, in *The Formation of the Gospel Tradition,* Taylor had written a very balanced reflective study on form criticism. He was convinced that a reaction like Schmidt's was too extreme, since it too easily dispensed with the witnesses of the early community.

> If the form critics were right the disciples should have been taken up to heaven immediately after the resurrection of Jesus.

The memories of Jesus were not handed to an anonymous collectivity, but to a structured community. However, the early Christians were in no hurry to write a life of Jesus in its early days.

> Christian hands were full of jewels, but there was no desire to weave a crown (p 175).

Form criticism did not necessarily lead to skepticism but could give a very valid confirmation of the historical trustworthiness of the gospels which he clearly saw were theological documents. He considered the title "Son of God" as beyond question representing the most fundamental element in Mark's Christology which he considers as high a Christology as any in the New Testament, not excluding John.

> The sheer humanity of the Markan portraiture catches the eye of the most careless reader; and yet it is but half seen if it is not perceived that this Man of Sorrows is also a Being of supernatural origin and dignity since he is the Son of God. The same conception lies behind the use of the title Son of Man, for he is not only the Suffering Servant but also the one who will sit at God's right hand and come with power upon the clouds of heaven (14:62). . . . It may be held that ultimately it implies a doctrine of pre-existence, but this idea is nowhere suggested in Mark. The claim that, according to Mark, Jesus becomes the Son of God by adoption has often been made, but it probably rests upon a superficial reading of the Gospel. The evangelist's idea is rather that Jesus is by nature the Son of God and that the Voice at the baptism declares him as such. Mark has no theory of the incarnation, but his assumption appears to be that Jesus is "Deus absconditus," the hid-

den God. This view is not docetism, since the humanity of Christ is conceived as real. It is rather the view that, behind a fully human life, Deity is concealed, but is visible for those who have eyes to see in his personality, teaching and deeds. In so describing this christology we are probably expressing it with a precision greater than that in which it appeared to the mind of the evangelist. It is uncertain, indeed, whether he had reflected upon it at all . . . (p 121).

For Taylor not all Mark's stories are Petrine, as some were probably known to Mark from primitive Christian tradition (1:1–15) and others describe incidents when Peter was not present (7:24–30; 14:53–65; 15:1—16:8). However, he finds good reason to trace to Peter's testimony the call of the first disciples, the departure to a lonely place, the call of Levi, the rejection at Nazareth, the confession of Peter, the transfiguration, the rich man's question and the two narratives attached to it, the request of James and John, the entry, the cleansing, the anointing, Gethsemane, the arrest and the denial, and perhaps also many of the miracle stories and some of the traditions which the evangelist himself appears to have constructed. However, he did not hesitate to propose a rationalizing position with regard to some of Mark's stories, e.g., the fig tree in 11:1–25 and the Passover preparation in 14:12–16. Taylor proposed a much simpler classification of the gospel stories than Bultmann or Dibelius, making two divisions of pronouncement stories and miracle stories (Mk 5:22–43). He also subdivided his first group into controversy stories (Mk 2:1–12; 3:1–6) and conversations with Jesus on the part of inquirers, ending with a memorable dictum of Jesus (Mk 11:17–22; 12:28–34).

Taylor's commentary on Mark (1952) quickly became a standard work, provided an alternative interpretation to Wrede's skepticism. Far from being an editorial imposition on tradition by the evangelist, Taylor considered the "messianic secret" to be an historical fact, an integral part of the material itself. Jesus, since he did not want to be known as a mere wonder-worker, played down his miracles and forbade both the demons and his disciples to make known his messiahship. At the time it would have had false political implications, whereas Jesus interpreted his messiahship in terms of the suffering servant. Only after the passion and resurrection could it be proclaimed without misinterpretation.

Like Rawlinson (1925) he dated the publication of Mark in the years 65-67 because it does not appear that the Jewish war had already broken out and the references in Mark 13 are rather vague and imprecise. For Taylor Mark's role was that of an editor and compiler who took over a series of "complexes" which had an independent existence and added his own comments, connecting them with some simple literary bridges.

> Mark's predecessors were not only teachers, but also preachers and evangelists, men who had received, reflected upon, and proclaimed the good news of the kingdom of God. His gospel is far more than a private undertaking; it is a product of the life of the Church inspired by the Spirit of God (p 104).

He used the important studies of H. B. Swete (1908) and C. H. Turner (1928) to provide what is still regarded as the best discussion of Mark's supposed semitic style, and he concludes (p 56):

> We have very good reason to speak of an Aramaic background to the Greek of the Gospel; there are grounds for suspecting the existence of Aramaic sources, which may, however, be oral; and we can speak of the evangelist's use of a tradition which ultimately is Aramaic; but to say more is speculation.

1953

In an October lecture, one of Bultmann's pupils, Ernst Käsemann, launched what has become known as *The New Quest for the Historical Jesus.* He published his criticism of Bultmann in an article, *The Problem of the Historical Jesus.* Käsemann saw the danger of reducing the Jesus of Galilee to a cipher, a symbol or abstract idea like a mathematical point which has position but no magnitude and of ending up like the gnostics or even the docetists. The existence of the four gospels shows that the early Christians were interested in the historical Jesus. Further, a Christian's faith requires confidence in the continuity between the earthly and risen Jesus while at the same time recognizing that the gospels are a product of the Easter faith of the Church.

In a survey of twentieth century interpretations of Jesus, John H. Hayes (*Son of God to Super Star,* Abingdon Press, 1976) finds four primary aspects of Jesus' life which have been the focus of the modern phase of the quest to understand:

1. Jesus within the context of his place in history in the first century Jewish community which was part of the Roman Empire.

2. The teachings of Jesus, his central concern, his newness, his

vision of life—whether it was ethically, socially, religiously and/or politically oriented.

3. The *why* of Jesus' death. Was it the culmination of his life and career? A misunderstanding or a miscarriage of justice? How did he himself understand it?

4. What was there in Jesus' career which accounts for the development of the Christian community? Hayes suggests three basic categories of problems which make it impossible for scholars to reach agreement on the nature and character of the historical life of Jesus: (a) the extent and character of the source materials; (b) problems of methodology in approaching the reconstruction; (c) the pre-suppositions and objectives of the researcher.

1954

H. A. Guy, in *The Origin of the Gospel of Mark,* investigates Papias' comment that Mark, although accurate, did not however record the "sayings and doings" of the Lord "in order." He examines such meanings of order as chronological, rhetorical and calendrical. Guy finds different kinds of disorder such as interruptions in the narrative (e.g., 3:22–30; 4:10–25; 5:25, 34; 11:18–27a; 14:27–31); repetitions, e.g., the doublets of 6:34—7:37 and 8:1–26; the haphazard arrangement of the circuitous route in 7:31; lack of topical or logical connection between successive statements, e.g., 2:28; 11:23–25. According to Guy the basic document of Mark consisted of papyrus leaves which contained stories about Jesus that were useful for early preachers. An unknown editor brought these together though not in a coherent pattern and added teaching of his association with Peter, the final compiler.

6
Marxsen and the Redaction Critics

1954

H. Riesenfeld, the Swedish scholar, published an essay with the significant title *Tradition und Redaktion im Markusevangelium* in which he almost simultaneously produced many of the results of the more famous Marxsen. He argued against the form critics that Mark's gospel was the deliberately executed work of one man. The arrangement of the gospel was the result of either Mark's theological reflection or that of his predecessors. Mark's plan is the result of the imposition of a dogmatic plan based on 8:27–30 upon a pre-existing geographical plan. He suggested such titles as The Son of Man and Israel (1:1—8:26) and, up to 10:52, The Messiah as Teacher and Judge. In an earlier work[199] Riesenfeld had suggested that the fear which Mark attributes to the disciples in 4:41; 9:6, 32; 10:32 and to the women in 16:8 is to be interpreted not so much as psychological but a theological phenomenon, the equivalent of a lack of faith or of spiritual insight. As fear and anguish characterize the Messiah himself in Gethsemane, the spiritual insensibility of the disciples is indicated by fear.

In 1957 Riesenfeld proposed an interesting thesis, *The Gospel Tradition and Its Beginnings,* which was later expanded by his student, B. Gerhardsson, in *Memory and Manuscript* (Lund, 1961), a thesis which they carried to extremes although it does provide a certain valid corrective to some of the extremes of form criticism. This thesis proposed that the fidelity of the early community in transmitting the message of Jesus was like the holy tradition of the rabbis in which the disciples of the rabbis scrupulously strove to repeat exactly the teaching of their master. This theory, while it has a certain validity, proves too much and does not account for the obvious differences between the gospels. Thus it ignores the important influence of the Easter faith and the conversion of the disciples in the reinterpretation of the Jesus tradition, not to mention the new problems and differing situations of the early Christian communities which produced the gospels. The fidelity of the early disciples did not rule out a certain creativity. One can point to Paul's quotations of Jesus' words (e.g., 1 Th 5:2; 1 Cor 7:10f; 9:14; 11:23–25; 13:2; Rom 14:14).

1956 (a)

W. Marxsen in his *Mark the Evangelist: Studies on the Redaction History of the Gospel* gave a new direction and emphasis and title to Marcan studies. Basically the redaction critics were not content to view the writers of the gospels as simple collectors of units but, as Jülicher put it, "a creative personality." They see the evangelists as creative artists guided by their theological concepts and community problems. This search for the authors' viewpoint and sociological world was an important development in gospel studies and provided a complementary method to that of form criticism both of which when used without prejudice help to provide an invaluable and deeper understanding of the historical Jesus. There was a tendency to transfer the "assumed creativity" of the gospel materials from the early community of the form critics to the evangelist. But creativity rightly understood and practiced gives a deeper understanding of the historical reality and is not to be rejected a priori. Before form criticism the gospels were mainly considered as sources for the life and teaching of Jesus. The form critics tended to focus on the Christological significance and development of the individual pericopes and to ignore the whole and in particular the literary framework which they regarded as secondary. They did not consider the evangelists as very serious theologians, as they had only primitive traditions and community sources at their disposal. However, form criticism inevitably paved the way for the redaction critics who tended to see the individual evangelists primarily as representing different theological approaches while playing down their role as historians and literary authors.

Marxsen was the main pioneer of the application of redaction criticism to Mark although traces of the method can be found long before him in Lightfoot, Wrede and even as far back as Reimarus. Instead of seeking to discover the historical tradition behind Mark he attempts to locate the point of view of Mark's "representation of Jesus" by an examination of Mark as a whole, in particular his program and his scenic framework. His book consisted of four separate studies, all of which show Mark's theology dealing with a particular subject: (1) John the Baptist; (2) geographical references in Mark's narratives; (3) the concept of "euangelion" (gospel) in Mark; (4) the apocalyptic discourse in Mark 13.

Marxsen begins with a study of the way Mark uses and presents the John the Baptist tradition. His thesis is that Mark, an individual, an author-personality who pursued a definite goal in his ministry, composed his gospel backward.

> The passion-story represents the first text of the tradition of Jesus to be fixed in writing. This then grew backward.

Mark puts 1:1 before his description of the Baptist, putting him in his place in the gospel of Jesus Christ (p 31). Mark's method in the early parts of the gospel is determined by a theme which he will develop later. He only includes people and events because of their connection with Jesus, not because of any interest in them as such. Thus any statement about anyone is a statement about Jesus. His description of the Baptist (1:4–8) is modeled on the ministry of Jesus and leads up to 1:14—the whole gospel leads up to the key statement in 16:7. Mark only quotes those words of John which concern the one who was coming after him. His purpose in telling of John the Baptist is not because of any special historical interest in John or to give an historical account of John but to use this event to say something about Jesus.

> The Baptist does not have any independent significance of his own; there can be no teaching about the Baptist or about baptism; rather, all that is said about the Baptist is in effect something said about the interpretation of Jesus as the Christ (p 33).

Such is the main purpose of his whole work. His method is to begin with Mark's statement and then to compare it with its development in the other synoptics, tracing the differences to the different concepts of the evangelists when composing their gospels. Marxsen made his own the theories of Lohmeyer and Lightfoot concerning the evangelist's geographical interest.

For Marxsen the geographical statements in Mark are not geographical references but theological statements, e.g., the wilderness in 1:4:

> The wilderness is not a geographical location. It is not permissible to reflect as to where it could lie. This reference is not intended to

> give a location for the work of the Baptist. . . . Rather "in the wil-
> derness" qualifies the Baptist as the one who fulfills Old Testa-
> ment prophecy. It might almost be said: The Baptist would even
> be the one who came "in the desert," even if in his whole life he
> had never once been anywhere near the desert (pp 37f).

Similarly, the time reference in v 14 does not necessarily mean that
Jesus' ministry began only after John had been arrested but that
theologically speaking John was the forerunner and Jesus the one
who came after. Therefore John is "delivered up" in v 14 and his story ends before that of Jesus begins.

Similarly Galilee is more a theological concept than a geographical place. He notes that all Mark's references to Galilee throughout
his gospel are found in his editorial sections and therefore are important for the evangelist.

> Galilee is obviously the evangelist's own creation. Mark does not
> intend to say: Jesus worked in Galilee, but rather: Where Jesus
> worked, there is Galilee. . . . Further, Jesus has already gone
> ahead to Galilee (14:28; 16:7). There he is hidden: there he will be
> seen at the parousia. Galilee is thus Jesus' "home" in a far deeper
> sense than the merely historical.

Again Mark represents Jesus as entering Jerusalem for the first time
during the last week of his life to make a theological point. In fact
there are several passages in Mark which show that Jesus has already
been in or about Jerusalem since he had friends there or they describe him as familiar with the locale (e.g., 10:46f; 11:2f; 14:3, 13ff,
49; 15:43).

For Marxsen the form critics who were chiefly concerned with
the individual units of a gospel could never do justice to Mark's bold
new step in collecting the units together while creating something
new—a gospel which Matthew developed into a chronicle and Luke
into a life of Jesus. While the form critics tended to focus on the formation of the oral tradition, redaction criticism focused on the completed written gospel. Marxsen investigated the framework of the
gospel, its seams, interpretive comments, summaries, modifications
and selection and omission of material. He distinguished three levels
of life situations within the gospel tradition, the first level during Jesus' historical activity, the second in the early Church when the units
of tradition began to circulate, the third, the situation in the community in which the evangelist wrote his distinct work to meet its prob-

lems. Mark according to Marxsen introduced the word "gospel" into the synoptic tradition (e.g., 8:35; 10:29). Apart from Paul, Mark is the only New Testament writer who uses the word gospel quite frequently (Mk 7, Mt 4, Lk 0, John 0, Acts 2, Paul 60). Normally he uses it absolutely and without further modification (except 1:1 and 1:14). This indicates to Marxsen "the proximity of Marcan to Pauline usage." One can substitute "Jesus Christ" for gospel in Mark (e.g., 13:9f). It is not the message which Jesus proclaimed but

> the form in which Jesus is made present. Jesus is the content of the gospel in the sense that he is preached.

Marxsen concludes that for Mark the gospel presents the risen Jesus. He insists that the opening verse is a title to the whole gospel deliberately chosen. Thus Mark transfers the noun "gospel" from the area of oral proclamation to that of a written composition. The word "beginning" does not cover the opening part but the entire work of Mark and means origin or principle and in a sense God himself as the author and originator of all that is—just as Genesis 1:1 opens the Bible on a similarly important note.

Marxsen is interested in Mark 13 in its final form as a totality and what it teaches about the historic situation of Mark's community, e.g., the command to flee in 13:14 is a reference to the flight of the Jerusalem Christians into the mountains of Galilee (which he broadly interprets to include Pella). This chapter does not consist in words of Jesus to his disciples, but for Mark it is words of the risen Christ to the waiting community to go to Galilee where the Lord will appear (13:14; 16:7). The parenthetical remark "let the reader understand" is Mark's way of focusing his readers on their present situation. Marxsen searched for what he called a catalyst or an occasion which caused Mark to write and make public in written form his work. Mark, he assumed, had before him a loose collection of narrative and teaching sections. This impulse to construct a coherent pattern Mark found in the controversial situation occasioned by the outbreak of the Jewish War in A.D. 66. Thus Mark is "a published appeal 'eine Programmschrift' as H. Conzelmann labels it," a polemical or "adversary theology," whereas Matthew is more a pastoral writer and Luke is concerned with apologetics,[200] although why Mark had to write such a complicated appeal as his gospel is not made clear by Marxsen. He sees the composition of Mark as determined by opposing movements, i.e.,

> the broadening of the *kerygma* which moves from the passion sto-
> ry backward, and the movement of the *history* which runs from
> John the Baptist forward (p 120)

and thus Mark tries to avoid the historicizing process which sets in
with Matthew and Luke. Mark maintains the original intention of
the individual traditions which were aimed exclusively at proclamation by an extreme "condensation" which the other synoptics break
up and disperse.

For Marxsen Mark's work is a direct address, a preaching written for Palestinian Christians to urge them to go to Galilee to await
the parousia there at a time when eschatological expectations were
very much in the air. Yet Mark is trying to dampen the apocalyptic
speculations caused by the Jewish War. The fact that there are no
resurrection appearances in Mark is deliberate. Because what the disciples are told to go to Galilee to see is not the resurrection appearances but the parousia, the command to go reflects the flight of the
Jerusalem Christians in A.D. 66. The unusual absence of a conclusion in Mark is an invitation to read Mark as much as a prophecy of
Jesus' return to Galilee as a reminder of his earthly life. Mark concluded his gospel at 16:8 because this prophecy had not yet been ful-
filled.

> Briefly put the gospel declares: "I am coming soon" (p 134).

The time was immediately preceding the fall of Jerusalem (A.D. 70),
thus making Mark into a sermon, an exhortation contemporary with
the events of 66–70. Mark saves Paul's message from mythologizing
by joining the Pauline kerygma and the (so-called) synoptic tradition
holding together "the eschatological and the historical event." For
Marxsen Mark is simply proclaiming in a different form and situation Paul's Christology that Jesus Christ is Lord (Phil 2:5–11). He is
not giving a report about Jesus but his aim is to provide an encounter
with the risen Lord. It is only after Marxsen's study that the suggestion would arise that Mark was providing a corrective Christology.

Marxsen, in pioneering fashion, opened up new worlds in Marcan studies, yet few are prepared to follow him as far as he went, particularly in making the whole interpretation of Mark depend on two
verses (14:28; 16:7). It is not necessary that the verb "see" in 16:7
should be related to the parousia. Further the passion predictions in
Mark only refer to the resurrection but not the parousia. Also it has

been pointed out that Mark 13 contains indications that the parousia is delayed rather than the imminent expectation of the parousia.

1956 (b)

J. M. Robinson, in *The Problem of History in Mark,* criticized many other analyses of Mark as "not built upon what Mark clearly and repeatedly has to say" (p 12). Thus for example he notes (p 74) the importance of the attitude of faith in Mark as the attitude which Jesus calls forth and praises while reproaching disbelief (4:40; 6:6; 9:19), exhorting to faith (5:36; 11:22), and attributing praiseworthy action to faith (2:5; 5:34; 10:52). He saw the overall structure of Mark and his editorial insertions in the light of his parallel theology. Jesus' own combat with Satan is paralleled and continued in the struggle of the Church in history as it is prompted by the Holy Spirit. For Robinson Mark 1:1–13 is a theological prologue announcing the theme of his whole gospel. Thus whereas Marxsen saw the key to Mark in the historical situation of his own time, for Robinson Jesus' struggle with Satan was central. He sees the entire earthly ministry of Jesus as the final struggle between the Spirit-endowed Son of God and Satan and the demonic powers in the sphere of history, the powers of the cosmos and the power of hardness of heart (3:5; 6:52; 8:17). Jesus' baptism initiates God's challenge to demonic authority. The temptation is the opening round of the war. It is followed by a series of conflicts, e.g., the exorcism struggles, healings, debates with Jesus' human opponents such as the Pharisees, altercations with the crowds, and the blindness and stupidity of the disciples. The crucifixion is the climax of the struggle, and the decisive victory over evil is achieved in the resurrection through which the power of evil is definitely broken and God's powerful reign established in history. In all these stories we find what Robinson calls "cosmic language."

It is worth noting that the French writer, E. Trocmé, accuses both Marxsen and Robinson of trying to fit Mark's message into the framework of modern theological categories. He accuses Marxsen of using Bultmann's existentialist theology and Robinson of borrowing from O. Cullmann's theology of the history of salvation.[201] In brief, Robinson sees Mark's understanding of redemptive history as in three successive periods. The first period of the preparation began in the Old Testament which culminates in John the Baptist. The second is the earthly ministry of Jesus. The third which is stressed in Mark's apocalypse is the period between the Christ event and the parousia and is marked by the Church's mission and the messianic woes. The first two have in common the prophetic significance and are separated by the point of John the Baptist where the fulfillment is initiated. The second two have in common the battle between the Spirit and Satan but are separated by the point of decisive victory found in the death and resurrection of Jesus.

Robinson himself in an article, "The Problem of History in Mark" in the *Union Seminary Quarterly Review* (1956, pp 132ff), saw a methodological weakness in his own work. His conception of the evangelist's work was based rather on the tradition which Mark had used with its mythic and cosmic notion rather than on the redaction which Mark himself made. In *Trajectories through Early Christianity*[202] Mark's model is suggested to have been an aretalogy, a widespread literary phenomenon from the Graeco-Roman world which was used to describe in particular the miracles performed by "divine men." Such a cycle of stories about an heroic teacher with divine powers was often involved with hostile powers and authorities and ended in martyrdom and apotheosis.

In this study Robinson and Koester have suggested that instead of thinking of the "backgrounds" to the New Testament images one should think in terms of "trajectories." The idea of a "trajectory" is taken from the term for the curving path of a planet or rocket in space. Thus such categories as Judaism or Hellenism or theology or heresy have been wrongly conceived as static entities (cultural background) as if a fixed, unchanging essence were involved. A particular New Testament text should be located by its point on the trajectory. Since a text takes on a life of its own, its place can be defined as much in terms of what comes after its writing as in terms of what comes before as part of a process of ideas. Thus Koester and Robinson attempt to trace a trajectory of the kind of literature which collects the sayings of wise men. Such collections they find in Egypt and Mesopotamia and then in such Jewish writings as Proverbs, Ecclesiastes, Enoch, the Apocalypse of Adam and the Testaments of the Twelve Patriarchs, and then in early Christian collections of Jesus' sayings, e.g., Q, the parables in chapter 4 of Mark, the exhortation in the Didache, and Jesus' teachings ordered as in Matthew, and finally in Gnostic collections such as the Coptic gospel of Thomas from Nag Hammadi.

Koester finds three kinds of gospels that were taken into Mark's unique creation which stressed Jesus' death and resurrection. First there is a "sayings gospel" like the gospel of Thomas which contains no future apocalyptic Son of Man sayings or predictions such as

Mark 13 but which focuses on the presence of the kingdom. Second, he finds an aretalogy or a pre-gospel "miracle gospel" which consists in collections of miracle stories that lie behind Mark and John (Jn 20:30f). Third, there is a "revelation gospel" which can be traced to a secret revelation of Jesus to his disciples on a mountain and which can be traced behind the "little apocalypse" of Mark 13 and also the farewell discourse of John 13–17.

1957–1958

G. Schille,[203] commenting on the Formgeschichte of the Gospels, proposed that Mark was a catechist and a teacher whose plan was based on the "agreed outline" of the Church (i.e., Phil 2:6–11; Heb 5:5, 7–10; 1 Tm 3:16), although critics point out that only the first part describing Christ's debasement is paralleled in Mark. This outline Mark filled out with the help of the esoteric teaching that the Church gave to its catechumens. Schille proposed that the whole gospel showed an elaborate parallel between the life of Jesus and that of a catechumen who entered the Church through baptism, received instruction and the eucharistic meal, and was warned of the coming temptation and the likelihood of martyrdom, a sequence found in Hebrews 6:1ff and the Didache.

On the formation of the passion stories Schille suggests that it was not due to purely historical motives but that the annual commemoration in Jerusalem of Good Friday and Easter provided the setting and the necessity to crystallize the memories of the passion. In particular, this crystallization took place around three poles in the living worship of the Church at Jerusalem: (a) an "anamnesis" of Jesus' last night, probably joined to an annual "agape" or love feast (Mk 14:18–72); (b) an annual liturgy, a solemn commemoration of the crucifixion modeled on the Jewish three hours of prayer (15:2–41): the execution begins at the third hour (15:25), darkness covers the earth from the sixth to the ninth hour (15:33), at the ninth hour Jesus utters his last articulate cry (15:34) and dies (15:37); (c) an Easter morning liturgy which may have included a visit to Jesus' tomb (15:42—16:8). Even before Mark's editing the three were dovetailed together with the help of a few editorial passages such as 14:1f, 10f, 17; 15:1.

1958

R. Morgenthaler in his *Statistik des neutestamenthichen Wortschatzes* collected some very useful statistics which help in an analysis of Mark. Of a total of 11,242 words, Mark uses 1,345 different words. This gives a far richer vocabulary than John (1,011 in a total of 15,240), slightly richer than Matthew (1,691 in a total of 18,305) but somewhat less than Luke (2,055 in a total of 19,404) and much less than the author of Hebrews (1,038 in a total of 4,951). All but 79 of Mark's 1,345 different words are found in the rest of the New Testament (Lk 250, Mt 112). Of these 79, some 41 are found in the Septuagint (Mt 76). In all Mark has 7 "hapax legomena" (1:35; 2:21; 7:37; 9:25; 12:4; 13:11; 14:31).

1960

S. E. Johnson, in *The Gospel According to St. Mark*,[204] holds that the earliest date for its composition is the 40's after the composition of the "little Apocalypse." But Johnson sees the great fire of Rome and the martyrdom of Peter in the background, thus excluding a date before 64. He considers the predictions of Mark 13 vague enough to accept Rawlinson's date of 65–67. On the other hand it can be argued that the unique terror of the war is well known and the conflict is nearing the end, as the Lord has shortened the days (13:19f) and false prophets described in Josephus[205] have arisen in Jerusalem (13:21f).

> It is therefore possible to think of the gospel as having been written after the destruction of the Temple but before the conclusion of hostilities in Palestine. Although Titus celebrated his triumph in 71, the fortress of Masada did not fall until April in 73. At any time in this period the evangelist might expect that the woes would end with the triumphant coming of the Son of Man.[206]

In contrast to Marxsen's idea that Mark was written in Galilee, Johnson argues that only the traditions behind the gospel have an authentic Palestinian flavor which are attributable to Peter and the "old pericopes" (e.g., 2:4). On the other hand there are many indications that the evangelist is not acquainted with Palestine (e.g., 6:17; 7:31; 8:10, 15, 26; 10:12; 12:13; 14:64) and is hostile to Judaism.

Johnson sees Mark as

> not a naive and fortuitous collection of incidents but the result of a long tradition of preaching and teaching.

To him, Mark is Oriental in contrast with Hellenistic and Roman writers and has no obvious break except at 8:27. Mark is like

> an Oriental rug in which many patterns cross one another . . . not made up with mathematical certitude but developed spontaneous-ly . . . a colorful piece of folk art . . . exhibiting the vitality of early Christianity.[207]

1961

J. Schreiber, in *The Christology of Mark's Gospel* (Z.T.K., 1961, pp 154–158), attempted to work out the following procedural principles as a help to interpret Mark's gospel correctly:

1. The point of departure in establishing Mark's theology is the verses which can be ascribed to Mark's redaction. Although scattered all over Mark's gospel they can provide a unified theology. This would include the messianic secret, the blindness of the disciples, a suffering Christology and discipleship.

2. Whenever Matthew or Luke or both alter a text of Mark we probably can discover a specific Marcan theology or prejudice.

3. Mark's selection and arrangement are a guide to his redaction. However, we have little idea of the material available to Mark.

4. A Marcan theology must not only be consistent but also meaningful in terms of a given historical situation.

Schreiber can be listed among the scholars who see Mark as taking his main ideas from Paul: J. Weiss, A. Loisy, B. W. Bacon, C. G. Montefiore, B. H. Branscomb, and W. Marxsen. Mark adapted Hellenistic theology with its three stages of pre-existence, humiliation and exaltation. He made the cross, understood as exaltation, central, using Philippians 2:6–11 as his model. However, it is difficult to find clues to pre-existence in Mark. Schreiber derives it from the designation of Jesus as the "only Son" and the idea of "sending" in 12:6. He explains the messianic secret by using 1 Corinthians 2:8:

> None of the rulers of this age understood this, for if they had they would not have crucified the Lord of Glory.

Jesus is a divine being who accepts a human existence yet remains divine, passing through life by going the way of a victim in Jerusalem to die as a divine redeemer (15:39). His moment of defeat is his triumph as he is exalted by God and installed in the heavenly sphere as judge over the already defeated powers of evil. The secrecy commands according to Schreiber are made so that Jesus will not be recognized by the demonic powers. However, contra Schreiber, it is precisely the demonic powers who really recognize Jesus, and he is put to death by human powers (3:6).

Joachim Rohde in his summary notes some six points about Schreiber's Christology:[208]

1. Mark shows in his "passion narrative with an extended introduction" that, like the way of Jesus and his proclamation of the gospel, similarly the life of Christians is determined by God's loving will and may lead to the sacrificing of one's life.

2. His messianic secret presentation shows that the will of God takes both redeemer and redeemed through suffering and concealment to life.

3. Jesus' death is his exaltation and enthronement. Rejection or confession of the crucified one means judgment or deliverance.

4. By his description of Jesus as a miracle worker and exorcist Mark is showing that Jesus, although hidden in the messianic secret in the sign of the cross and in his unconditional love, is the one who is now exalted and acting with authority.

5. As teacher and proclaimer of secret mysteries and the gospel, Jesus is simply giving testimony to the love of God that summons men to life with Jesus and thus to true life in love.

6. Discipleship means following Jesus' call unconditionally and experiencing his presence which now bestows a share in the divine spirit even in suffering (13:11) and gives life in love (10:29f).

Noting Mark's special interest in such areas near Galilee as Tyre, Sidon and Decapolis, he sees Mark as a call to mission from Galilee, a polemic aimed at the blind Peter and the Palestinian Jewish Christian Church who failed to go to Galilee and engage in the Gentile mission (14:28; 16:7), unlike the Hellenistic Christians. He sees 16:7 as an indirect rebuke for Jewish Christians showing the risen Christ already at missionary work in Galilee.

Like Bultmann in *History of the Synoptic Tradition* (p 258) and later T. J. Weeden (1968), Schreiber sees the criticism of "the twelve" in Mark as aimed at his contemporary Jewish Christians. Schreiber, developing suggestions of Conzelmann, seems to have been the first to develop the idea that there were two competing Christologies in Mark, a divine man Christology and Mark's own Christology of the Son of God who dies on the cross. This approach became very popular due to the studies of Dieter Georgi's study of Paul's Corinthian opponents and Schweizer's Marcan studies.

1962 (a)

John Marsh, in "The Theology of the New Testament" in *Peake's Commentary on the Bible,* asserted:

> Christian theology is distinguished from all other theologies by one unparalleled feature. From the metaphysical systems of Aquinas and the schoolmen on the one hand to the exclusively scriptural position of Calvin on the other, there is a consensus of opinion that the distinctively Christian assertions made by Christian theology can be made only because certain things have happened, things to which the New Testament is the only adequate witness (p 756).

For Marsh it is only an approximation to the truth to say that the New Testament contains the story of Jesus Christ. Only five of its twenty-seven books can be considered as narrative. It is the theologian's aim to draw out and systematize the truths contained in or implied by the story. When the story of Jesus has been told the theologian asks what truths it implies about God, Jesus Christ, the Holy Spirit, the Church, the ministry, the sacraments, man and his universe, time and history and the eternity which lies beyond.

But the New Testament no more tells us what exactly took place than the Old Testament. This is evident from its use of the exodus and other Old Testament elements in providing the narrative form for many events. In the Old Testament the exodus is the fundamental and pervasive event which can only be understood theologically in the light of what had been done before and afterward and what was yet to follow. The center of the New Testament is the Christ event which is deliberately related to the Exodus account as both fulfilling and transcending it. The New Testament, to use Luther's distinction, a distinction which must not be overstated, does not seek to impart "history knowledge" but faith knowledge. All New Testament theology can be reduced to one word—Christ. Each and every New Testament writer is concerned to present a Jesus of history who is the Christ of faith. The gospels which seem to deal especially with the Jesus of history tell the story of faith.

Marsh accepts the view that Mark was the first of the four gospels to be written. He begins his theology with a theological evaluation of Mark, finding a sound clue in Mark's opening words "The beginning of the gospel of Jesus Christ, the Son of God." He then gives a summary of the basic theological themes of Mark:

> The Gospel tells the story of the beginning of a new Israel or Son of God in the divine human person of Jesus. It brings the story of the exodus to provide categories of interpretation to the life and death of Christ. It tells of the proclamation of the kingdom of God as a present reality, and reports the miracles which are signs of its presence. It recounts how the power of the new Son is adequate to withstand the Adversary, to work effectively beyond what sin and death can do to men, and how, finally, he can defeat the assault of death upon himself. It tells how the Son from the beginning was the center and the life of a community, of how the community was disintegrated at Christ's death and awed by his resurrection. As a book which is intended to explain the Christian community to itself, it has the seeds of all later theology in it, as it sets the seal upon all that had been wrought hitherto.

In the rest of his article Marsh shows in quite an interesting fashion how these basic themes of Mark are expounded in other New Testament writings.

1962 (b)

C. E. B. Cranfield, who had published the *Cambridge Greek New Testament Commentary* in 1959, wrote the Marcan article in *The Interpreter's Dictionary of the Bible* in 1962. He finds in the whole gospel of Mark a Christology which is every bit as high as that of John's gospel and which presupposes the early Church's faith that Jesus is Lord (cf Rom 10:9; 1 Cor 12:3; 2 Cor 4:5). If Mark had not shared this faith he would never have written his gospel. Cranfield conveniently considers this Christology under four headings:

1. The Lord who "was rich." In 1:3 an Old Testament passage in which "Lord" stands for "Yahweh" is applied to Jesus. This points to a belief in his pre-existence (cf Enoch 46:1–3; 48:27; 62:7), and likewise the "I came" or "the Son of Man came" sayings (2:17; 10:45). The Son of God title which is prominent in Mark is not a mere messianic title, as the evidence for such a use in pre-Christian Palestinian Judaism is scanty and doubtful. It is best explained as having its origin in the filial consciousness of Jesus (13:32).

2. The Lord who "became poor." Mark's history is the story of the hidden Lord who laid aside every outward compelling evidence

of his divine glory. His self-dedication led him on the road of the servant into the lowest depths of human anguish and shame, including not merely death but death under the curse of God.

3. The Lord who is exalted. The whole gospel implies the existence of a Church living by faith in a risen and exalted Lord, greeting his presence in the celebration of his supper and experiencing his power to save in the midst of trials and persecutions.

4. The Lord who is coming from beginning to end. Mark breathes the hope of Jesus' coming. God's kingly rule had come in the person, words and works of Jesus but is a veiled mystery which could only be recognized by faith (4:11). As sowing is followed by harvest, so the present obscurity will be followed by the glorious manifestation at the parousia.

1962 (c)

T. W. Manson in a posthumous work, *The Foundation of the Synoptic Tradition: The Gospel of Mark,* in Studies in the Gospel and Epistles, defends Streeter's idea that the gospels preserve local church traditions, e.g., Mark, the Roman tradition. For Manson:

> The quest of the historical Jesus is still a great and most hopeful enterprise [because] in the gospels we have the materials—reliable materials—for an outline of the ministry as a whole ... [which] will fit into what we otherwise know about contemporary Jewish faith and life in Palestine ... and it will give an adequate explanation of the existence of the Church. We shall not be able to fit in all the details ... the gaps are enormous. But we have some details; and I think it is true to say that these short stories, parables, sayings, poems and so on, which go to make up the gospels themselves, epitomize the whole story. Each of them is, as it were, a little window through which we can view the ministry as a whole: a vantage-point from which we can take a Pisgah-view of the authentic kingdom of God (pp 11f).

Manson concludes from the various allusions to Mark's acquaintance with the early Christian leaders (Acts 12:12, 25; 13:5, 13; 15:37, 39; Col 4:10; 2 Tim 4:11; Phlm 24; 1 Pet 5:13):

> Mark had considerable opportunities of gathering knowledge of the kind that would later be useful in the composition of the gospel (p 37).

He sums up the early tradition about Mark's relationship to Peter:

> If Peter had paid a visit to Rome some time between 55 and 60, if
> Mark had been his interpreter then, if after Peter's departure from
> the city Mark had taken in hand—at the request of the Roman
> hearers—a written record of what Peter had said, then the essen-
> tial points in the evidence would all be satisfied (p 40).

Interestingly, Manson, following an argument that can be
traced back to F. Spitta who wrote at the beginning of the twentieth
century, asserted that the original beginning of Mark is missing (pp
31ff). In fact Mark as we have it seems to begin and end his gospel in
the middle of a sentence. Manson gives a somewhat exaggerated view
of the difficulties of Mark's opening verses.

> Verse 1 offers a subject with no predicate; verses 2 and 3 a subor-
> dinate clause with no main clause; and verse 4 gives a statement of
> fact about John the Baptist which seems to have some links with
> the thought of what has gone before but no obvious grammatical
> connection.

Recent researches have suggested that the flat book codex may have
been introduced as early as A.D. 70 and that the first and last leaves
may have been lost.[209] Manson argues from the observation that unlike the case with Mark 1:1 it was normal to describe the event before
giving the Old Testament proof text. But this practice is not certain.[210]

In the introduction to his *The Teaching of Jesus,*[211] Manson described Mark as "a biographical sketch" (p 12), noting that for great
stretches of Jesus' ministry, however short its duration was, no detailed record has been preserved. During Mark's account of the ministry "there are changes of emphasis, emergence of new ideas and
dropping of old ones." To understand Jesus' teaching, it must be fitted as far as possible into the framework of his life. This cannot be
done for writings of a Spinoza or an Amos, since we know almost
nothing about their lives. The life of Jesus interprets his teaching,
and the teaching interprets his life. This life, like that of the great
masters in music and literature, falls into periods. Peter's confession
marks a turning point—the close of one period of teaching and the
beginning of another. Manson suggests that one could draw up a list
of important terms which appear in only one or the other period.
Thus the phrase "Son of Man" (excluding places where it simply

means "man") was not used by Jesus before Peter's confession. Again, words which imply a demand for understanding on the part of his hearers belong in the first period. Manson points out that a careful study of Mark shows that Jesus did not have a uniform strain of teaching delivered to all and sundry. He finds three different teaching methods, determined by the personal relation between Jesus and the scribes and Pharisees, the crowds, and the disciples. To the disciples Jesus gives his confidence and speaks without reserve. To the scribes and Pharisees he is critical and even hostile. To the crowds who have little real grasp of his message Jesus uses parables which are intended as a spur to religious insight. In Mark 7:1–23 there are three short speeches based on the incident of the unwashed hands. The first is impatient and addressed to the scribes and Pharisees, using legal terms. The second is an epigram addressed to the general public. The third is spoken to the disciples.

1963 (a)

T. A. Burkill authored *Mysterious Revelation* (1963) and *New Light on the Earliest Gospel* (1972). In his second volume Burkill remarks that since 1963 the whole matter of Marcan priority has been seriously called into question but still maintains that Mark is the earliest of the four canonical gospels, written perhaps at Rome soon after the fall of Jerusalem in A.D. 70. He concludes that Mark did not pass through two editions but that the evangelist composed the first thirteen chapters to provide

> a propaedeutic to a suitably adapted form of the traditional passion narrative (p 264).

The evangelist is averse to the Jewish leadership generally but regards the Pharisees as the principal opponents of Jesus. He finds a series of fundamental doctrinal antinomies or contrary viewpoints in Mark, e.g., predestination and freedom, optimism and pessimism, retributive justice and factual truth, universalism and particularism, ritualism and ethics, reason and revelation. Burkill finds two central themes in Mark, the secret fact of the messianic status of Jesus which dominates the earlier part up to Peter's confession (8:29) and the mysterious meaning of that fact which dominates the rest. On the first part Mark is mainly concerned to represent the words and deeds of Jesus as esoteric manifestations of the secret fact of the messiahship. Burkill sees the two healings of blind men (8:22–26; 10:46–52) as not only marking important transitions in Mark's narrative but as having a symbolic function. They are in sharp contrast to the adjacent accounts of the disciples who are taught the truth about Jesus' suffering and death but are unable to understand it as God's purpose for Jesus. In the second part Jesus is mainly concerned to show that his messiahship mysteriously meant that Jesus had to endure the shame of the crucifixion to fulfill his redemptive mission.

Burkill and other scholars such as Peter Ellis have noticed Mark's propensity for "thinking three" while admitting that most of the triads are in the passion account and may be due to Mark's source material.[212] The passion narrative is arranged in two sets of three days: first set, chapters 11—13; second set, chapters 14—15. Jesus prays three times in Gethsemane and exhorts the apostles three times to watch (14:33, 35, 37). Peter's denial is foretold three times and thrice recounted (14:29–31, 53f, 66–72). During the crucifixion three hours are mentioned (15:25, 33–34). Three groups, the passersby, the chief priests and scribes, and those crucified with him mock Jesus on the cross (15:19–32). Three women watch the burial (15:40) and three go to the tomb (16:1).

The prologue is triadic: the Baptist (1:1–8), the baptism of Jesus (1:9–11), and the temptation (1:12f). There are three parables in 4:1–34. Three apostles accompany Jesus at the raising of Jairus' daughter (5:37), the transfiguration (9:2), and the agony in the garden (14:33). In chapters 11—12 Jesus is in controversy with three groups of Jews—the chief priests and elders (11:27–33), some Pharisees and Herodians (12:13–17), and the Sadducees (12:18–27). The apocalyptic discourse of chapter 13 is divided into three (13:5–13; 14:23, 24–37) and the exhortation to watch is given three times (13:33, 35, 37). Some three times in all Mark repeats in his gospel the triadic pattern of (a) introductory summary, (b) apostles, and (c) narrative or instruction: (a) 1:14—3:6; 3:7—6:6a; 6:6b—8:30; (b) 8:31—10:52; (c) 11:1—13:37; 14:1—15:47; 16:1–8).

1963 (b)

D. E. Nineham, in his well-known Pelican commentary *Saint Mark*, asserts:

> It is possible to read the Gospels with both profit and pleasure without the help of any commentator, [yet] without some knowl-

edge of the various stages in their growth, it is impossible to appreciate them fully, from either the religious or the historical point of view ... positive misunderstanding is likely to be the result. For the nearest analogy to a gospel in the experience of the modern reader is the biography ... (pp 15–17).

For Nineham:

> The older view that the gospels were attempted biographies of Jesus, as adequate as the education of the evangelists and the circumstances of the time would allow, has given place to the recognition that each of them was produced to meet some specific and practical needs in the church of its origin, and that it is those needs which have very largely controlled each evangelist's choice, arrangement and presentation of material, and distribution of emphasis (p 29).

The fact that Mark contains a number of unrelated paragraphs with very little organic connection,

> like a series of snapshots placed side by side on a photograph album, shows that apart from an outline passion narrative, and one or two short collections of material on special subjects, what Mark had to work on was a series of essential, disconnected stories.

He criticizes Dodd's thesis about the framework of the gospels—that it is an expansion of the pattern of Acts 10:37–41—and concludes that there would be no compelling motive for preserving or even remembering the order of the events of Jesus' life and that the order of the events had no importance in the apostolic preaching (p 22).

In fact, like Lightfoot, Nineham would consider Mark as rather a community production than an individual author's. He begins from an examination of the gospel and tends to rule out such traditional evidence as that of Papias. He makes the somewhat illogical statement:

> Most contemporary scholars agree that in places St. Mark's material bears all the signs of having been community tradition and cannot therefore be derived *directly* from St. Peter or any other eyewitness. But once that admission has been made about some of St. Mark's material, it seems only logical to go on and make it about *all* his material ... (pp 26f).

Nineham remarks that Mark (Marcus) was the most popular Latin name in the Roman Empire, borne as a first name (praenomen) by such as Cicero, Brutus, Aurelius, and Antony, yet he forgets that for John Mark it is a second name (cognomen). One must be careful not to identify all the Marks in the New Testament with the author of the second gospel. However, they form a coherent picture, and no other candidate to fit the picture has been brought forward.

In an article[213] Nineham described Mark as like a tadpole with a large head (i.e., the passion narrative) followed by a comparatively short tail. His aim is quite singleminded—to help the reader to see Jesus on the Cross. Therefore his passion narrative has the position of preeminence and climax and all the rest is in some way introductory.

For Nineham Mark is writing, to quote J. Weiss' phrase, "from faith to faith" for fellow Christians who already know the story as well as he himself does, and therefore he has no need to introduce such characters as John the Baptist, Herod, and Pilate or to explain the wilderness (1:4) or such places as the Jordan. In fact he suggests that through such interpretations as that of Mark who stood back from the actual events, we get a better appreciation of Jesus' ministry than if we had an actual transcript of Jesus' ministry and teaching.

Nineham indicates four main concerns of Mark:

1. Mark was not primarily concerned to prove Jesus' messiahship, since it was taken for granted in his circle, but to reconcile the fact of Jesus' messiahship with his disgraceful criminal's death.

2. He wanted to answer the question why Jesus did not claim the title of Messiah earlier and why his messiahship was not more fully recognized during his life, especially by the disciples. Mark's answer is twofold: Jesus deliberately tried to keep his messiahship secret, and the crowds and disciples had shown an incredible obtuseness which was divinely ordained (4:10–12; 8:17f).

3. Mark emphasized three points to help his community which was suffering unpopularity and persecution:

   (a) Jesus had suffered in like manner.

   (b) Jesus had warned that a disciple would share his sufferings.

   (c) Jesus had promised great and sure rewards to those who would endure suffering without loss of faith (8:34–38; 10:28–30).

4. Mark in keeping with the ideas of his time saw Jesus involved in a great battle against the powers of evil (3:23ff).

1963 (c)

E. Trocmé in The *Formation of the Gospel According to Mark* asked some interesting questions about the redaction of Mark's gospel which

> has no known antecedent and which, because of its brevity and literary weaknesses, contains little within itself to show why it was written.[214]

Why at a time when the only Christian writings were letters and perhaps some handbooks of Jesus' sayings did Mark decide to write a semi-biographical narrative about Jesus and not a writing like the Rule of Qumran, an apocalypse, a biblical commentary or psalms? Since it is absurd to assume Mark's ignorance of them, why did he omit such beautiful elements of the Jesus tradition as the Beatitudes, the Lord's Prayer, and numerous parables? Yet, according to Trocmé, Mark seems to have added to the Church tradition such miracle stories as the possessed man at Gerasa, the deaf and dumb man, and the blind man at Bethsaida. He sees Mark as the voice of a progressive movement which had broken away from the mother church at Jerusalem and launched out on a widespread missionary movement among the peasants of north Palestine. He examines Mark's aversions, i.e., the Pharisees are "despised," the Jerusalem priests are "feared and hated," the temple is "execrated," and Christians are criticized for legalistic scruples and naive apocalyptic beliefs. Mark, according to Trocmé, does not regard the Pharisees as the principal enemies of Jesus. Rather regarding them as the upholders of the purity of personal morality, he still cherished a limited hope of their conversion to Christianity.

Mark's gospel has mainly a theological aim, since it is

> the work of a man who wished to reform the Church of his own day.

While ostensibly attacking the scribes and the temple authorities of Jesus' time, he is really criticizing the establishment of his own time, the leaders of the Jerusalem church who were hindering the progress of the gospel by their attachment to the temple and to Jewish customs. These leaders are easily identifiable: Peter (8:29, 32f; 9:2, 5f; 13:3), John (9:2, 38), James (9:2; 13:3) and Andrew (13:2). Trocmé finds a certain mixture of deference and caution with regard to Simon Peter who played a decisive role in Jesus' ministry. He finds James and all the family of Jesus deliberately attacked in 6:3f and 3:20f, 31–35.

The gospels describe a considerable activity of Jesus in Galilee: Nazareth (6:1ff), Nain, Cana, Bethsaida (11:12ff), Chorazin, Dalmanutha (8:10), the country of the Gerasenes (5:1), Gennesaret (6:53ff), Petraea (10:1), Caesarea Philippi (8:27), Jericho (10:46), Bethphage (11:1), Bethany (11:1). But the present community believed in the identity of the risen one, the crucified Jesus, and that he was no mere figure from the past or just a founder of a new movement but was still present with the disciples and the crowds. Mark has no clear account of the resurrection or christophanies, yet he several times mentions Jesus' rapid victory over death (8:31; 9:31; 10:34). For Mark the resurrection means a mysterious return of a presence no longer physical or limited to one place. The transfiguration according to Trocmé shows Mark's understanding of this presence of a Jesus whom the Father openly honors and who is guiding his community and assuring them of their communion with the Father. Thus a clear distinction is not made between the past and present acts of Jesus. Like the disciples he was not interested in merely recalling the past, but like them he worked for the edification of the Church to strengthen their communion with the risen Jesus.

Mark, which is far from the naive description with no clear theological tendency as it has sometimes been described, is an accusation to the Church of his time

of neglecting its missionary duties and of complacently assuming a security guaranteed by the possession of the tradition which comes from Jesus. To this end he appeals to history against tradition and presents Christians with a portrait of Jesus where the whole emphasis is placed on the boldness, the mobility and the success of the missionary Master, whose vigor has not even been brought to an end by his passion, since he has been raised from the dead, and his disciples continue his work. The portrait is never exclusively that of the historical Jesus, but it is valid for today, because the Christ is once again mysteriously present among his adherents. Mark eliminates everything which, in the tradition, has no direct relevance to his aim. He preserves all that can be integrated into his argument, but sometimes boldly corrects it, so obliging the other evangelists to restore the primitive form in a number of cases. In order the better to shake the false self-confidence of the official guardians of Church tradition, he went outside it for narratives concerning Jesus, and found them above all in the very region of Jesus' activity, in the villages round Lake Tiberias, where the famous healer of the past was still spoken of.[215]

Trocmé[216] finds among a number of scholars an essential agreement on Mark's plan and subdivision into six sections of approximately equal length which some divide again into two groups of three with the break after 8:21 or 8:30.

Section 1:   1:1 or 1:14 to 3:6 or 3:19. 1:1–13 is taken by some as an introduction to the whole Gospel.

Section 2:   3:7 or 3:20 to 6:6, 6:13 or 6:29. The problem is the placing of 6:17–29, the death of the Baptist.

Section 3:   6:7, 6:14 or 6:30 to 8:21, 8:26 or 8:30. Peter's confession (8:27–30) is the hinge, and the episode can be attached to section 3 or 4.

Section 4:   8:22, 8:27 or 8:31 to 10:45 or 10:52. The healing of Bartimaeus (10:46–52) is difficult to place.

Section 5:   10:46 or 11:1 to 13:37.

Section 6:   14:1 to 16:8.

For Trocmé the original Mark which was more or less Mark 1—13 stopped at the end of the synoptic apocalypse so that the story of the passion is only a disturbing appendix. He criticizes writers like Kähler, Bultmann, Taylor and Cranfield who describe the passion story as the center of gravity and the Easter story as the conclusion. The original Mark was written in Palestine by the group of seven and their circles whose ideas in Acts 6—8, 11:19–21 and 22:20 he finds close to Mark. Thus he gives a fairly early date closer to the time when Jesus lived on earth. The earliest date is 40 when the collusion of the Pharisees and Herod Agrippa (died 44) posed a threat to the Christians and justified their association in 3:6 and 12:13. Also Caligula's plan in 39–41 to set up his statue in the temple is reflected in 13:14. The latest date A.D. 57 is Luke's discovery and use of the original Mark during his two-year stay with the prisoner Paul in Caesarea (before 57). He argues that chapters 14—16 belong to a second edition of Mark c. 85, i.e., after Luke (A.D. 80?). It was an anonymous ecclesiastic of the Roman community who put the two documents together. To Mark was attributed the second document, a liturgical document used perhaps for the annual commemoration of the passion. His name was transferred to the final document, thus putting it under the quasi-apostolic patronage of Peter.

In a 1973 article[217] Trocmé asks: "Is there a Marcan Christology?" Jesus is evidently radically different from the ordinary man and greatly superior to the most prominent people as a teacher, healer, debater, and leader of men (1:7f, 22, 27; 2:12, 27f; 3:11, 27). Trocmé sees Mark as centered on the person of Jesus and "the behavior of those who came face to face with him." Christology is less important than the constant call to follow, to learn from Jesus in order to become the Church for the world. None of the titles in Mark is used as a vehicle for his Christology. Neither Son of God, Son of Man nor teacher is used to give expression to a new image of Jesus. For Mark the right Christology is primarily an acceptance of suffering for the sake of Christ. He is reacting against some Christians whose spokesman is Peter and who know quite well who Jesus is and like saying it but are afraid to risk too much to spread the gospel. The messianic secret vanishes for lack of evidence, e.g., the stupidity of the disciples is due to ambition, pride, narrow-mindedness and heartlessness; the private teaching they receive is not Christological in most cases.

1964 (a)

S. Schulz[218] maintains that Mark's purpose is not to record history pure and simple but rather to give a kerygmatic and edifying interpretation of history to proclaim a message. Mark in fact is the only person to write a gospel. Before him the word gospel meant a message of good news in an oral or letter form. After him Matthew and Luke wrote rather "Lives of Jesus." The important question in understanding Mark is to try to discover what theological problems he was facing and trying to correct. Jesus in Mark's gospel is shown as a divine man, as God himself in human form, the God-man incognito. Mark in fact reinterpreted the traditions about Jesus which he had received

> by means of an epiphany-Christological pattern of humiliation and exaltation.[219]

He united the traditions from the Palestinian community with the Hellenistic Christian tradition, especially Paul's kerygma of the cross, thus putting the emphasis on the passion and a Son of God eschatology. However, not many perhaps would agree that the pre-Marcan traditions should be dichotomized into either Q traditions of a future Son of Man or the Pauline gospel which Mark used to reinterpret them.

1964 (b)

Philip Vielhauer published a study of Mark's Christology.[220] He notes that the title "Son of God" is proclaimed at three key points in Mark's narrative, unlike 1:24, 3:11 and 5:7 where it leads to rebuke. It is his chief title as can be seen from Mark's superscription in 1:1. Thus Christology is the key concern of Mark who bases his gospel on the structure of the triadic scheme of the enthronement ceremonial, the ancient Egyptian rites used for the installation of a king. These are reflected also in 1 Timothy 3:16, Hebrews 1:5–13, and Revelation 5. This drama contained three acts: (a) the king receives the divine gift of the Spirit from the Father and is adopted, i.e., Jesus' baptism (1:11); (b) then he is presented to the pantheon of the gods, i.e., the transfiguration (9:7); (c) finally he is proclaimed as the ruler of the world, i.e., the crucifixion (15:39) which is the actual enthronement when a world dominion is handed over to the Crucified One as is evident from the cosmic wonders, the acclamation of the centurion who represents humanity, and then at 16:6 by the word of the angel.

For Vielhauer the gospel is the story of the hidden mission of a divine Son who passes unrecognized through the world of men. The demons are rebuked for recognizing him. But three moments of revelation are given, leading to the recognition by the centurion. Vielhauer criticizes Wrede's messianic secret and sees it rather as the theology of the cross read back into Jesus' life on earth as the myth is historicized.

1965 (a)

Alfred Suhl in a study of the use of the Old Testament in Mark[221] concluded that unlike the other synoptics Mark did not use the Old Testament in a pattern of prophecy and fulfillment. Rather he describes his New Testament events in Old Testament coloring and echoes. He pre-supposes a close knowledge of the Old Testament on behalf of his readers all through his gospel as is seen from the Old Testament patterns which lie behind the announcement in the baptismal scene, e.g., the unmistakable allusion in 14:18 to Psalm 41:9 which does not emphasize fulfillment but stresses the divine will in all that happens to Jesus.

1965 (b)

E. Best in *The Temptation and the Passion: The Marcan Soteriology*[222] sees the temptation of Jesus in Mark as the binding of Satan referred to in the parable of the strong man which Best takes as an allegory, unlike Matthew and Luke. Like J. M. Robinson, he stresses the exorcisms in Mark. However, he sees Jesus therefore not as the champion of man who has to win anew each battle against the demoniac forces. Rather Jesus is the strong Son of God who has bound Satan in the temptation, whom the demons already recognize as their master and who is now plundering Satan's possessions and releasing man from Satan's underlings. The temptations which Jesus resists and the evil which he overcomes in his ministry are the result of human sin, not of Satanic interference. Evil for Mark includes the seductive power of wealth, fear of persecution, enticements of other men and man's inner weakness; all these cause man to sin. Mark is interested in Jesus as the bearer of forgiveness and as teacher rather than as exorcist. Jesus shows men a new way of life and the truth of the cross as redemptive. In the parable of the sower Best has difficulty in interpreting the birds to represent Satan as still active and suggests that Mark is somewhat inconsistent.

Best examines the term "Christ" (Hebrew "Messiah") and notes that it is rarely found in significant passages (1:1; 8:29; 9:41; 12:35ff; 13:21; 14:61f; 15:26), and he concludes:

> Mark leaves the title, so far as we know, in the material as it comes to him; he does not deny that Jesus is the Christ, nor does he stress it. In itself the title tells us nothing about the achievement of Jesus; it may even suggest a false conception of the central figure of Mark's gospel.

Best emphasizes Jesus' training and teaching of the Twelve:

> The main purpose of his teaching is to bring his followers to an understanding of his own cross, not only as redemptive, but also as a way of life for themselves: they must take up their crosses as he did and serve as he served (p 190).

For Best, Mark's understanding of Jesus' death is not based on the Hellenistic redeemer model as scholars such as Bultmann have claimed. It is a development of the Jewish tradition about the obedient son, especially Isaac whose obedience unto death was considered in first century Judaism as

> the one perfect sacrifice by which the sins of the people of Israel were forgiven.

Best notes that Mark's emphasis on the suffering rather than the triumph of the Son of Man is already found in Daniel 7:13, 21, 25, 27.

1965 (c)

J. Bowman in *The Gospel of Mark: The New Christian Jewish Passover Haggada*[223] takes up some suggestions of David Daube[224] that the form of the Passover Haggada explains some of the sequences of material in Mark. Bowman criticizes the "calendar" hypotheses for not providing an adequate explanation of the gospel as a unit, as a published whole based on internal data. He presupposes that it is not a biography but is

> highly stylized and rigorously subordinated to a certain pattern (p xiv)

and he asserts that

> Mark devoted three-eighths of the gospel to events immediately leading to his [Jesus'] death (p 312).

He suggests that the Passover festival, the archetype for Israel's redemption with its past and future aspects, provided the occasion. The Passover had a retelling of the exodus liberation, a haggada (Ex 13:8).

> This Passover haggada with all its diversity but underlying unity provided the pattern not merely for the Last Supper, but for the whole of Mark's Gospel form.

It would explain the emphasis on Jesus' passion in Mark and according to Bowman his episodic narrative which was an imitation of the Jewish haggada.

1966

R. H. Fuller, in *A Critical Introduction to the New Testament,*[225] sees all four gospels as products of the sub-apostolic age. They are then "primarily" evidence not for the history of Jesus nor even for the theology of the apostolic Church but for the theology of the sub-apostolic age. Thus at the Jesus level of the parable of the sower we have the "pure parable itself" (4:3–8). The allegorical interpretation was added at a later stage in the Hellenistic missionary Church (4:14–20). Finally the evangelist Mark added from another tradition the interpretation passage (4:10–13). According to Fuller a homilist would have to decide which of the three levels speaks most directly to the situation of his congregation and treat the parable at that particular level.[226] He finds the clue to this "sub-apostolic" theology in the redaction of traditional materials, their order of the units, the links that they construct, and their overall shape and structure (p 104).

Fuller sees Mark as a powerful reassertion in terms of "a life of Jesus" of the Pauline kerygma of the cross emerging likewise from the Hellenistic church. His church is tempted by false teachers (13:6, 22) to think of Jesus as a divine man. Yet he sees the evidence which Bacon found of Pauline influence in 10:45 and 14:24 as part of the common stock of apostolic Christianity going back to the early Palestinian community. Paul often has Mark's favorite Christological title "Son of God." Both seem to presuppose the pre-existence of the Son of God and his descent into the world, e.g., Mark 1:35ff: "for this purpose came I forth," i.e., from the Father of heaven, 12:6, where God sends his beloved son. He sees the presentation of the miracles as epiphanies implying pre-existence, and in particular the transfiguration is an unveiling of Jesus' divine nature. Fuller points out that both were concerned to tone down this Hellenistic emphasis: Paul by his "kenosis" concept (Phil 2:6ff) and his emphasis on the cross (2 Cor 10—13), Mark, by his messianic secret, thus opposing the same kind of Hellenistic man Christology as Paul by his three devices which Wrede noted were not in the tradition but in the redaction and thus give a clue to Mark's theology. These three are the injunctions to silence in the exorcisms and healings, the disciples' misunderstanding of Jesus, and Mark's theory that the parables were deliberately told to provoke misunderstandings. Fuller sees Mark as clearly trying to reduce the emphasis on miracles while not rejecting them and also to tone down the reader's impression that the miracles, teaching and activity of Jesus are complete revelations of Jesus' messiahship. Mark's point is that Jesus can only be properly confessed as Son of God in the light of the crucifixion and resurrection. The miracles and episodes of Jesus' Galilean ministry can be seen and treated by the homilist only as pre-figurations (in Austin Farrer's words) of the supreme messianic miracle which is the death and resurrection of Jesus. Fuller agrees that Jesus did not make any "explicit" messianic claim. Yet against Wrede he sees the life of Jesus as implicitly Christological through and through. It only became explicit with the rise of the Easter faith.[227]

According to Fuller Mark has his own distinctive "theologia crucis" which is different from Paul's. Jesus is forsaken by all, finally even by God, and he dies saying "My God, my God. . . ." Yet Fuller notes the confidence, grace and almost ease with which Jesus in Mark's gospel moves, with a sense of the inevitability of his victory.

1967 (a)

E. Schweizer, who had written several articles since 1962 on Mark's theology and his contribution to the quest of the historical Jesus, published a commentary on Mark. What is interesting in the English translation[228] is that the text of Mark in English is taken from the Good News Bible which, not unlike the Jerusalem Bible, uses the modern translation theory of dynamic equivalence.[229] This philosophy of translation which is not a paraphrase seeks the closest natural equivalence to the original language (source language). It tries to state accurately the meaning of the original text in a language which is widely understood in today's English, avoiding "biblical English" or "Semitisms." Its aim is to make the reader forget he is using a translation and to produce the same effect on him as the original produced on its audience. This is a wonderful ideal but not so easily realized. Most scholars would agree that for a scholarly study of a biblical text a translation such as the Common Bible (R.S.V.) or the New American Bible should be compared. These keep closer to the form of the original text whereas the "dynamic equivalent" texts often make decisions about the interpretation of the original which need to be justified.

Schweizer's interpretation is based on his study of word statistics by which he identified Mark's typical vocabulary which he has worked into his redaction and on his analysis of the gospel's structure. Both show Mark's theological outlook. For Mark, the time of the kerygma which he reserves to Jesus to proclaim (1:15; 6:12) is the age of salvation prophesied in the Old Testament. It begins with the Baptist, and is continued by the disciples, and leads to the universal mission of the Church. Mark stresses the universality of the gospel by using the words "all" (1:5; 2:13; 4:1; 6:33, 39, 41; 13:10) and "whole" (1:28, 33, 39; 6:55). The kingdom which Jesus proclaims is not a teaching but rather the mystery which Jesus himself embodies and reveals only to his disciples who seem incapable of understanding it. Jesus' ministry and teaching which is almost indistinguishable from his miracles and exorcisms is a revelation of his own identity and function in the kingdom. The structure of Mark shows the progressive revelation of Jesus' status as Messiah and Son of God (1:1—8:30) and suffering Son of Man (8:31—16:9). Jesus deliberately concealed this status during his ministry and the disciples only imperfectly understood it, but at his death it was understood by the Roman centurion.

While it is evident that Mark is writing for believers who lived after the time of Jesus, he directly speaks only of the time of Jesus and the kind of relationships possible during his life. For Schweizer Mark is criticizing inadequate views of Jesus which were quite prevalent in his day. First the Jewish Christian community honored Jesus primarily as a human person, an outstanding ethical teacher. However, enthusiasts such as at Corinth tended to ignore Jesus' humanity. They overemphasized the resurrection and the heavenly Christ so much that Paul found it necessary to stress the cross (1 Cor 1—2). Another group, perhaps in Syria, put the emphasis on Jesus' mighty deeds, looking on him as a kind of incarnation of divine powers and his death as a tragic end due to man's failure to recognize him. Mark, creating a new literary form, steers a course between this Charybdis and Scylla, accepting the basic truth of each but insisting that in the real human life of Jesus God encountered man. There was a danger that Jesus as a real man might fade into a mere symbol or a cipher that says nothing and that therefore the kerygma might lose all roots in history. Yet Mark was not attempting to give a transcript of Jesus' life. He wants to show the difficulties which revelation encounters with men. Mark, who estimates miracles highly, stresses Jesus' refusal to give demonstrable proofs on the one hand and his readiness to suffer rejection and death on the other. Visible proof would turn faith into nothing more than

> a logical conclusion which anyone ultimately might draw without becoming involved (p 174).

Thus for Schweizer Mark's emphasis is not on the miracles and exorcisms which he received from tradition. He insists that one should not speak of a divine-man Christology in Mark or before him. He doubts that the so-called Hellenistic "divine-man" in the sense of miracle worker ever existed in the first century A.D. and points out that the "man of God" who worked miracles without becoming divine is found already in 1 Kgs 17:16ff; 2 Kgs 2:14ff. Mark, who is avoiding a docetic Jesus and also a false reliance on history, has above all an apologetic purpose to defend the true nature of the Christian faith and discipleship, its corollary, and to write a gospel about the unbelievable love of God who seeks man, all men in Jesus. Mark especially emphasizes the teaching of Jesus since the frequent use of both the verb and noun (teach, teaching) is due to the evangelist himself. Yet it is chiefly in the second part of Mark, in the prophecies of Jesus' suffering, death and resurrection, that Mark gives a content to this preaching. This emphasis on teaching distinguishes Jesus from John and the Church, both of whom are said to proclaim.

Schweizer accepts the priority of Mark, the use of Q by Matthew and Luke, the theory of form criticism that the gospel material circulated in small isolated units, sometimes already grouped before Mark (e.g., 2:13–17; 3:7–12; 6:21–43; 9:41–50), and that

> the passion narrative was told as a continuous story at a relatively early date.

Schweizer notes that from the beginning of the passion the sequence of events corresponds closely to the sequence in John's gospel and that many of the particular pericopes in the narrative would be meaningless outside their context in the narrative. He suggests that the earliest items are those found in the same order in both Mark and John.

With many contemporary scholars, Schweizer discounts Papias' tradition of Mark the interpreter recording Peter's memories. Unlike many scholars he gives three reasons, however unconvincing they may appear:

(a) It is very unlikely that Peter carries on missionary work with the help of an interpreter.
(b) The expression "memories" is fitting neither for Peter's preaching nor for Mark's book.
(c) The primary objection is that there is no evidence of any particular Petrine tradition in Mark.

On the contrary many of Mark's vivid and detailed episodes such as the possessed man, the woman with the hemorrhage, and the epileptic boy can easily be described as "memories," and there is an obvious Petrine theme in Mark, however one explains it. Schweizer does not think that Mark is to be associated with the John Mark of Acts 12:25, since he does not seem to know the geography of Palestine and writes in a very polemical way against Jewish customs which he explains to his Gentile readers (7:1–23).

Schweizer, in an article "The Portrayal of the Life of Faith in the Gospel of Mark,"[230] insists that one must first of all look at the totality of Mark's gospel to see what he tries to convey. Mark is the first to have written this new literary form, although John who is not directly dependent on the other three shows that there probably was a pre-Marcan tradition moving toward this new literary genre. Schweizer summarizes in three main points what he considers most scholars would agree regarding the structure of the whole gospel:

1. Jesus is rejected by men all through Mark's gospel. The first half consists in three complexes each of which ends with his rejection by the authorities (3:6), by his fellow citizens (6:1–6), and by his own disciples (8:27–32a; 9:30–32; 10:32–34), and even in this period of open revelation of his destiny his disciples misunderstood him.

2. Man is called to follow Jesus—with the call in 1:16–20 Jesus' work starts and the call is repeated at the beginning of the next two subdivisions 3:13–19 and 6:7–13. Three times the call is Jesus' answer to the disciples' misunderstanding in part two (8:34—9:1; 9:35–50; 10:41–45). Finally in the pericope of the blind man which connects the passion story the blind man is said to "follow him on the way."

3. Jesus cannot be understood without the cross. For Mark nobody can understand Jesus in a non-demonic way unless one follows Jesus personally on his way to the cross (8:34; 10:52), i.e., a life of faith. Mark's miracle stories are different from the Hellenistic ones not only in the structure but particularly in his placing of faith at the beginning of the story. Mark stresses that Jesus refuses a sign to those who seek one (8:11–13). Mark underlines the painful inability to understand Jesus of even those closest to him. There is obvious need for the divine gift of perception and faith.

The verb "to follow" is found in Mark, Q and John but always connected with the earthly Jesus. In the Old Testament it is used of following idols or Yahweh, e.g., in holy war. This following Jesus

> means to be with him (3:14) in such a way that he remains the
> Lord who goes ahead and breaks the way for his followers.

It means following him to the lonely places where he prays (1:35f; 14:32f; 6:31f), to the tribunal (14:53f; 13:9), into the midst of the storm (4:37–39; 6:47–51) and being trained in faith by such experiences (4:40f; 6:51f). It means a life of service to others (1:31; 5:20), to the little ones (9:41f), with the poor widow as an example (12:42–44). It means giving God the love which belongs to him (12:13–17, 28–

34). It means the kind of conflict which brings Jesus to the cross. For Mark such love only becomes possible for those who follow Jesus, who

> in his perfect love to God his Father and to the many for whom he has opened this new way to real life, has "shed his blood of the covenant for many" (14:24).

Schweizer, on the title Son of Man, criticizes much recent opinion and insists that as the title is found only on Jesus' lips it must have been used by Jesus himself. It is not some apocalyptic figure other than Jesus himself, for:

> It is hardly possible that Jesus who avoided anything of an apocalyptic nature would have used to denote the coming of a heavenly figure a title which at that time was familiar only to small separated groups.

Surprisingly, Schweizer rejects the widespread opinion that Jesus took over the title from the apocalyptic reference in Daniel 7:13 and rather sees its origin from Ezekiel where it is a characteristic used no less than eighty-seven times. Analyzing these references he finds an emphasis on humble service of God through suffering with an assurance of final vindication. This explains the association of the title with the Suffering Servant of Isaiah and suggests that the Son of Man sayings about the earthly Son of Man are the original ones.

For Schweizer Mark's aim is to proclaim Jesus as the Son of God but not to produce a description of the inner and outward development of Jesus. Thus he has no interest in exact chronological and geographical data. His message is to be found in the framework which he contributed as he arranged the traditions which he collected. The cleansing of the temple is put into the framework of the cursing of the fig tree to symbolize the judgment which is threatening Jerusalem and the temple. Similarly he explains Jesus' sayings by the setting into which he puts them. He maintains the historicity of the empty tomb because, if it had been developed later as a proof of a "concrete" resurrection, the story would have included a large number of good witnesses. The decisive factor in the miracle stories is Jesus' encounter with the person, his faith. The reason for the Marcan device of "the messianic secret" is

> that the time for proclamation has not yet come, since the secret of Jesus will become really apparent on the cross, and one must follow him in the way of the cross to really understand it (p 56).

According to Schweizer one of the most peculiar features is that for Mark the time after Easter is a time without Jesus. Nowhere does he speak of the presence of the exalted Jesus in his church (13:34). Even during his earthly life Jesus was never simply available, e.g., Jesus asleep during the storm. The "powerlessness of Jesus" continues after Easter, a period of wars (13:7), persecution (13:9), betrayal and hate (13:12f), tribulation (13:19) and deception (13:21f). Yet Jesus is present in his word as the final parable of this chapter shows; each servant has been given his work as all wait for the final salvation in the parousia (13:24–27).

1967 (b)

H. Conzelmann, in *An Outline of the Theology of the New Testament*,[231] makes some brief but interesting reflections about Mark. He criticizes Marxsen's use of Mark 13:14, suggesting that it was improbable that anyone who saw the catastrophe of A.D. 70 rushing toward him would calmly write a book to summon his readers to an urgent flight (p 144). He suggests that Mark is making a published appeal ("eine Programmschrift") to his Galilean community. For Conzelmann Mark's contribution does not consist

> in his forcing non-messianic elements into a framework of christological belief but rather in his putting together a mass of materials already understood christologically in such a way as to conform to the kerygma.[232]

He thinks that the traditions about Jesus arose from a need to protect his humanity, to clothe the bare facts of Jesus and his cross as the instrument of salvation with sufficient personal detail, to prevent the assertion of an unreal incarnation. Mark's gospel is focused on the idea of revelation and his concern is directed toward the period between Jesus' baptism and crucifixion. Conzelmann finds Mark's concept of revelation astonishingly well thought out from a theological point of view and agrees with the aptness of Dibelius' description of "a book of secret epiphanies." The opening title "gospel" shows that Mark is shaped by the Easter faith and is quite simply a commentary on the kerygma. The kerygma has the same imbalance as Mark in whom the last weeks of Jesus' ministry occupy as much space as the whole ministry (e.g., Acts 2:22–24). Jesus in Galilee is surrounded with mystery as he preaches and works his miracles. For

Conzelmann the theory of a failure in Galilee is exclusively the result of an unhistorical combination of the Marcan and Johannine accounts (Jn 6:66–67). The true motive for withdrawal is the messianic secret. When the true nature of Jesus is presented by Peter's confession, the transfiguration scene and the passion predictions, the way is open to Jerusalem where Mark has compressed the final events into a few days. The "messianic secret" suggests that the proclamation of the crucified-resurrected Lord can only be understood from the standpoint of resurrection. Mark is giving a message to his community not to be frightened by what they see and endure as they try to carry out Jesus' missionary mandate to the Gentiles, for Jesus foretold such things and will be with them in the Holy Spirit.

> What does the Exalted One do in the intermediate period? He strengthens those who confess him under persecution (p 141).

1967 (c)

R. P. Meye authored *Messianic Secret and Messianic Didache in Mark's Gospel*[233] and *Jesus and the Twelve: Discipleship and Revelation in Mark's Gospel.*[234] For Meye, Mark and his community in which his gospel originated worshiped Jesus as the Son of God.

> The narrative of Mark's gospel and its origin with the worshiping Church, as well as its continual use by the worshiping Church, makes this abundantly clear (p 30).

He sees the call scene in 1:16–20 as programmatic in Mark's whole plan anticipating the call of the Twelve (3:13–19) and their mission (6:7–13) and looking forward to the conclusion of Mark's gospel. He sees Mark's honest portrayal of the disciples as having the theological point to show that it was through such unpromising people that God was pleased to establish his mysterious kingdom and communicate his teaching. It is impossible, he concludes, that Mark's community did or could have loved the Messiah and hated his chosen disciples.

1968 (a)

T. J. Weeden, in *The Heresy That Necessitated Mark's Gospel,*[235a] attempts to begin thinking like a first century reader and to be guided by the same principles and procedures of literary analysis. These he finds in H. I. Marrou.[235b] Study of a literary work began with a summary from a teacher who used graphic techniques and pictures to annotate dramatically the important characters and events. When the content was quite familiar attention was turned to interpretation which included a careful investigation of the vocabulary and terms and a meticulous investigation of the characters. Therefore Weeden concludes that a reader would have instinctively turned to the Marcan characters, their portrayal and the events which engulfed them. A careful reflection on the attitudes, speeches and behavior would have led him to extrapolate insights so as to understand the intention and message of Mark.

Weeden places Mark's gospel in a world of the 80s captivated by the idea of "divine men" ("theioi andres") who paraded their powers as wonder-workers. He notes how in chapters 1—8 Mark presents Jesus as such a "divine man" but in the second part of his gospel stresses that Jesus is the Suffering Servant. Like R. Bultmann, J. Tyson, J. Schreiber and A. Kuby, Weeden sees Mark as using the Twelve as a polemical target so as indirectly to correct his community of a false Christology. Thus, in Mark, Jesus is a surrogate for Mark himself and the disciples are surrogates for his "divine men" opponents. The delay of the parousia had led to the appearance of a group of "illuminati," of spirit-filled "divine men" (13:6, 22; Mt 7:21–23; 2 Cor 11:13–15; Acts 8:9ff; 19:13–16) who claimed to be Jesus figures in the churches and to have esoteric knowledge of Jesus as a "divine man" and to be his personal envoys on earth. The community is full of eschatological excitement awaiting impatiently the return of Jesus (13:30). Mark, who is hostile to the Twelve, presents them as false teachers. He contrasts the true picture of Jesus the Suffering Servant with the false picture of the triumphalistic wonderworker in chapters 1—8. This is evident from the way Peter's confession is rebuked and from his insistence that Jesus is the gospel and his the only message to be preached (1:15; 13:9f). By ending his gospel at 16:8 he shows that Jesus is absent from his suffering Church. Weeden concludes from a literal interpretation of 16:8 that the women actually said nothing to anyone and therefore that the Eleven did not learn from them about the resurrection and further that they did not learn from "anybody" that Jesus was going ahead to Galilee and that he expected to see them there.

Weeden describes as a good example of hermeneutical intransigence Rawlinson's comment on the reflection of a friend who said: "How Mark does hate the Twelve!"

> The remark betrayed, no doubt, an exaggerated impression: The Twelve are certainly not spared in this Gospel, but it would be a mistake to regard Mark as cherishing any animus against them.

In the light of 14:38 Weeden claims that the Twelve are men lacking in the Holy Spirit. The Holy Spirit, Mark insists against his opponents, provides continuity between the earthly Jesus and the Lord of the Church (13:11). The Spirit commissioned Jesus in the task of suffering messiahship (1:10), and this is the only path along which he guides Jesus' community now. However, Weeden goes too far, since there is no evidence that the Twelve ever claimed a divine man status at any time. Such texts of Peter's behavior as Acts 5:3ff can easily be balanced with texts about similar behavior of Paul (2 Cor 12:1ff; Acts 19:11ff; 28:1ff). The criticism of the Twelve in Mark for staying in Jerusalem seems clear, but the problem is the interpretation, and many agree that Weeden's "vendetta" of Mark against the Twelve is too extreme (see 14:28; 16:8). Yet Mark, unlike the other gospels, does not conclude with a solemn commissioning of the Twelve (Mt 28:16–20; Lk 24:36–49; Jn 20:19–23; Acts 1:8). Weeden sees the gospel structured in three stages, reflecting the deterioration in the disciples' relationship to Jesus from the first stage where they are imperceptive to Jesus (1:16—8:26) to the second (8:27—14:9) where they misconceive his person to the third where they reject him (14:10–72) and are themselves rejected (8:38). Most scholars would however side with the view of E. Best[236] that the disciples in Mark are "examples" through which Mark teaches his community about the love and power of God. In the preface to the 1979 edition, Weeden admits that the term "divine man" has been significantly challenged and may prove unsatisfactory for describing the triumphalist Christology and discipleship of Mark's opponents.

1968 (b)

Rudolph Pesch wrote *Naherwartungen Tradition und Redaktion in Mark 13* (Dusseldorf). Like Marxsen Pesch finds chapter 13 of Mark of key importance and he gives it a similar date, although he interprets it quite differently. He finds an elaborate structural pattern in Mark of six sections, each in three parts with 6 + 2 + 6 pericopae. However, since chapter 13 does not fit into this carefully ordered plan, Pesch concludes that it was a later addition which Mark inserted when he was concluding his gospel. It was so important to Mark that he allowed it to disturb his order. Originally it was a kind of apocalyptic broadsheet which derived from the time when Caligula endeavored to set up his image in the Jerusalem temple. It was revived in Christian circles during the Jewish war when excited expectations of the coming of Christ were aroused, expectations which led naturally to disappointment. Mark made some changes in this prophecy and inserted it at the most striking point in his narrative just before the passion story. His aim was to meet a twofold danger of too enthusiastic a hope and on the other hand the disappointment of unfulfilled hopes. His aim was to teach watchfulness and a more cautious hope of the coming parousia (13:37).

Pesch followed up these studies with a two-volume commentary on Mark completed in 1977. This detailed commentary has received high praise from reviewers who called Pesch

> "our foremost technical authority on the literature and the state of critical study" and praised his "superb treatment of the text, judicious discussion of exegetical methodology, comprehensive listing of pertinent literature," his "undaunted criticism of the received tradition and 'opinio communis,'" and his "concern for the expression of the earliest gospel and freedom from dogmatic defensiveness.[237]

Pesch gives a fivefold exegesis of each sub-section, ranging from textual information to genre and from critical information, a verse by verse commentary, to a history of traditional information to redactional critical remarks. He uses the structure developed in his 1968 work, dividing the gospel into six parts at 3:6, 6:19, 8:26, 10:52, and 12:44, while considering chapter 13 as an interpolation.

For Pesch, Mark, the author, is a Jewish Christian living in Rome soon after 70. He has no demonstrable connection with Peter, since Pesch considers the similarity in name with the Mark of 1 Peter 5:13 responsible for the traditional association. Mark created a new literary genre in which

> missionary and catechetical interests were united in a presentation of the basis of the gospel in their historical origin.

Pesch is critical of the extremes of the redaction critics' attribution of creativity to Mark. He considers Mark as rather a somewhat conservative collector of traditional units, collections, cycles and complexes whose aim is to secure continuity through a careful preservation of earlier traditions. Thus, since Mark gives only minimal redactional intrusions, it is impossible to expect a unified theology in his collection of different traditions. He regards the kerygma or history dilemma as a false choice. Mark is giving an epiphanic history, an evangelical portrait, a narrative theology to serve the missionary and catechetical needs of his Christian audience. His aim was to arrange the traditions which he received so as to inform his church about the roots and foundation of the gospel in the age of Jesus and to provide the basis for their mission to the nations. Pesch gives valuable separate treatments of the messianic secret, the pre-Marcan catechetical elements of chapter 10, the pre-Marcan passion narrative, the passion chronology, the Last Supper tradition, the trial of Jesus, and the resurrection narrative.

1968 (c)

G. Minette de Tillesse wrote *Le secret messianique dans l'evangile de Marc,* a French study on the messianic secret in Mark. De Tillesse sees Wrede as the beginning not only of form criticism but also of Bultmann's demythologization and the recent research about the historical Jesus. While Wrede posed the problem, the others attempted to provide the solution. For Wrede the messianic secret was the projection of the paschal faith back on the earthly life of Jesus so that he becomes the Christ of faith, the glorified risen Christ, not the Jesus of history. For De Tillesse the messianic secret in Mark plays the same role that the developed account of the temptation scene plays in Matthew and Luke. Jesus could have had a triumphant career with dignity and power, but he chose the way of humiliation through which he would accomplish man's salvation. Thus the messianic secret is not Jesus' messiahship but the manner in which it is achieved. Nevertheless, Jesus' glorious sonship shines through despite his attempts to conceal it and his imposition of an ambiguous and impossible silence. The spiritual beings understood it immediately, and the people who benefited from Jesus' activity recognized that someone extraordinary was present before their eyes.

7
Mark Restored: 1969 Onward

1969 (a)

A new era began for Mark's gospel in this year when it was given an equal place with the other three gospels in the Church's liturgy. A new series of lectionaries for Sundays, weekdays and holydays was issued for the Catholic Church: *Ordo lectionum pro Dominicis, Feriis et Festis Sanctorum.*[238] This was the product of some five years of study and the cooperation of a large number of liturgical catechetical and scriptural experts with some 6,600 pages of criticism sent into the commission from all over the world. The commission was set up in response to such statements of the Second Vatican Council as the following from the *Constitution on the Sacred Liturgy:*

> The treasures of the Bible are to be opened up more lavishly so that a richer fare may be provided for the faithful at the table of God's word. In this way a more representative part of the Sacred Scriptures will be read to the people in the course of a prescribed number of years (n 51). . . . The sermon, moreover, should draw its content mainly from scriptural and liturgical sources . . . (nn 35, 52).

We have little precise information about the early Jewish synagogues and the early Christian readings of the Bible (see Lk 4:16–21; 24:31–15; Acts 8:26–40) apart from the occasional reference in writers like Justin. From the fourth century up to the Council of Trent the picture is one of great variety and freedom at the beginning but moving toward a greater uniformity at the end. From the thirteenth century the mendicants and the Roman churches began to use missals containing all the required readings for the eucharistic celebration. In 1570 in obedience to the wishes of the Council of Trent (1545–1563) Pope Pius V imposed a uniform missal on the whole Western Church which lasted until the reform of Vatican II. The lectionary section was not the result of careful planning but was an assembly from various liturgical books from different traditions. Mark in particular was rather neglected in the previous lectionary. A rapid survey of a pre-Vatican missal shows Mark being read in the gospel of the Mass only fifteen times in the full year, although it should be noted that Mark was read on the feast of Easter (Mk 16:1–7) and the Ascension (Mk 16:14–20) and on two other Sundays, the Sixth Sunday after Pentecost (Mk 8:1–9) and the Eleventh Sunday after Pentecost (Mk 7:31–37).

The new lectionary for Sundays has a three year cycle. The essential feature differentiating one year from the other two is the particular synoptic which is read semi-continuously, avoiding some duplications: Matthew in year A, Mark in year B, Luke in year C, thus giving Mark a full place in the liturgy. In the separate weekday lectionary the three synoptics are all read annually in the significant order of Mark, Matthew and Luke.

1969 (b)

K. G. Reploh's title shows that he regards Mark as *Teacher of the Community*.[239] What is particularly interesting is his careful analysis of the gospel to show the distinctive features of Mark's community. It seemingly was developing a hierarchy of leaders, with some seeking power and others becoming rich. There was a general lack of understanding of Jesus' teaching, particularly his parables and a reluctance to face suffering although persecution was imminent or had already broken out. The disciples with their lack of understanding, particularly in 1:14—8:26, represent Mark's readers and all believers. His redaction of such pericopes is intended to lead his readers to a proper faith. In 8:27—10:52 Mark shows that true discipleship leads to taking up one's cross and becoming last of all and servant of all. Mark is also teaching his community on the importance of children, the danger of riches and the necessity of prayer in the struggle against evil. He presents Bartimaeus as the example of how to follow Jesus on the way to Jerusalem. Thus Reploh's thesis is that Mark's aim was not to give an account of the past historical Jesus but to address his own Christian community and show it its obligations through an account of the Jesus tradition. However, he probably overstresses the typological aspect of the Twelve. More recent scholars such as G. Schmahl (1974) and K. Stock (1975) stress their unique historical importance and the fact that due to their unique experience of Jesus' life only they can properly mediate Jesus and his life's work to others.

1969 (c)

Quentin Quesnell's *The Mind of Mark: Interpretation and Method through the Exegesis of Mark 6:52*[240] sees Mark's gospel as a rather sophisticated technique for teaching his community. Quesnell endeavors to view the whole gospel through the prism of one enigmatic verse,

> For they had not understood about the breads, but their heart was hardened

in which Mark comments on the amazement of the disciples at the end of his description of Jesus' miraculous feeding and coming to them over the water (6:51f). However, Quesnell gives no convincing reason why he begins his interpretation of Mark's gospel at this verse. He advises caution in the application of redaction criticism to Mark because we do not know either his precise audience or his relation to them or his mastery over the material available to him.

For Quesnell Mark's intention is to lead the reader who feels superior to the disciples and their constant misunderstanding of Jesus in the first half of the gospel to realize in the second part of the gospel that the reader himself has not fully or properly understood because he has not fully accepted all the consequences of living the Christian way of discipleship.

Quesnell notes how Mark has gathered his universal, moral exhortations, directives and positive teachings (e.g., 8:35, 38; 10:24, 25, 29f) into the second half, especially into 8:27 to 10:45, although he notes that

> the entire gospel is concerned somehow with moral questions (p 137).

When Mark describes Jesus as teaching or speaking the word in 1:15, 21–22, 39; 2:2, 13; 4:1, 2, 33; 6:2, 34 he could have used the opportunity for Jesus to expound at length on any of the themes which he received from tradition: Jesus' revelation of himself as the predestined Son of Man, his destiny to lose his life, his passion, death, resurrection and coming, his moral teaching and exhortation for Christ's followers present and future. All these Mark must have known before writing his final draft and must have consciously restrained himself from mentioning until the second half of his gospel when, for example, the moral directives are often directly dependent on Jesus' own destiny. Also in Mark's plan his theme and problem of non-understanding which reaches a climax in the long exhortation and cure of the blind man in 8:17–26 must have something to do with pointing the reader toward the revelation to come. For Quesnell, Wrede overstates his case badly when he denies that there is any change in the disciples' understanding of Jesus' messiahship, and he quotes Wrede's remark:

> If the confession of Peter stood in chapter 2 or in chapter 12, the passion-prophecies were scattered through chapters 3—8 and 12—14, and the transfiguration were read in chapter 6, it would not make any real change at all, as far as I can see, in the thought of Mark.

According to Quesnell any child will grant a great difference between 4:41: "Who then is this, for the winds and the sea obey him?" and 8:29: "You are the Christ."[241]

Mark's plea for understanding, addressed to the reader to go beyond a superficial understanding of the teaching, work and identity of Jesus as the Son of God, takes as its starting point the ignorance of the disciples about God's message of salvation. They fail to appreciate the meaning and mystery of the breads, the eucharistic implications of the story of the feedings.

> The full meaning of the Eucharist is the full meaning of Christianity. It means death and resurrection with Christ. It means the union of all men in one Body. It means his abiding presence. It means his satisfaction of all wants in faith. None of this could be seen before the event, and before the central Christian reality which clarified the event as salvific (p 276).

1970

In the *Cambridge History of the Bible*[242] C. F. Evans gives a brief survey of the lack "of any great consensus of opinion in the search for a key" to Mark's gospel.

> The most diverse views have been held of its purpose and arrangement—that it is primarily historical, and aims to trace a genuine sequence of historical cause and effect (F. C. Burkitt); that it is

largely topical, with material arranged to illustrate different aspects of Christian truth (K. L. Schmidt); or that it is both (C. H. Dodd); or that it is numerological and typological, with each cycle preparing for the next and the whole gospel prefigured in the part (A. M. Farrer); or that it was intended to provide a church with a lectionary for the calendar year (P. Carrington). Is the work, "the apostolic kerygma—Old Testament evidence and all—built up into a vivid narrative form" (Moule, *The Birth of the New Testament,* p 92), and if so should the word kerygma be taken to mean that it was a missionary work addressed to outsiders? Or was it for internal consumption to explain Christians to themselves, or to arouse them to action in view of an imminent parousia in Galilee (W. Marxsen)? Was the emphasis on the passion of Christ and the disciple's suffering with him directed to those who at any time might expect to suffer martyrdom at Rome (A. E. Rawlinson)? Is it a simple, artless work in which it is fruitless to try to find any pattern, or a highly theological one to be classed with the Gospel of John (J. H. Ropes)? Was it a revolutionary departure from the tradition, or a criticism of certain tendencies in the Church (E. Trocmé), or such a faithful transcript of tradition that its appearance may have made very little stir (R. H. Lightfoot)? It is evident from the diversity of scholarly opinion that something of the mystery and secrecy which are distinctive features of Mark's presentation of the acts, teaching and person of Jesus hangs over the book itself (T. A. Burkill, *Mysterious Revelation: An Examination of the Philosophy of St. Mark's Gospel,* N.Y., 1963). Its abrupt beginning is matched by an even more abrupt ending; it combines brevity with prolixity; its poor Greek serves a vivid narrative style; the forceful, pregnant utterances which provide the sharp points of the individual pericopes triumph over a general poverty of form. The predominance of stories of mighty acts of healing, exorcism, restitution and provision, the preference for teaching in the form of controversial dialogue, and the part played by the passion and the approach to it, leave a strong impression of the Gospel as one of divine power and authority in the epiphany of the Son of God who is also the Son of Man, whose hiddenness, rejection and death are the predestined way to an ultimate sovereignty. But for whom all this was written down (the absence of citations from it in I Clement points away from Rome), at what date (except that it must be before the writing of the Gospels of Matthew and Luke) and for what purposes, remain obscure.

In four lectures on the redactional approach to the passion Evans has some interesting observations on Mark[243] whom he sees as a pioneer combining a passion narrative with a Galilean ministry to produce

> a remarkable, not to say puzzling document [as is evident from] the fact that after a century or more of concentrated study of it there should be so little consensus of opinion amongst scholars as to what exactly it is that he wrote and why it is what it is.

He agrees that Mark, like some of the apocryphal writings, approximates and exhibits certain features of the Hellenistic "aretalogy," a kind of literature which deals

> with the exploits of gods, sons of gods, prophets, ascetics, or other holy or ideal men, in which one scene is strung after another with no particular connections, except that they relate to the same person (p 114).

Yet he finds the synoptics on the whole so different in tone due to three causes. First the Old Testament language in which the stories are told ties them firmly to the Old Testament idea of the one God who manifests himself in power and action. Second,

> the compulsion which the evangelists feel to bracket the succession of narratives between at the one end the story of the baptism of Jesus (or his birth), and, at the other end, of his resurrection, with the transfiguration in the middle—

these stories secure that Jesus is seen

> as the God who stands behind him, sees him, and as the instrument of that God.

Third,

> the whole narrative of incidents, miracles, parables and sayings is so told as to move toward crucifixion, ratified by resurrection, and so the Messiah is not presented as an independent "lord" in his own right, upon whom attention comes to rest, but as one who is Messiah because he is "capax resurrectionis," and faith in him issues in faith in the God who stands behind him (p 115).

Evans describes Mark as

> built up as far as chapter 10 of a series of accounts of the type
> misleadingly called "miracle," interpreted at chapters 2, 4, and 7
> with sections of teaching, the first and last of which take the form
> of conflict and controversy. This first part would seem to have
> been constructed around the ideas conveyed by two Greek words
> which occur not infrequently in it: "dunamis" and "exousia."
> "Dunamis" is one of the Greek words for power and at one point
> (5:30) is said to be what Jesus perceives to go out from himself
> when he performs one of these actions. In the plural the word is
> used to designate such actions as words of power (6:2, 5, 14; 9:39).
> "Exousia" is a synonym for "dunamis" and it is the word used for
> the power when transmitted to disciples (6:7), but since it has the
> additional nuance of authoritative power it can also be applied to
> teaching (1:27). . . . From this beginning there follows in 1—9 a
> succession of such actions of power with respect to fever, leprosy,
> total paralysis, partial paralysis, storm, demon possession, hemor-
> rhage, death, food, water, demon possession, deafness and dumb-
> ness, blindness, demon possession, blindness. From time to time
> editorial notes are added to the effect that this kind of thing is
> constantly happening (1:32–34, 38–39; 3:7–12; 6:53–56). At one
> point such activity is connected with the unexplained term "the
> Son of Man" when the healing of the paralytic is said to be evi-
> dence that the Son of Man has "exousia" to forgive sins (2:10),
> and in a dispute with Pharisees over the disciples' contravention
> of sabbath regulations their conduct is defended on the ground
> that the Son of Man is lord of, or has power over, the sabbath.

From chapter 8 onward the narrative begins to change in direction and tone, and in this the Son of Man again figures:

> We have long been accustomed to speak of the "passion" or "suf-
> fering" of Christ, and to our sensibilities—partly as a result of tra-
> ditional piety of the cross—suffering tends to denote primarily
> physical or mental pain. The gospels would appear, however, to
> show little or no concern with this, if indeed they are even aware
> of it. In the Greek language the verb "to do" ("poiein") does not
> possess a passive with the sense "to be done to." What did service
> for this was another verb "paschein" (from the Latin equivalent
> of which the English word "passion" is derived), and the first
> meaning given in the dictionary for this word is "to have some-
> thing done to one," the opposite of "to do."

For Evans, Matthew's passion is just a transcription of Mark
with legendary accretions. Mark's story is predominantly a Jewish

matter with a comparatively protracted examination by the Sanhedrin in contrast to the Roman examination by Pilate in five verses. Luke has a better balance, with the Jewish side shorter and the Roman expanded to include official charges and Pilate's threefold protestation of Jesus' innocence. In John the whole is concentrated on the other side in the confrontation of Pilate with Jesus and the Jews. Mark describes a strongly kerygmatic proclamation of the action of God as is seen from the Old Testament language with which the crucial points in it are underlined. Mark's language (e.g., 14:33) indicated that he has in mind those for whom Christian discipleship involves an extreme of persecution. Mark

> proclaims an isolated event done by God on a gallows in the midst of total incomprehension and as the sole basis of anything that may follow from it (p 48).

Luke, for whom the passion is, not as in Mark, the reverse of a series of acts of power, gives a predominantly didactic version emphasizing the love of Jesus which Christians should imitate. In Luke the cross is, in Augustine's words, "the chair of the Master teaching," a pulpit from which Jesus preaches his last sermon based on his previous teaching, "Love your enemies. . . ." In Luke Jesus is the agent, whereas in Mark he is the patient, "though God is mysteriously active in his passivity." The dramatic John is the archetypal passion play. Evans contrasts Mark's dominant note of mystery and realism with Luke's pathos and humanity and John's majesty and irony.

1971

Joachim Jeremias authored *New Testament Theology* (SCM). For Jeremias, since Mark writes the most primitive Greek and is the least sophisticated of the evangelists in content, e.g., Christology, the censuring of the disciples, etc., his is the earliest of the four canonical gospels and the basis of the other two synoptics. The gospels arose from "complexes of tradition," not from the arrangement of individual stories and individual "logia." He believes that the whole of Mark consists of complexes of tradition (1:1–15; 1:16–39; 1:40—3:7a; 3:7b–19; 3:20–35; 4:1–34; 4:35—5:43; 6:1–32; 6:33—7:37; 8:1–26; 8:27—9:1; 9:2–29; 9:30–50; 10:1–31; 10:32–45; 12:1–44; 13:1–37) and that therefore "the search for a systematic structure of the gospel is a lost labor of love" (p 38).

1971–1972

F. Neirynck wrote a series of three articles which were published together in 1972[244] under the title *Duality in Mark.* It is an examination of the familiar Marcan phenomenon of duplicate expressions of time and place, pleonasms and repetitions, double questions, antithetic parallelism, grammatical and lexical redundancies. Neirynck gives a comprehensive list of this Marcan feature, setting out the Greek text with appropriate underlinings and other indications. Mark's duality had often been understood as the combination of two sources and in particular as clear evidence for the double stage of tradition and redaction. However, Neirynck, developing the reflection of an earlier investigator, J. C. Hawkins, who noted that the second half of a Marcan duplicate expression was no mere repetition but actually added something to the first part, concluded that there was considerable homogeneity and unity in Mark. Mark, in his progressive two-step expressions, has a process of refining and making more precise, as is evident from his temporal expressions (1:32, "that evening, at sundown"), local expressions (1:28, 38; 5:1; 11:1; 13:3), double questions (13:4) and the antithetical parallelisms which are recognized as a feature of Jesus' own style (2:19f; 9:37; 13:11). He notes also Mark's tendency to make a statement about Jesus' teaching activity (oratio obliqua) and to follow it immediately with a direct personal statement of Jesus (4:2; 9:31; 11:17; 14:35f). One could add what is considered a typical Marcan redaction, the scheme of public teaching and private explanation given to the disciples (4:1–9; 7:14f, 17, 28; 9:14–27, 28f; 10:1–9, 10f). This is such a pervasive phenomenon in Mark that it is impossible to separate tradition from redaction. It is a phenomenon which is often part of conversational style and oral tradition.

1972 (a)

Ralph P. Martin authored *Mark, Evangelist and Theologian.*[245] In his study of Mark's theology and Christology in particular, Martin gives a very useful survey of recent Marcan scholarship which has frequently been drawn upon here. Martin himself develops the ideas of E. Schweizer and T. J. Weeden and S. Schulz. He tries

> to offer a suitable background in early Christianity for Mark's publication and to place it in an appropriate Sitz im Leben (p 156).

Building on 1 and 2 Corinthians Martin suggests that heresies developed from Paul's preaching which proclaimed a spiritual, gnostic Christ or Jesus as a "divine man." These heresies Paul himself had opposed by emphasizing the cross. Mark, however, is dealing with a situation which

> arose after Paul's death or at least in areas where the influence of Paul's kerygmatic theology had sufficiently been diluted as to suggest a loss of grip on the historical events underlying his kergyma (p 161).

He sees the need to stress the earthly rootage of Jesus the man for Christians who were only too conscious of Christ's contemporary spiritual presence. His aim is to establish a continuity of this figure with the Jesus who shares man's life in Galilee and Jerusalem, and to this extent Mark is a historian if not a biographer. One of his purposes was to edit and tone down the magical associations which were so evident in the miracle stories and had led to a docetic Christology by deliberately stressing faith and avoiding the impression that Jesus was like the common Hellenistic magicians.

According to Martin, Mark's Christology is that

> of a teacher who has caught the essence of Paul's thought yet expressed it by use of language and terminology to which Paul had no access (the Jesus-tradition) and did so in order to compensate for what he believed to be a serious distortion of his master's thoughts as apostle par excellence (p 161).

Mark is no speculative thinker, but he bypasses the question of Jesus' prior existence just as Romans 1:3f and 4:25 and 1 Corinthians 15:3ff do. Mark offers a dramatization in the life of Jesus of the twin elements in Paul's teaching, the humiliation and enthronment of the Lord. This he achieves by

> a selective use of the materials at his disposal and by his innovative joining of a Jesus-tradition and a passion narrative.

Mark has a practical interest because the pattern of his Christology is the same as the nature of the Christian discipleship which consists in taking up the cross and following the Lord who entered his glory through the suffering defeat of the cross (e.g., 8:35; 10:45, Mark's distinctive notes).

Martin finds it impossible to give a final answer to the "where" and "for whom" of the gospel. However

> the external and internal evidence do offer some pointers to the conclusion that Mark wrote in Rome and for some Gentile constituency,[246]

e.g., Mark's explanations of Jewish customs and practices (7:3f), his interpretation of Aramaic expressions (14:36), his Latinisms. Mark's church faced the hostility of persecution in Rome in the years following A.D. 64. Martin rejects Marxsen's attempt to place the gospel's origin in a Christian community in Galilee. He can find no independent witness to this Galilean community in the 60's and wonders why Mark would have written a full-length gospel if all were directed to the parousia in Galilee. He sees Mark on the one hand firmly detached from the apron strings of Peter and standing on his own feet as a gospel writer and no mere compiler. Yet he can present (pp 52–60) a strong case for the traditional dependence of Mark on Peter. He puts his finger on one of the weaknesses of Wrede's "messianic secret" theory. He asks how Mark could have left traits of messianic publicity if he was determined to insist that the secret was only made public at the resurrection and was observed throughout the ministry.

1972 (b)

Jose O'Callaghan, S.J., a papyrologist of the Biblical Institute in Rome, caused considerable excitement with an article "New Testament Papyri from Cave 7 at Qumran."[247] O'Callaghan claimed to identify at least two fragments of the gospel of Mark, 6:52–53 (7Q5) and 4:28 (7Q6,1). All these fragments are quite small—7Q5 is only $1\frac{1}{2}$ inches long and $1\frac{1}{8}$ inches wide. The important point is of course the date of the fragments, approximately A.D. 50, a date which was first established for the fragments by scholars other than O'Callaghan. The evidence is admittedly quite tenuous and inconclusive, but if correct would pose a radical challenge to the dating of Mark and the whole New Testament. The fragments if correctly identified are too small to prove that they actually came from Mark's gospel. Further, there is a time span of at least twenty-five years in the dating of such papyri by means of palaeography. Even our modern revolution in dating which began in 1949 with the radio-carbon technique had to be corrected with the second revolution in 1966 through the evidence of tree-rings (dendrochronology).

1972 (c)

Leonardo Boff, in *Jesus Christ Liberator: A Critical Christology of Our Time,*[248] offers some very interesting remarks about Christology and hermeneutics in this Brazilian Christology which is a refreshing alternative to many of the "armchair," abstract Western Christologies. On the problem of the so-called hermeneutical circle from which no one can escape, not even the evangelists themselves, Boff insists that one cannot reconstruct a history without interpreting it. Therefore since no one can escape the self and arrive at the object no matter how much he tries to abstract from himself, every life of Jesus will of necessity partly reflect the life of its author and his concept of scientific scholarship. Each sacred writer seeks within his pastoral, theological, apologetic and vital preoccupations to respond in his own way to the question: "Who do men say that I am?"

Further, Boff points out that

> any attempt to reconquer or reclaim an historical Jesus at the cost of a dogmatic Christ merely confuses the dimensions and erroneously understands the faith as an inadequate and imperfect form of knowing. Can the historical Jesus himself be understood outside of the dimension of faith, if he himself, Jesus of Nazareth, understood his entire life as a life of faith? Is it not precisely faith itself that gives the proper atmosphere and perspective that enables us to understand the historical Jesus? It was not without reason that the primitive community identified the fleshy historical Jesus with the Christ risen in glory. History always comes to us in unison with faith and consequently any docetist watering down, be it reducing Jesus to mere word (kerygma, preaching) or to a mere historical being that ceased to exist in death, ought to be rejected a priori.
>
> The Word was made flesh. This means there is a history of a new and eschatological being, inaugurated with full, global clarity, in an epochal and unique manner, in the person of Jesus of Nazareth. This is the fundamental nucleus of the Christian message.[249]

For Boff, Mark, writing probably between 65 and 69, portrays a Jesus who is above all the hidden Messiah and, not surprisingly for a South American theologian, the great liberator. Mark emphasizes Jesus' actions and miraculous deeds rather than his words and parables. Jesus, who exorcises the earth wherever he appears, is

> the cosmic victor over death and the devil, liberating the earth of
> its alienating forces and inserting a divine peace, though he refuses to reveal himself explicitly and publicly as the Messiah.[250]

The meaning of the so-called messianic secret in Mark is that Jesus did not come to preach but to live in words and actions as the Son of God, the Christ, the Messiah.

> Jesus was far too simple, sovereign and original and attached to
> the lowly classes and the socially disqualified to give himself titles
> of honor and excellence and even divine titles (p 147).

1973 (a)

John R. Donahue, S.J. authored *Are You the Christ? The Trial Narrative in the Gospel of Mark.*[251] Since the pioneering studies of Wrede and in particular Dibelius, two principles of Marcan criticism were quite popular, namely that Mark's theological purpose influenced the arrangement of the gospel, yet to a large extent his passion narrative was unaffected as it had reached its present form prior to its inclusion. Donahue, using the modern methods of redaction criticism, endeavors to reduce the tension between these two principles. He finds widespread use in Mark of what he describes as "insertion." By this literary device a text is called to the reader's attention by being sandwiched between two identical phrases, e.g., 3:20–25 where the Beelzebul controversy and the saying about the sin against the spirit are sandwiched into narratives dealing with Jesus, his disciples and relatives. Donahue finds the same technique in the trial before the Sanhedrin (14:55–65). This scene is framed by the denial of Peter (14:54–72). According to Donahue, who like several of the redaction critics transfers the creative activity from the community of the form critics to the evangelists, Mark composed the trial scene and intercalated it in the context of Peter's denial. It does not reflect historical factuality but is a historicization of Old Testament traditions (especially Pss 27 and 35; Is 53) and proclaims the innocence of Jesus, showing his fulfillment of Scripture in the role of the silent (vv 60f), innocent one, assailed by false accusers (vv 56f) and mocked by his enemies (v 65).

In Mark it brings to a climax his Christological concerns. Similarly the presentation of Peter as a representative disciple—confessing (8:29), misunderstanding (8:32), at the transfiguration (9:5), at Gethsemane (14:37)—reaches a climax in the betrayal as had been predicted at the Last Supper (14:30f), leading to Peter's collapse (14:72) in a scene which an Aristotle would have described as "cathartic." The trial scene in Mark brings to a climax his anti-temple tendency and is used both to correct false interpretations of Christ the Son of God and to give an unambiguous and definitive interpretation of the title Son of God through the insertion of sayings concerning the Son of Man. The high priest challenges Jesus as "Christ the Son of the Blessed," i.e., Son of God (14:61). This brings together two titles which have separately been placed alongside the title Son of Man earlier in Mark. Jesus, by responding "I am," accepts the titles and abandons the messianic secret. This formula of self-identification used in the ancient Near East at an early stage (Ex 3:14f), and used also for deities, divine men and redeemers in the Hellenistic world, had been used earlier by Jesus himself (6:50) and by the "parousia pretenders" of Mark's day (13:6). Now the messianic secret is revealed, as Jesus is both Christ and Son of God according to his explanation in terms of the Son of Man.

In a more recent essay Donahue seems to have changed his position on Mark's Christology due to the Qumran studies of Fitzmyer who published an Aramaic fragment from the last third of the first century B.C., using the title Son of God for an enthroned king who was possibly Davidic. This title had too easily been seen as a Hellenistic title with divine man association. Donahue suggests that Mark's Christology should be examined in the light of Jewish royal messianism.

> For Mark the final assumption of total power and the handing on
> of royal authority will take place when Jesus returns as Son of
> Man.

Jesus, the new Son of David, like the older one, Solomon, builds a new temple, i.e., the future community. Among the Davidic references which he lists is the fact that Peter, James and John recall David's three generals, two of whom were brothers. He concludes that Mark's passion story

> owes its final form and coherent structure and meaning to Mark

and that it is the final product of a varied and complicated development.

Mark's purpose was to establish an ideal paradigm of trial behavior and also a theological rationale for Christians who were facing trials (13:9ff) as a result of the Jewish wars in the late 60's. His problems caused by messianic pretenders and a false eschatology were the result of Zealot activity in Jerusalem. He intercalated the trial within the denial scene to warn his Christians against faltering during trial like Peter.

An interesting consequence of such a reconstruction is that John must have known Mark's gospel since he has the trial scene in the same place. But if one accepts John as an independent witness, then the thesis fails to convince. Similarly, scholars like H. Schurmann and C. H. Dodd argue that Luke preserves independent traditions of the passion which would put important question marks against too facile an approach to the gospels such as that Mark created the gospel tradition and the other three knew and used Mark.

In a fascinating article, "Jesus as the Parable of God in the Gospel of Mark,"[252] Donahue makes the interesting proposal that Mark who is the first New Testament author to hand on an explicit Christological question "Who do men say that I am?" (8:27) should be read as a narrative parable of the meaning of Jesus' life. Donahue approves of contemporary scholars who have broken with Jülicher's view of parable as aligned with allegory and who study parable in the context of literary studies on metaphor, e.g., Robert Funk's description of parable as metaphor which "because of the juxtaposition of two discrete and not entirely comparable entities produces an impact upon the imagination and induces a vision of that which cannot be conveyed by discursive prosaic speech" and Keck's description of a parable as "a metaphoric life situation with disclosure potential." Donahue does not claim that Mark's gospel is

> a product of a sophisticated and subtle imagination which weaves metaphor throughout the text

but that like any literary or religious text it

> is the product of an author's imagination in the sense stated by Dame Helen Gardner: "By the time we have read through the Gospel of St. Mark nothing has been proved and we have not acquired a stock of verifiable information of which we can make practical use. In that sense reading the Gospel is like reading a poem. It is an imaginative experience. It presents us with a sequence of events and sayings which combine to create in our

minds a single complex and powerful symbol, a pattern of meaning."[253]

Using C. H. Dodd's definition of a parable:

> At its simplest the parable is a metaphor or simile drawn from nature or common life, arresting the hearer by its vividness or strangeness, and leaving the mind in sufficient doubt about its precise application to tease it into active thought,

Donahue tries to show how major aspects of Mark correspond to the characteristic features of a parable and work on the readers an analogous effect. Mark has no perfectly unified or dominant picture of Jesus but rather gives a multi-dimensional portrayal which allows and calls for a reading that is always open and repeatedly calls for revision and restatement. Like a parable it is so composed as to provoke the reader to question its precise meaning and draw him into a process of active interpretation and the appropriation of it into a life of discipleship. Donahue quotes Wolfgang Iser's observation that what gives a literary text its enduring and aesthetic quality is its ability to engage the active participation of the reader, e.g., the unwritten part of the text, the necessity of choosing between various perspectives, the hidden significance of apparently trivial and schematic scenes, the inevitable omissions through which the story gains its dynamism, the process of retrospection and anticipation, and the formation of illusions.

1973 (b)

W. G. Kümmel, in *Introduction to the New Testament* (SCM), concludes from his survey that a clear explanation that takes into account all the facts concerning Mark's Christological aim has not yet been found. He believes that Mark's objective is best determined correctly

> if his portrayal of the Son of man, who wants to be hidden yet cannot remain so, is understood as an expression of faith which perceives—already in the earthly life of Jesus—the hidden dignity of the Son of God who goes through death to resurrection, and which can account for the unbelief of the Jews, and the misunderstanding of the disciples, only as resulting from intentional concealment (p 92).

Further, Kümmel sees Mark as defending Jesus against the accusation of abandoning the Jewish law and against the suspicion of Jewish nationalism. All human guilt in Jesus' crucifixion is ascribed to the Jewish leaders (2:6–8; 3:6; 7:7f, 13; 12:13ff, 28ff; 14:1f, 55). Mark's apologetic is intended to make his Gentile readers aware of the riddle of the Jewish unbelief and their own grace. While Mark's gospel pursues no biographical-chronological goal, yet it is not correct to say that Mark had no interest in the history of Jesus as an event of the past, e.g., 9:9; 6:17ff; 11:30; 1:14. Mark represents the history of Jesus as a chronological sequence between John's coming and the crucifixion.

1974 (a)

Werner H. Kelber, in *The Kingdom in Mark: A New Place and a New Time,*[254] concentrates on the gospel as a structured whole and not just on Mark's seams and summaries like many redaction critics. Kelber's thesis is a modification of the well-known theories of such as Lohmeyer, Lightfoot and Marxsen about a Galilean Christianity opposed to a Jerusalem Christianity. The latter founded on Peter and the Twelve had led to Jewish hopes of a parousia in connection with the Jewish-Roman war and had consequently suffered a great blow in the fall of Jerusalem. Kelber sees Mark as a polemic against a false eschatology whereas a Weeden saw him combating a false Christology. Thus, unlike Weeden, he does not see Mark including the miracles to reject them but rather sees Mark as combining in a positive way the dimension of "exousia" and passion. He goes so far as to suggest that the original disciples never heard of the resurrection and are ultimate failures, with the Marcan Jesus discrediting the notion of apostolic leadership and succession.

For Mark the place of the parousia and the kingdom is not Jerusalem but Galilee. The time is not Jesus' generation but Mark's own—hence Kelber's title, *A New Place and a New Time*. He sees Mark as an unknown Christian writing a tract for his time in Galilee shortly after A.D. 70, using bits and pieces of earlier tradition and as full of symbolic meanings as Bunyan's *Pilgrim's Progress*. Mark is writing to explain the extinction of the Jerusalem church and the abolition of Jewish legalism to vindicate the Gentile mission and to emphasize the way of the cross as the only true Christian way of life. While one can accept that Galilee has more than a mere geographic meaning for such writers as Mark and Matthew and that it has theological and symbolic overtones, nevertheless it is important to remember how little we know of first century Galilean Christianity and that the Gospel emphasis is based on Jesus' actual ministry to the poor and despised in what was often regarded as a despised northern province of Israel. Further W. D. Davies well remarks:

> There is no Galilean idyll for Jesus in Mark or Matthew. For them both Galilee found much to object to in Jesus, as he found much to condemn in it.[255]

Kelber also, it might be remarked, seems to forget that Judas was the "evil" betrayer of Jesus, not Peter who is not condemned by Jesus in Gethsemane and ends up weeping.

For Kelber then the most surprising feature of Mark's theological enterprise is his elimination of the three mediating authorities between Jesus and his reader: the relatives of Jesus whom he relegates to the outside, the messianic charismatic prophets whom he describes as false prophets, and the disciples whom he describes as failures who adopted a whole system of self-serving values. Like the Reformation theology it is a rejection of tradition and a return to the fundamentals with a strong emphasis on the theology of the cross. Both Mark and the Reformers wrote at a time of considerable cultural and political crisis. All Christian churches with time run the risk of growing apart from Jesus and his original message, of developing an exaggerated sense of the importance of their institutions, of practicing faith as the way of self-improvement. Mark's refreshing and abiding value is that he invites us back on Jesus' journey through a series of unexpected experiences and crises to consider what Christianity was meant to be. Jesus is constantly on the move journeying through Galilee, making six boat trips across the lake of Galilee, traveling from Galilee to Jerusalem, and making three trips into the temple, and near the end he signals a return to Galilee. Mark's deepest concern is to reinterpret the past for the present. He, an anonymous Jewish Christian author, is writing in Galilee or southern Syria and shows an unusual preoccupation with the Jerusalem temple and its destruction, which indicates its composition in the aftermath of the Roman-Jewish war. Kelber remarks that both in study and in worship Mark has been treated as a collection of short stories and that because of this focus on the individual stories we have not come to know the story of Mark. Rather Mark must be approached from a literary perspective like any other story in his own terms without injecting Matthean, Lucan or Johannine elements and read as a single coherent story:

> to read the whole story from beginning to end, to observe the characters and the interplay among them, to watch for the author's clues regarding the plot, to discern the plot development, to identify scenes of crisis and recognition, and to view the story's resolution in the light of its antecedent logic.[256]

1974 (b)

J. Rademaker's *La bonne nouvelle de Jesus selon Saint Marc* (Brussels) provides a text of Mark in this first of two volumes in which he indicates thematic, structural and redactional links and emphases by the use of different kinds of type. He finds Mark's structural elements in his repetitions, inclusions, synonymous and antithetic parallelisms, and summaries (e.g., 14:1–11). He also discerns frequent concentric patterns (i.e., a, b, c, b', a') in Mark. Thus he finds the key to the prologue (1:1–13) in 1:7f. He divides the gospel into six "étapes" in addition to a prologue (1:1–13) and a "pivot central" (8:27—9:13) and conclusion (16:1–20). The first three "étapes" (1:14—3:6; 3:7—6:6; 6:6—8:30) describe first the approach of the kingdom in the coming of Jesus, second the mystery of the kingdom, Jesus and his own, and third the spread of the kingdom with Jesus as the bread for all men. The second three are the way of Jesus—entry into the kingdom (8:31—10:52), the kingdom of David—judgment over Jerusalem (10:32—13:37), and revelation of the Son of Man and Son of God (14:1—15:47). Each of his nine chapters has four phases in his study of the text. First, a careful reading of the text in the context of the gospel is given, noting the signs of composition, explaining the vocabulary and indicating the echoes of the Old Testament. Second, an examination of the sources and a comparison with the corresponding parts of Matthew and Luke are given. Third, the structure of the unit is considered, and its literary composition, chronological and topographical indications, and interaction of dramatis personae are investigated. Finally, an explanation of Mark's message for a twentieth century Christian is given in modern language. This study which was the product of teacher-student interaction gives lists of stimulating questions for further study (pp 74–79). The more original part of this commentary is its emphasis on structural investigation. However many will question the too frequent discovery of concentric patterns in section after section.

1974 (c)

W. Lane, in *The Gospel of Mark,*[257] accepts many of the more traditional opinions about Mark's gospel. Such a commentary is quite useful, especially in questioning many of the more radical interpretations of Mark which are current. He criticizes Marxsen's programmatic study, insisting:

> The assertion that Mark made historical events subservient to his theological purpose demands the affirmation that there were historical events (p 7).

Mark is based on the testimony of eyewitnesses (p 12), a pastoral response to the critical situation of Christians in Nero's Rome facing suffering and martyrdom. It is a witness document prompted by the apostolic preaching. The gospel is actually anonymous but unbroken tradition puts forth as its author John Mark, a Jewish Christian (1 Pet 5:13). The Papias tradition stressed Mark's initiative and independence from Peter. He was a theologian of the first rank and

> ultimately responsible for the selection, arrangement and structure of the tradition (p 12).

One can sketch an intellectual portrait of Mark the evangelist from the form and content of his work (p 23). Evidently he was a charismatic teacher. The wilderness motif (1:1–13, 35–39; 6:30–34) shows a significant grasp of the relevance of the Old Testament revelation.[258] His parenthetical clauses introduced by the use of "for" to evoke the biblical background to an event (e.g., 1:16; 11:13) and the allusive qualities of his use of rare vocabulary (e.g., 7:32; 8:3) give evidence of an agile mind. He perceptively recognizes that historical events possess cosmic significance in the battle between God and Satan (1:4–13; 3:7–12; 4:35–41; 8:34–38; 11:27–33). With pastoral concern he indicates the significance of particular events for his readers (2:10, 28; 7:19; 13:9–13, 32–37). He subtly designs his writing with rhetorical questions and parentheses to keep his audience from being merely spectators. Rather he calls them to get involved in the crisis of decision, prompted by Jesus to stand where he stood (e.g., by juxtaposing the contrasting accounts of 3:7–19 with 3:20–35). He can address his audience directly, e.g., 2:10a: "Know that the Son of Man has authority. . . ." Such Marcan parentheses are in contrast to the reserve with which Jesus spoke of himself.

1974 (d)

W. R. Farmer wrote *The Last Twelve Verses of Mark*.[259] Farmer, who is well known as a capable defender of what are generally considered lost causes, argues that the case against the authenticity of Mark 16:9–20 is not as strong as is widely assumed. His study is a response to Kenneth Clark's presidential address to the Society of Biblical Literature.[260] Clark drew attention to

> a most significant event of our day . . . the publication of the New Testament in English bearing the mutual approval of the Protestant National Council of Churches and the Roman Catholic Church.

While Clark in his review of the alterations made in the R.S.V. disapproved of the restoration of the "adulterous woman" to its traditional position in John's Gospel, he saw that

> the restoration of the traditional ending of Mark is a wholesome challenge to our habitual assumption that the original work is preserved no further than 16:8.

From the fact that Justin, Irenaeus, Tatian and the earliest translations in Latin, Syrian and Coptic all witness for inclusion, Clark concluded that the question was still open as the witness both for and against were early and impressive.

Farmer examines the Marcan and non-Marcan words and phrases. He suggests that the contradictory elements and the difficulties as regards the references to serpents and poison led to the suppression in Alexandria of the longer ending. Parallels to these can be found quite early in Acts 27:8, in the Acts of John and in Eusebius' treatment of Papias. However, Farmer admits of no final results although he leans toward authenticity.

1974 (e)

E. Schillebeeckx in his massive work *Jesus, an Experiment in Christology*[261] sees Mark as sounding a fairly solitary note within the New Testament as a whole. Mark is

> the gospel of Jesus' absence and above all the gospel of the earthly Jesus recollected and the expectation in hope of the coming heav-

enly son of man, an expectant awaiting of his exaltation which is
to usher in the eschatological kingdom (pp 421f).

Jesus is completely absent from his suffering and sorrowful Church
and in no way operative before the parousia. There is of course the
present gift of the Spirit (13:11) but the Spirit and Jesus are in no
way identical (3:28f). Jesus' absence is symbolized polemically by the
conspicuous absence of any appearance.

Schillebeeckx agrees with Weeden that Mark linked the exaltation not with the resurrection but with the parousia and that Mark
8:38, 9:2–8, 10:37, 13:26 and 14:62 are to be interpreted in the light
of 13:14–27, 14:6 and 13:26. The resurrection is not primarily seen as
God's correcting the scandal of the cross but as providing grounds
for expecting the parousia, a confirmation of Jesus' status as the Son
of Man soon to come.

Like the Q theology, Mark represents a maranatha Christology.
Schillebeeckx sees Mark's negative theology as an anti-triumphant
Christology which puts the rejected Jesus at the center. Mark is cam-
paigning against different forms of a premature "power Christology"
vis-à-vis both the earthly Jesus and the exalted heavenly Jesus, risen
but not yet invested with power. Since Jesus' death we find ourselves

> living in a rather drab but necessary interim period (13:9–13) in
> which Christian faith will be severely tested. But anyone who ac-
> cepts this Christology will be saved (13:10–13).[262]

For Schillebeeckx the search for a storm-free area for faith
which is independent of the proper degree of permanent uncertainty
of the historical result is unjustified. He finds scholars like Bultmann
and Tillich wrong in their contention that judgments concerning or
involving faith must be completely detached from historical judgments. The Christian faith can find ground in historical data.

The major part of this massive study is devoted to an exegetical
examination of Jesus' public ministry, death and resurrection. Schillebeeckx finds a fundamental misunderstanding in recent discussions
about the continuity and discontinuity between Jesus on this earth
and Christ in the preaching of the Church which sees the "breakage
point" with on the one side the death of Jesus and on the other the
Church's subsequent preaching of the resurrection. This point is
rather to be located within the ministry of the historical Jesus. According to Mark, Jesus' going about as the one who offers God's es-

chatological rule meets with initial success in Galilee. Mark amplifies the veiled ambiguous character of Jesus' historical manifestation, yet he only makes more plain what had already been consciously articulated in the pre-Marcan tradition. He thematizes the rejection of Jesus' message and ministry as early as the start of his gospel (2:1—3:5).

Jesus in fact rejected both the Aramean-Pharisaic exposition of the law and the high-handed Sadducees' devotion to the cult, striking at the very heart of the Judaic principle of performance in religion, in particular with his solidarity with the "unclean" and the tax gatherers and sinners. But from Mark 7 on the allusions to a great crowd diminish as well as the positive reactions. There is a growing consensus with regard to a hard core of history in the mission of the disciples (6:7–13), but Jesus does not seem too certain of the disciples' success. He plainly insists on a rest for the disciples far from the people, so they cross the lake, but unfortunately they run into a large crowd. This story not only is found in all four gospels but two have dual accounts of it. Jesus feeds the crowd in miraculous fashion. Mark's comment "They did not understand it" is especially significant (6:52; 8:17–18, 21). Jesus offers a meal of fellowship to sinners; they want to proclaim Jesus king. According to Mark, Jesus is obliged to constrain the disciples to keep away from the enthusiasm of the crowds and to return by boat to the other side even though it was night and a storm was threatening. Jesus himself withdraws to a solitary mountain. From then on Jesus regards his message as having failed in Galilee and decides to make an exodus journey toward suffering and death in Jerusalem. This is deliberate, since according to Schillebeeckx one would have to consider Jesus a simpleton if he went to Jerusalem in all innocence without any idea of the deadly opposition. Everyone was aware of the Roman punishment of crucifixion, the Sanhedrin had the right to stone (e.g., Stephen) and Herod Antipas had the right to behead someone. The beheading of the Baptist must have been vividly present in Jesus' mind.

Schillebeeckx's central thesis is that Jesus' unique "Abba-experience" caused him to see himself as the eschatological prophet. Thus a prophetic Christology, not a Davidic-Messiah or divine Son of God Christology, is a central aspect of Jesus' self-consciousness. Schillebeeckx plays down the Davidic dynastic messianism although he does accept a Davidic wisdom Christology. He plays down the Davidic significance of Palm Sunday and ignores the distinction between the prophets and the son in the parable of the wicked husbandmen, not to mention the transfiguration scene which he omits completely.

What actually took place between the two historically accessible elements of Jesus' death and the preaching of the apostles was a process of conversion which is presented in the form of an appearance vision. This hypothesis which is cautiously put forward is seen clearly by Schillebeeckx (p 710) as constituting a break with the centuries-old hermeneutical tradition. The disciples arrived at evidence for belief that the Lord is alive after having experienced the grace of forgiveness after Jesus' death, discussing and meditating on Jesus' sayings about the gracious God. The appearances are the result rather than the cause of the new-found faith of the disciples. False problems are to ask whether this Christological mode of seeing was a sensory seeing of Jesus, an objective or subjective seeing, a manifestation or a vision. There is no inference from an empty tomb to the resurrection but the reverse. The "He has risen, he is not here" (16:6) narrative presupposes Christian belief in the resurrection and points to the practice of venerating Jesus' tomb in Jerusalem and to the fact that some women were witnesses to the site of the tomb.

Schillebeeckx sees a basic vision with a fundamentally single identity at the root of the different Christologies which are merged in the New Testament.

> In spite of the not inconsiderable distinctions Jesus "comes across" everywhere in the early Christians in the self-same way. The unity turns out to be more universal and profound than the pluralism. . . . Broadly speaking, the New Testament is a true to life (faith-motivated) reflection or mirroring of the historical role enacted by Jesus of Nazareth (p 515).

1974 (f)

Norman Perrin in *The New Testament: An Introduction* gives the fruits of some twenty-five years of teaching and writing on the New Testament. He gives an exegetical survey of Mark which includes the insights of such students of his as Robbins, Kelber and Donahue.

Perrin thus summarizes his conclusions from his research into the accessible historical facts about the life of Jesus (pp 288ff):

> He was baptized by John the Baptist, and the beginning of his ministry was in some way linked with that of the Baptist. In his own ministry Jesus was above all the one who proclaimed the kingdom of God and who challenged his hearers to respond to the reality he was proclaiming. The authority and effectiveness of Je-

sus as proclaimer of the kingdom of God was reinforced by an apparently deserved reputation as an exorcist. In a world that believed in gods, in powers of good and evil, and in demons, he was able, in the name of God and his kingdom, to help those who believed themselves to be possessed by demons.

A fundamental concern of Jesus was to bring together into a unified group those who responded to his proclamation of the kingdom of God irrespective of their sex, previous background or history. A central feature of the life of this group was eating together, sharing a common meal that celebrated their unity in the new relationship with God, which they enjoyed on the basis of their response to Jesus' proclamation. Jesus challenged the tendency of the Jewish community of his day to fragment itself and in the name of God to reject certain of its own members. This aroused a deep-rooted opposition to him, which reached a climax during a Passover celebration in Jerusalem when he was arrested, tried by the Jewish authorities on a charge of blasphemy and by the Romans on a charge of sedition, and crucified. During his lifetime he had chosen from among his followers a small group of disciples who had exhibited in their work in his name something of his power and authority.

That, or something very like it, is all that we can know; it is enough.

Perrin finds four aspects of the synoptic material where we can come close to Jesus' historical words—

(a)   The proclamation of the kingdom of God which was the central aspect of Jesus' message (Mk 1:15a; Lk 11:20; 17:20f; Mt 11:12).

(b)   Parables which the early Church readily translated into allegories (e.g., Mk 4:13–20).

(c)   Proverbial sayings, e.g., the most radical sayings (Lk 9:60a; Mt 5:39b–41), the eschatological reversal sayings (Mk 8:35; 10:23b, 25, 31; Lk 14:11), the conflict sayings (Mk 3:27; 3:24–26), the parenetical sayings (Lk 9:62; Mt 7:13f; Mk 7:15; 10:15; Mt 5:44–48).

(d)   The Lord's Prayer in Luke's version.

Perrin's general view of the gospels can be seen from his statement in his *Rediscovering the Teaching of Jesus:*[263]

The most that the present writer believes can ever be claimed for a gospel narrative is that it may represent a typical scene from the ministry of Jesus.

This conclusion is based on his negative remainder approach by which he eliminates whatever can be derived from contemporary Jewish sources or from the kerygmatic proclamation and controversies of the early Church, thus arriving at the tradition as it emanates from Jesus himself. However, it is evident that this approach only attributes a minimum of material to Jesus. Evidently Jesus used sayings and opinions which were current in Judaism and others which the early eyewitnesses would have repeated in their controversies. Other criteria are also proposed such as the principle of multiple, independent attestation (i.e., does the material appear in more than one source, e.g., Mark, Q?) or the criterion of coherence (i.e., does the material form a coherent pattern with the material already decided upon?). Such criteria will never yield complete certainty and are often open to the accusation of circular reasoning and producing the absurdity of a Jesus who was a non-Jew and had little or no connection with the early Church. Any reconstruction must produce a first century Palestinian Jesus and explain his followers—why a Peter would leave his nets to follow him—and above all what led to his crucifixion by the Romans.

According to Perrin Mark is addressing the Church of his own day in the form of a story of Jesus teaching his disciples. Jesus is not just addressing the disciples in Galilee but also the members of Mark's church who are shocked by the destruction of the temple and

> in a situation like that of the women at the tomb, aware of the resurrection and awaiting the parousia in trembling and astonishment (16:8) (p 148).

Mark does not write a direct discourse like a letter of Paul or tell of visions like John of Patmos or give a mixture of remembering, interpreting and creating like Q. He has taken a daring and imaginative step of telling the story of Jesus' ministry in such a way that the concerns of the risen Jesus for Mark's present Church are in the forefront. Thus Jesus' past ministry in Galilee and Judea, his present ministry in and through his Church and his future ministry when he comes as Son of Man—all three are blended together in the narrative of Mark's gospel. His gospel is

> a narrative blend of proclamation and paraenesis, of myth and history, a literary type distinctive to Christianity.

Mark's teaching is characteristic of apocalyptic writers. He strongly holds the early Christian apocalyptic hope for the imminent coming of the Son of Man and sees his Church caught up in the final events of history. Thus Mark's gospel is cosmic drama unfolding in three parallel acts—

(a) John the Baptist "preaches" and is   "delivered up."
(b) Jesus   "preaches" and is   "delivered up."
(c) The Christians   "preach"   and are to be "delivered up."

When the third act is complete the climax of the coming of the Son of Man will take place. Mark indicates the movement of his narrative by geographical references and summary reports. Perrin notes that every major section of the gospel ends on a note looking toward the passion (3:6; 6:6; 8:21; 10:45; 12:44) while the central section 8:27—10:45 is concerned with interpreting the passion. However, Mark, writing shortly after A.D. 70, is not concerned with Palestinian but Gentile readers. This is seen from Mark's concern for the Gentile mission and his symbolic use of Galilee. Mark's concern for Gentiles and the mission to them is seen in such texts as 12:9–11; 13:10, 27; 14:9 and the many references to Gentiles in the miracle stories in chapters 5 and 7. The centurion, at the Christological climax, is a Gentile (15:37), and the prominent title Son of God is Gentile rather than Jewish. Galilee (14:28; 16:7), the location for the parousia, is likely to be symbolic rather than literal. It has come to symbolize especially the mission to the Gentile world.

With time Mark's apocalyptic purpose came to be lost and what remained was the vivid nature of his narratives which are

> so realistic that as perceptive a modern literary critic as Eric Auerbach[264] ascribes their realism to the personal reminiscence of an eyewitness and participant.

The realism shows that Mark intends his narratives to be understood, e.g., his explanations in 12:42 and 15:16. It draws the reader into the story as an involved participant so that he can hear the voices and take part in the action.

Three further surveys of Perrin in the Supplementary Volume (1976) of the *Interpreter's Dictionary of the Bible* on Mark's gospel and the messianic secret and the Son of Man should also be noted. In his review of Marcan studies Perrin notes that while there is no scholarly consensus about Mark's purpose in writing, nevertheless there is some consensus that the evangelist writing shortly before or after the fall of Jerusalem is addressing Christians caught up in a period of apocalyptic fervor to help them face suffering as they prepare for the imminent coming of the Son of Man. Mark is an author who systematically pursues thematic concerns. Perrin names five themes being studied:

1. The messianic secret is a theme introduced into the tradition by the evangelist to correct the tradition which depicted Jesus as a wonder-working Son of God. A distinction must be made between the commands to secrecy already present in the tradition, e.g., 1:25a, a typical element in an exorcism story, and redactional commands, e.g., 1:34; 3:12; 8:30; 9:9. These latter are a literary device by which the evangelist stresses that the titles are not to be used unless they are adequately explained as in 14:61 and 15:39.

2. Christology—probably the major concern of Mark who is writing against a Christology of glory whereas for Mark the suffering and the glory are equally real.

3. Discipleship—two different treatments are given by Weeden and Meye.

4. Galilee, symbol of the Gentile mission—two major concerns as Lightfoot and his pupils Boobyer and Evans have shown.

5. Eschatology—Kelber has investigated the theme of the kingdom of God.

According to Perrin Mark develops further and makes the most significant use in the New Testament of the three uses of the title Son of Man which was the most used designation of Jesus in earliest Christianity. The apocalyptic use was already fully developed in his community, and he only adds his characteristic touches (8:38; 13:26). But the other two, which were previously only tentative, he develops into major Christological uses. Mark has created the three passion predictions which provide the core of his central interpretative section (8:27—10:45:8:31; 9:31; 10:33f). In the third use, as a reflection on the earthly ministry of Jesus, Mark makes the ransom saying (10:45) the climax of his central interpretative section. He also gives a new emphasis to the title to establish Jesus' authority on earth as an anticipation of his authority as Son of Man (2:10, 28).

1975

P. J. Achtemeier's *Mark*[265] is a very helpful discussion of many of the issues which contemporary scholarship has discerned in the Marcan material. The twelve brief chapters discuss such issues as the intention in Mark's gospel, Mark's method of creating a narrative, his structure, and Christology, Jesus as preacher, teacher and miracle worker, his passion, the disciples in Mark, and the parousia.

Achtemeier points out that it is not self-evident that a gospel should have been written. The early Christians were focused on the future and expected this world to pass away and God's rule to be visibly established instead of the contemporary political structures. The early Christians collected traditions about Jesus not to provide information about the past but

> to announce that this same Jesus would very soon return, this Jesus who now lives with God (p 3).

He concludes that the author intended to be anonymous, making no effort to identify himself or the place and date of his writing but content to let Jesus' story unfold and stand to be judged on its own merits. He does not see Mark as providing an extended introduction to an already formulated passion account. Rather Mark skillfully composed and arranged the entire narrative from independent traditions in such a way that the historical climax of Jesus' career becomes its theological climax also and the key to its meaning as his basic themes reach their fulfillment, e.g., his use of John the Baptist, his juxtaposition of traditions, the conflicts with the religious authorities, the disciples' lack of understanding, and the repeated suffering predictions. The hermeneutical key that Mark chose is the passion, death and resurrection of Jesus. There is no real comprehension of Jesus apart from his final fate and apart from faith. Only faith can penetrate the risen Jesus and anticipate the final day of the harvest. There is no Jesus without the cross, no Jesus without faith and no faith without a cross. Mark tries to deny the possibility of seeing Jesus as primarily a wise teacher, a compassionate friend or a miracle worker, although he was all three but more. Primarily for Mark Jesus was the crucified and risen Lord. He gives no resurrection appearance, only a promise that the disciples will see Jesus at some future time. Thus the same ambiguity which cloaked the earthly Jesus remains until his return in glory. Only faith can penetrate this ambiguity in these hard times of persecution and other ways of interpreting life (4:16–18) when there is a desire to find in Jesus an easier way to God, a surer way to personal fulfillment and happiness. Only faith can anticipate the abundant crop of the final day of the harvest when the tiny seed becomes the tree (4:30–32). If a disciple has faith, Jesus, not self-interest, will become the center of his life.

Achtemeier incites his reader "to look over the author's shoul-

der as he writes his gospel" (p 91) and to distinguish the three levels
or kinds of material he provides, i.e., actual historical events, existing
traditions and Mark's personal theological understanding. Mark has
no set kind of literary form to which he could turn as Paul and others did when using the epistle form. Why then a gospel? Achtemeier
provides some hints for this first understanding of the Jesus tradition
as a "story arranged in rough chronological sequence," e.g., the crisis of A.D. 66 which was imminent or recent, the needs of the wider
mission,

> the disappearance through death of those who had known Jesus
> and who served as the wellspring and check on the traditions
> about him (p 6),

to meet the growing desire to know more about Jesus. The most subtle crisis he finds was the radical acculturation of Jesus and the potential loss of the traditions to interpretations that would conform
Jesus to the mold of the more popular Hellenistic religious heroes,
miracle workers, magicians or philosophers (Acts 8:9–19; 17:18–21).
The resurrection about which Mark certainly knew (p 91) is God's
vindication of the suffering way of Jesus. The same power which ani-
mated Jesus who now guides his Church through his Spirit is still
available to his Church which he invites to follow his divinely ordained path of suffering.

1977 (a)

H. C. Kee wrote *Community of the New Age: Studies in Mark's
Gospel* (SCM). Whether anything new can be said about Mark is a
legitimate question which might be asked at this point after we have
had source, form and redaction criticism. Kee takes us back to a suggestion which the form critic Dibelius made but never developed,
pointing out that the form-critics were content to define the social
setting of the gospel in little more than vague, general terms. Kee's
pioneering work aims to recover the situation of Mark in its social,
political and cultural as well as theological dimensions in which the
Jesus tradition was grasped and interpreted afresh. He admits that
the transmission of the Jesus story was shaped by the individual writers, but this was

> not a matter of aesthetic preference or even simply of theological
> conviction.

Rather the compelling factor which differentiated one gospel from another, one writer from another, was

> the outlook on the world which he shared with his community. This life-world framed the questions with which he dealt and the responses which he represented the tradition as providing him and his community.[266]

Kee then attempts to discover the full range of social and cultural factors which shaped Mark's community, their ideas, their horizon and understanding of themselves and their place in the universe. Mark must be interpreted against a Greek-speaking community background which reads its Bible in Greek and uses Hellenistic type narrative forms, yet has the perspective of Jewish apocalypticism.

Kee's multidisciplinary approach is to use modern sociological writers, e.g., Max Weber and K. O. L. Burridge, who are concerned with similar questions as an aid to using the internal evidence of Mark's gospel to describe his community. In particular, he uses Bryan R. Wildon's study of millenarian movements and his suggestion that the most useful criticism for the classification of a sect

> is in terms of a movement's response to the world [which] may be manifest in many relatively unfocused, unpurposive activities . . . also in life-style, association and ideology.

Whereas orthodoxy accepts the world and its values, religious deviants are marked by

> concern with transcendence over evil and the search for salvation and consequent rejection of prevailing cultural values, goals and norms and whatever facilities are culturally provided for man's salvation.

These are precisely the factors which Kee finds operative in the Marcan community's definition of itself over against contemporary religious, political and cultural institutions (pp 162f). Unlike the passive acceptance and contemplative life of the Pharisees, who accepted the social and political order, or the zeal for God, despair of human institutions and withdrawal and waiting for God's time, characteristic of the Essenes, Mark's community is at once "esoteric and evangelistic," carrying on clandestine activities. It is both "inclusive and voluntaristic," affirming both divine determination and hard decisions to be made by its members. Its attitude to the state is neutral but is negative toward religious authorities (p 147). It is a community which found confidence in wealth a problem. It practiced fasting (p 160). Kee finds rough but useful analogies between Mark and some of the Qumran writings. Both have esoteric interpretations of the Jewish Scriptures

> which point to the coming of the founder of the community of the new covenant and promise that beyond his suffering and death lies divine vindication.[267]

The scroll of the Rule has regulations for the on-going life of the community. The War Scroll and the biblical commentaries at Qumran like Mark 13 have references to the struggle with worldly and demonic powers. In brief Kee sees Mark as a foundation document for an apocalyptic community.

Kee begins with a study to determine the horizon which defines Mark's intention as a whole. Then he carefully outlines his own method as he tries to avoid imposing a sociological scheme on Mark. He begins with the literary questions and concludes that while Mark was influenced by Hellenistic culture he did not try to write an aretalogy. The gospel is a completely new kind of literature. Yet it shares many features with the literature of Jewish apocalyptic, with the overwhelming importance of Daniel who alone of all the Old Testament books is quoted from every chapter and underlies the ending of the gospel, the transfiguration scene and the apocalyptic section. Mark, he concludes, has been

> influenced directly by Daniel in his representation of the career and intention of Jesus (p 45).

Mark's community is not unlike the Qumran Hasidic movement which was alienated from all the other Jewish sects. Mark is also influenced by Cynic-Stoic itinerant preaching, teaching, healing and exorcisms (pp 105, 146).

Next Kee focuses on the socio-cultural features—What sort of person, in what sort of primitive Christian group, would have been motivated to produce this kind of writing?—the Jewish models, and in particular the disciples, as the model of Mark's community, e.g., their prophetic, charismatic ministry and avoidance of political involvement.

A constitutive element in apocalyptic is that the community regards itself as a colony of the end time, as the recipient of a revelation through a God-sent prophet. For Kee, a proper understanding of the meaning of Jesus for Mark's community is not gotten from an assessment of the Christological titles, but especially from the revelatory and redemptive roles assigned to Jesus by the community—the prophet, the mightier one, the holy one of God, the cosmic agent, Son of God, Son of David, Son of Man, Jesus and the Holy Spirit.

In his final chapter, Kee tries to produce a composite picture of the nature and self-understanding of the community that is presupposed by Mark, whose people were already living in the new age and awaiting the final consummation of the kingdom. It is an apocalyptic community of itinerant charismatics, with a Greek Bible trying to carry on the work of Jesus and ready to follow him to death. The time was just before the fall of Jerusalem. Mark was probably written in southern Syria as a challenge and guidebook for this community.

This is a challenging and highly original study full of interesting reflections and gospel information, however one may disagree with aspects and conclusions of it here and there. It seems to ignore the work of Reploh and others who sought similar reconstructions. What is new in Kee is his use of sociological models to help his investigation.

1977 (b)

John P. Kealy: *Who Is Jesus of Nazareth?*[268a] This is the present writer's attempt to see Mark's gospel as a question mark to the contemporary Christologies and the problem of projection in religion, i.e., of projecting one's own Christ based on one's own needs, desires and even prejudices. Four recent trends are considered, the existential, secular, historical and political approaches. The first half of Mark's gospel is seen as describing the encounter of Jesus with the various groups of his day. The religious and political currents in Palestine in the time of Jesus represent certain typically human options which exist in our time and are often mixed by well-meaning adherents with the way of Jesus. Mark is not just correcting a false Christology of his own time. He is presenting a picture of the disciples which he believes basically is historically accurate but which is typical of the human response in his own and every age. It is only when we contrast the way of Jesus with the differing ways of the Baptist, the Pharisees, the scribes, the Sadducees, the Essenes, the Samaritans, the Zealots, the Herodians, the tax collectors, the Greeks, and the ordinary people that we can understand the distinctive way of Jesus, i.e., Mark's functional Christology. Mark is particularly concerned with what Lonergan calls "scotosis," the capacity to exclude painful insights into the cost of discipleship and the realization that even a disciple needs to have Jesus open his eyes and gradually reveal himself. This study is a reflection on the ongoing quest of every man for Jesus and concludes with an adaptation from St. Augustine: "One seeks in order to understand but one understands in order to seek more." The answer which Mark is seeking from his reader to his key question "Who do you say that I am?" is not a purely intellectual understanding of Jesus but an answer of commitment to a person and his way of life. It is a covenant, a commitment to a deep personal relationship.

The present writer is rather skeptical of any solution to Mark's gospel which does not find some basis in the tradition about Mark in the early Church. Such a solution as the Galilean hypothesis is interesting but clearly not proven. The Roman community seems the best community which satisfies all the evidence and the time of the Jewish war seems the best date. However, it is all too often forgotten that Mark is a work of literature and art which typically cuts many of its ties with the particular situation in which it arose. Therefore it has been able to speak to different ages and cultures and like any great work of art give rise to an unceasing fascination and quite a variety of interpretations. There should be no strict theology or history dilemma. Mark is best taken as a pastoral presentation of Jesus' life to deepen the understanding of his community and especially its commitment to the way of the cross.

1978

St. Mark's Gospel was a hit in the West End Theater.[268b] Christopher Porterfield in *Time* magazine (September 18, 1978) wrote:

> The simple audacity of the enterprise is breathtaking. English actor, Alec McCowen, casually dressed in a sports coat and open-necked shirt, strolls onto a stage furnished only with a table and three chairs and recites, from memory, the entire Gospel according to St. Mark, then strolls off again. It is the sort of feat that is inevitably called a tour de force; yet a tour de force is precisely what it is not. The performance, quietly magnificent as it is, nevertheless is purged of all bravura. It is compelling theater that is at the same time non-theatrical. . . . The operative word for McCowen is tell. He tells Mark's story, he does not intone it. He clears away the ponderousness and singsong preachiness of centuries of Bible reading to rediscover the urgent, living voice of a

man who is recounting nearly contemporary events, many of them derived from eyewitness accounts.

It is interesting to note what this theatre critic picks out for comment in Mark:

> Through that living voice, living people begin to inhabit the stage: the scribes and Pharisees hardened by suspicion and orthodoxy: the disciples, stalwart but muddled: Jesus himself, patient and determined but often exasperated ("Perceive ye not yet, neither understand?").
>   McCowen sketches in these characters with a few gestures— flinging of his arms, walking a few steps, sitting, taking a well-judged pause for a sip of water. But mostly it is acting as the saying goes from the neck up. It rests on vocal virtuosity, powerfully abetted by the matchless pith and vigor of the King James version. McCowen's narrative throbs with excitement or drops to an astonished whisper during his recounting of the miracles. He stifles a yelp of laughter at supplicants removing the roof of a house to get at Jesus (one of several surprisingly humorous moments). He rises to a tipsy bellow as Herod offers Salome a reward for her dancing, then sheers off into girlish silliness when Salome, as if for want of anything better, asks for the head of John the Baptist. Only in the somber final chapter through Gethsemane and the crucifixion does McCowen abandon these shadings for an almost severely straightforward manner. With a sure instinct, he realizes that here a minimum of effects will achieve the greatest effect.

Actually McCowen, as he explains, has no theological reason for choosing Mark over the other evangelists. His concern is with words. Mark happens to be the shortest—the performance lasts two hours and ten minutes, with one intermission—and "the easiest one to tell aloud."

1979

M. Hengel wrote *Acts and the History of Earliest Christianity.*[269] Several remarks are worth quoting from this thoughtful study which may be described in words from one of its chapter titles as "Unfashionable Reflections" in which he questions the fashionable radical skepticism about the history of early Christianity although he admits the fragmentariness of our sources and the haphazard way in which they have survived, e.g., what the rats and worms have left of the scrolls in the caves of the Judean wilderness. He reminds us how little we know about Judea under the Roman prefects between A.D. 6 and A.D. 41, a period so important for the understanding of the New Testament.

For Hengel the author of Mark is not an unknown Gentile Christian but probably identical with John Mark (Acts 12:12; 13:5; 15:37) who was later associated with Peter (1 Pet 5:13). All the history writers of the New Testament have the one aim: "That you may believe . . ." (Jn 20:31). He considers decisive the degree of education, theological thinking, origin and school to which the evangelists belonged. Luke has the greatest degree of formal education. Matthew is indebted to the Pharisaic tradition whereas in John one finds an almost esoteric community indebted to Palestinian Jewish mysticism. In Mark, who is relatively closest to the original events, one can see the strong missionary impulse found also in Paul. Mark's attention is deliberately focused on Galilee, Jesus' homeland and the most important place of his activity. Jerusalem is the place of rejection and suffering. Hengel describes Mark as having "no literary education" but "a capable theologian and indeed a gifted narrator" (p 49). Marxsen's explanation of the word "gospel" in Mark's opening verse he finds as completely distorting—Marxsen had described Mark as a proclamation but

> not a report about Jesus [so that] it is almost accidental that something in the way of a report also appears.[270]

Hengel bluntly criticizes the cherished idea of the form critics that individual traditions freely circulated completely detached:

> The earliest stage was not the isolated individual tradition but the elemental wealth of impressions called forth by the meteoric appearance of Jesus. Then, still during Jesus' lifetime, there began a process of collection which at the same time meant selection and restriction (p 25).

The period of thirty to sixty years before the composition of the gospels was considerably less than for the rabbinic and Talmudic writings. Further, Hengel criticizes the idea that the gospels were

> the result of the anonymous, creative productive force of some Palestinian or Hellenistic communities [noting how amazingly few signs] the synoptic gospels show of the "needs" of the communities as we know them from the letters of the New Testament.

In essentials we know far less about such communities than we know about Jesus himself. In reality oral tradition was associated with well-known individual, authoritative bearers of tradition, especially Peter (Gal 1:17; Rom 16:7; 1 Cor 9:5). He sees Paul's allusions as a presupposition that his readers knew more (1 Cor 11:23ff; 15:3ff; Rom 1:3; 15:8; Phil 2:8; Gal 4:4). It would have been impossible in the ancient world to proclaim a crucified man as Son of God without a clear account of him, since people then were no less curious than they are today.

Concluding Remarks

One is tempted to conclude this survey of more than nineteen hundred years' study of Mark's gospel with the sympathetic concluding words of Qoheleth (Ecclesiastes) after his own exhausting and unsatisfactory survey:

> Of making many books there is no end and much study is a weariness of the flesh. The end of the matter; all has been heard. Fear God, and keep his commandments. . . .

A more positive view is that of the Syrian St. Ephrem in his *Commentary on the Diatessaron* (1.19). Ephrem tells us to drink what we need from the living water of Scripture but never to imagine that we have drained it dry. Not only can we come back again for more but there is plenty remaining for others also to discover.

However, we will leave the last word to some remarks from that modern Qoheleth, D. E. Nineham. He admits that

> scholars of very different sorts are increasingly agreed, not only about the fact of Jesus' existence but about the nature of his person and claims. With surprising unanimity, there comes from the pens of scholars in England, Germany and America an argument which runs something like this: None of the gospels provides a photograph, and the portraits in the various gospels, and principal gospel sources, when combined with certain striking similarities, are of a kind which suggest a single figure, a single sitter of whom they are all portraits. And by studying minutely the technique and style of each portrait and the kind of impression it was intended to give, you can begin to build up a picture of the sitter in considerable detail.[271]

Nineham's own somewhat skeptical view is that one joins the Church or remains a member if one finds in it in large measure

> what it claims to possess, peace and communion with God, community with one's fellows, the power to serve the world and the other elements of Christian faith and experience.

Nothing the historian can do will shake his conviction that God was at work in Jesus producing the community in and through which salvation should be available,

> whatever exactly the events may have been through which the Church came into being.

The application of modern historical methods suggests that some of these stories which are evidence for and part of the earliest Christian's response

> may be unauthentic, in whole or part, and forces us to admit that about the authenticity of some others we have no means of deciding.[272]

Nineham quotes with approval a modern literary critic who makes no attempt to "arrive finally at the meaning of" the play *Measure for Measure* but is content to leave the play more meaningful than it was before her study.[273] He is convinced by the brilliant study of Father J. S. Dunne[274] that it is possible to "pass over" into the faith and way of life of another culture, to return to one's own time and culture with one's outlook, faith and understanding both deepened and broadened. He remarks that any suggestion that in biblical theology we are "over the hump" or "into a post-critical phase" is dangerous nonsense. One of the disturbing or stimulating things which the cultural revolution in Western Europe for the last two hundred years

> has taught us, or should have taught us, is that there can never be definitive and timeless solutions of intellectual problems in the conditions of historical existence as we know it.[275]

There is a fundamental truth in the old adage "Omnia abeunt in mysterium." In scientific work ready-made answers on a plate are dangerous and even to be rejected as each person needs to do his research for himself, to find the mystery in a personal encounter.

Scientific research, we have learned in recent years, is not carried out with dispassionate objectivity in any purely objective mechanical or standardized way. It relies on imagination, flair, luck and creativity, yet it has its own often deeply hidden assumptions. It is not surprising that the Greek god Hermes, the patron of interpreters and young men's studies, who gave us our word "hermeneutics," is also the patron of thieves, tricksters, travelers and merchants. There is always a tension between imagination, creativity and the institution with its accepted conclusions, between theories and the detailed cross-checking which is essential for their validation. The interests and values of the researcher, his faith just as much as his absence of it, at least partially determine his conclusions.

In literature as in psychology or sociology one can never reach the categorical precision of abstract mathematics. Yet in a study like Mark the search is for the obvious, what in rabbinic terminology is called "peshat," the plain meaning of the text as contrasted with the unlimited number of other meanings which can so easily be read into the text. This is one of the paradoxes of modern theological thinking. Truth is simple and joyful despite the appearance of complications. So often in the history of religion the story is how simple, obvious and meaningful insights become with time blurred, complicated and obscured as man escapes into his rationalizations, theories, corruptions and institutions. Most interpreters are united in the belief in the search for the common sense theories which make sense of the whole of Mark. The aim of a gospel writer was probably multiple, and so the danger of over-simplification has to be avoided.

Yet on the other hand few would see his intention to be like Joyce's explanation that he put in his *Ulysses* so many enigmas and puzzles to keep professors busy for centuries and so ensure his immortality. Mark's meaning, like that of any great work of art, music or literature, is unending. Every time it is read it will suggest new ideas. For it is a mirror in which each can see and correct himself, and in a changing world every time we look we are different, and so the study of a work like Mark is a lifetime journey into mystery for each person, for each new generation. When correctly studied it is an encounter with the most human yet most mysterious person who ever lived.

It would be rash to predict the future of Mark's gospel. No one in the long history of the Church could have predicted the amazing revival of interest in Mark which has taken place now for more than a hundred years. Similarly, no one could have foretold the effect of Barth's commentary on Romans in 1919 when, to allude to his own image, while groping in the dark he grabbed a rope to discover that it was tied to a bell which roused the whole town. Mark has been such a rope which lay hidden for many centuries. One could say that, like the men and women in Shakespeare's *As You Like It,* the biblical books "have their exits and their entrances." But Mark has played such a tremendous comeback in modern biblical studies that it is hard to believe that he will ever take a back seat for so long again. Yet it may be correct to say that Mark's hand has been over-emphasized by scholars in recent years to the detriment of the other three gospels as if they were distortions of the gospel tradition. Mark needs to find his proper equal place as one among four equal gospels which form a unity. As an Orthodox scholar put it:

> Orthodox theology does not neglect the many differences but it lends more importance to the unity aspect, reflecting on the Gospels as if they composed an inseparable, complementary whole.[276]

Notes

1. For critical editions of the commentaries and relevant background information and articles consult a standard work such as *The Oxford Dictionary of the Christian Church, The New Catholic Encyclopedia,* W. G. Kümmel, *The New Testament: The History of the Investigation of Its Problems* (SCM); The *Cambridge History of the Bible.* Useful surveys of Marcan studies are R. S. Barbour, "Recent Study of the Gospel According to St. Mark," *Expository Times,* 1968, pp 324–329; H. D. Knigge, "The Meaning of Mark," *Interpretation,* 1968, pp 53–70, C. L. Mitton, "Some Further Studies in St. Mark's Gospel," *Expository Times,* July 1976, pp 297–301, H. C. Kee, "Mark as Redactor and Theologian," *J.B.L.,* 1971, pp 333–336; "Mark's Gospel in Recent Research," *Interpretation,* 1978, pp 353–368, J. D. Kingsbury, "The Gospel of Mark in Current Research," *Rel. St. Rev.,* April 1979, pp 101–107. For the Greek text of Mark see the very useful and reasonably priced edition of *The Greek New Testament,* published by the United Bible Societies (London, 1975) and edited by Aland, Black, Martini, Metzger and Wikgren. A companion volume edited by B. M. Metzger is *A Textual Commentary On The Greek New Testament* (London, 1971).

2. The English Open University's Humanities' Foundation Course studies Mark. The textbook *What Is a Gospel?* prepared by John Fergman describes Mark as "one of the most influential books of history" (p 3).

3. An example of this continuing interest in Mark and such themes of his as the mystery of the kingdom and the Marcan theory of parables is the fact that J. Lambrecht could list forty-four books and articles on Mark chapter 4 alone during the seven years from 1967–1974. See *L'Evangile selon Marc,* M. Sabbe (ed) (Louvain, 1974), pp 269–307.

4. Peter F. Ellis in *Biblical Studies in Contemporary Thought,* Miriam Ward Greene (ed) (Hodden & Co., Massachusetts, 1975), p 88.

5. An interesting example of a non-scholar view is the selection from an Australian aboriginal's plea made at the Australian Bishops' Conference, Sydney, 1977:

> When I read the Gospels, I read them as an aboriginal. There are many things in the Gospel that make me happy to be an aboriginal because I think we have a good start. So many of the things Christ

said and did, and the way he lived, make me think of the good things in our way of life.

Christ did not get worried about material things. In fact, he looked on them as things that get in the way and make it hard to get to our true country. He was born in the countryside in a cave, like many of us have been born. He walked about like us and with nowhere to lay his head. He died, with nothing, on a cross. So many of our people die with nothing. He had his own little group, like us. He was strong on sharing: "If someone wants your tunic, give him your cloak." We do a lot of things like that. Of course, he went a lot further. In the Eucharist, he shared himself as nobody else could. He liked the bush, as we do. He loved nature. He saw in the lilies of the field a glory greater than Solomon's. He loved the little things like the mustard seed and the grain of wheat and the corn, drops of cold water, and the little sparrows. We have similar things, like seeds and berries and yams, small waterholes, and we like the quietness of the hills and the bush. Like him, we have a deep sense of God in nature. We like the way he uses the things of nature to teach, and the important part nature plays in the sacraments.

6. See Gabriel Daly, "Prayer of Petition," *Doctrine & Life,* March 1980, p 143.

7. D. E. Nineham, *Explorations in Theology I* (SCM, London, 1977), p 3.

8. John A. T. Robinson, *Redating the New Testament* (SCM, London, 1976), p 360. Similarly Patrick Henry, *New Directions in New Testament Study,* pp 33f, mentions a classical historian who had carefully studied the second century evidence for the traditions that Mark directly reflects Peter's reminiscences and concluded that he would be delighted to find such solid evidence for some other ancient historical tradition and that the severe skepticism of nearly all New Testament scholars was a puzzle to him.

9. Gerald O'Collins, S.J., in *What Are They Saying about Jesus?* (Paulist Press, New York, 1977), pp 56f, finds a startling contrast between Bruce Vawter's *This Man Jesus* (New York, 1973) and Malcolm Muggeridge's *Jesus.* Vawter's book he concludes is technically correct and shows up the fundamental mistakes of the brilliant amateur Muggeridge who is horrified at the deserts and jungles of biblical criticism with its rows of new translations. Future historians according to Muggeridge will conclude that

the more we knew about Jesus the less we knew him, and the more precisely his words were translated the less we understood or heeded them.

O'Collins, asking why is such New Testament scholarship failing, concludes that Vawter's book which remains at one remove from religious commitment needs to be applied pastorally. Muggeridge's book has been much more successful in bringing believers and non-believers into contact with the living Christ. O'Collins applies to Muggeridge Augustine's dictum "Give me a lover and he will understand" and sees his book as a reminder that we are not saved by historical scholarship alone. Knowledge of Jesus Christ is far too serious a business to be left to theologians and exegetes alone. Since the Middle Ages these professionals have neglected art and the imagination as guides to religious truth. Muggeridge makes a very valid point in his hyperbole:

> Only mystics, clowns and artists, in my experience, speak the truth, which, as Blake was always insisting, is perceptible to the imagination rather than the mind.

C. F. Evans, *Explorations in Theology* (SCM, 1977), pp 77f, gives an interesting example of the practical problem of hermeneutics from *The Interpreter's Bible:*

> In the lay-out of this commentary the text is printed in English with a line drawn under it. Beneath this line is what is termed the "exegesis," which is of a historical kind and is done with a high standard of competence by recognized scholars. Under the exegesis a further line is drawn, beneath which is what is called the "interpretation," which is done by someone other than the scholar responsible for the exegesis. What makes this commentary difficult, even at times embarrassing, to us is the hiatus and contrast between the exegesis and the interpretation. A particularly ripe example is the comment on Mark 16:1–8, where the exegesis is what would be expected from a scholarly discussion of this very complex pericope, whereas the interpretation runs as follows: "Now and then on the bulletin boards of post offices we see presented the face of a man with this warning 'Dangerous man at large.' That is the message of the resurrection."

The famous biblical scholar Julius Wellhausen saw the problem when he asked to be transferred from the theological faculty to the faculty of philosophy and wrote to remind the Prussian Minister of Culture in a letter dated April 5, 1882:

> I became a theologian because I was interested in the scientific investigation of the Bible. It has only gradually become evident to me that a professor of theology also has the practical task of preparing students for service in the Protestant Church, and that in this practical task I have fallen short. Indeed, in spite of all reserve on my part, I am in fact making my hearers unfit for their ministry (H. J.

Kraus, *Geschichte der historisch—kritischen Erforschund des Alten Testaments,* Neukirchen, 1956, p 236).

For a brief review of the current dissatisfaction with the historical-critical approach to the Bible and such alternatives as structuralism and analytical psychology, see Dennis C. Duling, *Jesus Christ Through History,* pp 298ff; Patrick Henry, *New Directions in New Testament Study,* pp 56ff.

10. Robert C. Tannehill, "Tension in Synoptic Sayings and Stories," *Interpretation,* April 1980, pp 138f, 149f.

11. C. K. Barrett, *The Gospel of John and Judaism* (SPCK, London, 1975), p 42, notes that whereas Antiochus' profanation of the temple called forth the Book of Daniel and the less provocative Act of Pompey and the Psalms of Solomon:

> Yet there is scarcely any essentially Jewish Apocryphal material which clearly mirrors the events of the year 70 with the one exception of the Apocalypse of Abraham (par 27: ". . . a heathen people and they pillaged. . . . Lo, I saw them run toward them, through four entrances, and they burnt the temple with fire, and the holy things that were therein they plundered").

12. Paul J. Achtemeier, *Interpretation,* October 1978, p 339. Augustine well described the paradox of the New Testament as a book which offered itself to all

> in the plainest words and simplest expressions, yet demands the closest attention of the most serious minds (Confessions 6.5.8).

Gregory the Great in the preface to his *Moralia* described the New Testament as

> a kind of river in whose shallows a lamb may wade and in whose depths an elephant may swim about.

Patrick Henry, in *New Directions in New Testament Study,* p 37, gives a salutary warning for those who think that only ancient texts are difficult to interpret:

> Anyone who takes the trouble to read more than one local paper is quickly brought face up against the difficulty of interpreting contemporary texts.

13. Patrick Henry, p 63.

14a. A reproduction of one of the fragments of p [45] is given in Norman Perrin, *The New Testament,* p 142.

14b. Martin Hengel, *Acts and the History of Earliest Christianity* (SCM, London, 1979), pp 5f.

15. William Barclay, *The Gospel and Acts,* Vol One, p 25.

16. Ibid., p 25. Writing his commentary on the Corinthian letters (p 129) in 1954 he calculated that a book the size of the New Testament would have cost £40.

17. John Drury, *Tradition and Design in Luke's Gospel,* p 83, comments on Luke's redaction of Mark—that Luke

is out to make Mark more historically consecutive

and that most readers will agree that something of the sort is needed.

Incident is piled upon incident with no more apparent connection than a mere "and" or "and suddenly." The method certainly has power and is appropriate to Mark's approach governed by the idea of a divine invasion of human life working violently against the grain of all human aspirations. But if it impresses the reader it also disorients and tires him. If there are connections in many stretches of Mark's book they strain the poetic ingenuity of Austin Farrer to uncover. The ordinary reader is soon lost.

18. Others would consider the Valentinian Heracleon's commentary on John written about 170 as the first commentary on a New Testament book. A recent article on Papias and Irenaeus (*The Expository Times,* August 1980, pp 332ff) by A. C. Perumalil dates Papias' "Exegesis" (Interpretations) to about A.D. 100. It criticizes the tendency of modern scholars to belittle the testimony of the early Christian writers and points out that Irenaeus was sufficiently close to the authorities of Papias to have gathered reliable and independent information of his own.

19. Robinson, *Redating the New Testament,* p 109.

20. Eusebius Hist. 3, 37, 13.

21. Irenaeus Adv. Haer. 5.33.4.; cited in Eusebius Hist. 3.39.1.

22. Eusebius Hist. 3.39.3f.

23. Ibid., 3.39.15.

24. See the discussion in R. P. Martin, *Mark,* pp 80ff.

25. Note Acts 13:5 which may mean that Mark was a teacher in Paul's mission.

26. R. G. Heard, *The Old Gospel Prologues* (J.T.S., 1955), pp 1ff; W. F. Howard, "The Anti-Marcionite Prologue," *Expository Times,* 1936, pp 534–538.

27. Hippolytus Refut 7.30.

28. A fragment of the Diatessaron reads as follows:

And the day was Preparation; the Sabbath was dawning (Lk 23:45). And when it was evening, on the Preparation, that is the day before the Sabbath (Mt 27:57; Mk 15:42) there came up a man, being a member of the council (Mt 27:57; Lk 23:50), from Arimathea, a city of Judah, by name Joseph (Mt 27:57; Lk 23:50), good and righteous, being a disciple of Jesus, but secretly for fear of the Jews (Mt 27:57; Lk 23:50; Jn 19:38). And he was looking for the kingdom of God (Lk 23:51). This man had not consented to their purpose (Lk 23:51).

See W. Barclay, *Introducing the Bible* (The Bible Reading Fellowship, London, 1972), pp 61f.

29. See Leon-Dufour, *The Gospels and the Jesus in History* (Desclee, New York, 1968), pp 47f.

30. R. H. Grant, *A Short History of the Interpretation of the Bible* (Macmillan, New York, 1963), p 72.

31. Patrick Henry, *New Directions in New Testament Study,* p 54.

32. Irenaeus, *Against Heresies* 3.11.7.

33. Ibid., 3.11.8.

34. Eusebius Hist. 6.14.5.

35. Ibid., 2.15.2.

36. Adumb. in 1 Pet 5:13. See Robinson, *Redating the New Testament,* pp 108f.

37. See Supplementary Volume, *Interpreter's Dictionary of the Bible,* p 573.

38. Eusebius Hist. 6.25.4

39. Ibid., 6.25.5.

40. R. P. C. Hanson, *Allegory and Event* (London, 1959), p 360.

41. I. Howard Marshall (ed), *New Testament Interpretations* (The Paternoster Press, Exeter, 1977).

42. See Patrick Henry, *New Directions in New Testament Study,* p 48.

43. See the article in the Supplementary Volume of the *Interpreter's Dictionary of the Bible,* p 609.

44. Eusebius Hist. 2.16.1.

45. Quaest. ad Marinum I.

46. W. Barclay, *Introducing the Bible,* p 63.

47. Jerome, Ep. 120 ad Hedib. 11.

48. Ibid., 120.3.

49. Jerome, Adv. Pelag. 11.15.

50. Augustine on Christian Doctrine 1.36.40.

51. Augustine, *De Consensu Evangelistarum* 1.2.4. His remark on the language of the gospels is interesting also.

Of the four it is certain that only Matthew is regarded as written in the Hebrew language, while the others wrote in Greek.

52. A. Robert and A. Feuillet, *Introduction to the New Testament* (Desclee, New York), p 266.

53a. However, it seems not unlikely that scholars such as Origen had written one as he had written commentaries on most of the books of the Bible. See Jerome's not necessarily complete list in his *Letter to Paula* (Epist. 33).

53b. The Codex Bòdlerianus attributes it to Cyril of Alexandria.

54. Robert E. McNally S.J., *The Bible in the Early Middle Ages* (The Newman Press, Maryland, 1959), pp 105ff. Note also the mid ninth century Irish Introduction to Mark (*The Medieval Irish Contribution*, M. McNamara (ed) (Dominican Pub., Dublin, 1976), p 131, which deals with such questions as why Mark was written and explains how Peter was in Rome, the fact that Christ is a Greek translation of Messiah, that the mention of Isaiah in 1:1 of Malachi is in Jerome's phrase a "vitium scriptorum." An Irish scholar, Miss Maura Walsh, who kindly sent a copy of her M. Phil presentation (1977) on *The Study of the Gospel of Mark in Irish Monastic Schools c. 600–1000 A.D.*, had noted among published text some nine texts which consider Mark or his Gospel especially. In addition to those listed in our text these would also include a *Praefatio Secundum Marcum* (c. 750–775) which seems to be an outline on a lecture on Mark and his gospel (R. E. McNally [ed], cc. 1088, pp 220–224); *Excerpts from the Gospels* (cc. 1088, pp 213–219) which is a systematic investigation of the four gospels according to fourteen categories (locus, tempus, persona, lingua, demonstratio, conventio, qualitas, numerus, documenta, etc.).

55. Lightfoot, *The Gospel Message of Mark*, p 2.

56. Thomas Aquinas, *Summa Theologica* (1a.1.10).

57. Augustine, *City of God* 17.3.

58. D. E. Nineham (ed), *The Church's Use of the Bible* (SPCK, London, 1963), p 61.

59. H. de Lubac, *Exégèse Médiévale* (Paris, 1959).

60. C. S. Lewis, *Surprised by Joy* (Fontana, 1969), p 166.

61. R. E. McNally, p 63.

62. See Kealy, *The Changing Bible*, pp 6ff, 57ff.

63. R. M. Grant, *A Short History of the Interpretation of the Bible*, p 116.

64. Comment of Miss M. Walsh. See note 54.

65. *Corpus Christianorum*, Vol 120, 439. Translation given in *Interpretation*, 1978, p 404.

66. *Salimbene-Chronica*, M.G.H. Scriptores xxxii (1905–1908), pp 186f.

67. Erasmus, *Works*, (ed) Holborn, I, 142, 202ff.

68. C. F. Evans, *Explorations in Theology*, p 80.

69. Robert M. Grant, *The Interpretation of the Bible*, p 130.

70. Ibid., pp 132f.

71. Quoted in D. E. Nineham (ed), *The Church's Use of the Bible*, p 79.

72. See the *Oxford Dictionary of the Christian Church* sub Cajetan.

73. Latin 1555; English translation by W. Pringle, Edinburgh 1845, reprinted Grand Rapids, U.S.A. 1949.

74. See T. H. Parker, *Calvin's New Testament Commentaries* (Eerdmans, 1971).

75. See the *Oxford Dictionary of the Christian Church* sub Maldonatus.

76. Ibid. sub Cornelius à Lapide.

77a. *The New Catholic Encyclopedia* sub Calmet.

77b. Kümmel, p 48.

78. Ibid., p 50.

79. Ibid., p 49.

80. James P. Mackey, *Jesus* (SCM, London, 1979), p 17. A quotation from Bishop Butler's *Analogy of Religion* (1736) is an interesting indication of this age of unbelief, irreligion and self-centeredness so similar to much of Western society. Butler, the foremost philosopher in England, thought it unlikely that anyone would succeed himself as bishop and believed it improbable that Christianity would survive his own lifetime.

> It has come to be taken for granted by many persons that Christianity is not so much a matter for inquiry but is now at length discovered to be fictitious. Accordingly they treated it as if in this present age this were an agreed point among all people of discernment, and nothing remained but to set it up as a prime subject for mirth and ridicule, as it were by way of reprisals for its having so long interrupted the pleasures of mankind.

However, Michael Green (*Evangelism—Now and Then*, Inter-Varsity Press, 1979), p 30, pointed out that Butler's gloomy prediction would be proved wrong before the end of his lifetime by the preaching of Wesley and Whitfield.

81. Kealy, *Who Is Jesus of Nazareth?* pp 20ff.

82. This view has been vigorously revived by W. R. Farmer, *The Synoptic Problem* (N.Y. and London, 1964) and others. Farmer places Mark last of the synoptics by arguing that lifelike details, e.g., people's names and Aramaisms, are signs of lateness in contrast to the opinion of most scholars. In fact Griesbach's hypothesis is enjoying a remarkable revival in recent years when a bicentenary colloquium was held in Münster. See B. Orchard and T. R. W. Longstall, *J. J. Griesbach: Synoptic and Text-Critical Studies* (C.U.P.). A lively discussion of the nineteenth century German development of the Marcan priority which has often been drawn upon in this study is Hans-Herbert Stoldt's *History and Criticism of the Marcan Hypothesis* (Mercer University Press, Georgia, 1980). See B. Orchard, "Why Three Synoptic Gospels?" *Irish Theological Quarterly*, No 4, 1979, ₣ρ 240ff. A useful modern synopsis in English is Throckmorton's *Gospel Parallels* (Nelson) and, with Greek text, K. Aland's *Synopsis Quattour Evangeliorum* (Stuttgart).

83. B. Orchard, *Why Three Synoptic Gospels?* pp 240ff.

84. Kümmel, *The New Testament* (SCM, London, 1973), p 77.

85. R. P. Martin, *Mark*, p 33.

86. Kümmel, p 78.

87. C. F. Evans, *Explorations in Theology*, pp 89f.

88. Kümmel, p 80.

89a. Summary from Duling, *Jesus Christ Through History* (Harcourt, N.Y., 1979), p 148.

89b. See Sommervogel Bibl. de la c. J. II, 481ff (Brussels, 1891).

90. Quotation from Kümmel, p 148.

91. Kümmel, p 111. Cf. H. A. W. Meyer, *Critical and Exegetical Commentary on the New Testament.* This series was translated into English and published by T & T Clark.

92. Trocme, p 52.

93. Denis C. Duling, *Jesus Christ Through History*, p 162.

94. Strauss, it should be remembered, was not a believing Christian as early on his Christian faith was shattered. Not only did he see nothing in the whole idea of resurrection but he abandoned all belief in a personal and transcendent God and saw Jesus as a man and no more than that. See H. Harris, *David Friedrich Strauss and His Theology* (C.U.P., 1974).

95. Quoted by Nineham, *Explorations in Theology*, p 117.

96a. Duling, pp 180f.

96b. Ibid., p 182.

97. Kealy, *The Changing Bible*, p 40.

98. Mackey, *Jesus*, p 31.

99. Duling, p 194.

100. Ibid., p 195.

101. B. C. Butler, *The Originality of Matthew*, pp 62ff.

102. A. Schweitzer, *The Quest of the Historical Jesus*, p 125.

103. J. M. Robinson, *The Problem of History in Mark*, p 8.

104. Kümmel, p 149.

105. Mackey, *Jesus*, p 27.

106. Duling, pp 187f.

107. Marc Stephane, *The Passion of Christ* (Paris, 1959).

108. Georges Ory, *The Christ and Jesus* (Paris, 1968).

109a. John Allegro, *The Sacred Mushroom and the Cross* (Hodder & Stoughton, 1970).

109b. R. Bultmann, *Jesus*, pp 13–14.

110. C. F. Evans, *Explorations in Theology*, p 123.

111. Kümmel, p 222.

112. Neill, *The Interpretation of the New Testament*, p 261.

113. Kümmel, p 223.

114. M. Kähler, *The So-Called Historical Jesus* (Fortress Press, 1964), pp 48f.

115. Duling, *Jesus Christ*, pp 261f.

116. R. P. Martin, *New Testament Foundations*, Vol I, p 36.

117. Duling, *Jesus Christ,* p 260.

118. H. C. Kee, *Interpretation,* 1978, p 353.

119. Wrede, *The Messianic Secret* (Cambridge, 1971).

120. Wrede, *Paulus* (Tübingen, 1904), pp 5f.

121. Wrede, *The Messianic Secret,* p 185.

122. See Leonard Sabourin, *The Parables of the Kingdom* (Biblical Theology Bulletin, 1976), pp 130f.

123. In subsequent printings of the latter work in German to which Schweitzer made substantial additions not found in the English translations, he changed the title to *An Account of the Scholarly Study of the Life of Jesus.*

124. Nineham, *Explorations in Theology,* pp 123f.

125. C. K. Barrett, "Schweitzer and the New Testament," *Expository Times,* October 1975, p 6.

126. A. Schweitzer, *The Quest of the Historical Jesus* (Macmillan, N.Y., 1966), p 401.

127. Ibid., p 312.

128. S. Neill, *The Interpretation of the New Testament,* p 195.

129. See *The Kingdom of God and Primitive Christianity,* p 71.

130. See Kealy, *Who Is Jesus?* p 30.

131. Norman Perrin, *What Is Redaction Criticism?* (SPCK, London, 1970), p 14. Nineham, *Explorations in Theology* (p 198), quotes Evans to reject the popular view that methods of historical investigation were first perfected in secular studies and then somewhat reluctantly applied to the study of the Bible and Christian history. The great classical scholar Wilamovitz actually dedicated his Homeric studies to Wellhausen whom he describes as the pioneer of rolling back the history of the transmission of his text.

132. Norman Perrin, p 14.

133. Kümmel, pp 282f.

134a. Quoted in H. Cadbury, *The Making of Luke-Acts,* pp 93f.

134b. Quotations from Ralph P. Martin, *Mark,* p 39, who remarks that Burkitt had taken over, with some caution from the nineteenth century "lives of Jesus" people, notions of a flight from Herod and a failure of the Galilean mission after an initial flush of success and popularity. After 8:27 Mark gives the actual succession of events. At least nothing in the other gospels has a better claim to give the true sequence, as their differences are not due to superior chronological information but to editorial combination and rearrangement.

135. *Journal of Theological Studies,* April 1907, pp 454ff.

136. See S. Neill, *The Interpretation,* p 115, who comments that Burkitt's phrase "the stormy . . ." is exactly right:

What had this Jesus to do with the mild Galilean peasant of Renan's fancy? Here is a man of more than Napoleonic stature, who spreads around him astonishment and dismay; whose words are perplexing in the extreme; who goes on puzzling his disciples to the very end; who flouts the conventional piety of his day; and yet who all through remains human, without a single trait characteristic of the Greek hero, the "theios aner." Here are problems galore, if at any time we should venture to write a life of Jesus; and we may be certain that what we write will be wholly unacceptable to those who like their Jesus tamed and conventionalized and are not willing to be led away to the bleak uplands on which he moves in the Gospel according to St. Mark.

137. E. Trocmé, *The Formation of the Gospel According to Mark,* p 23.

138. Von Harnack, *The Essence of Christianity* (1900).

139. See P. F. Forsyth, *The Person and Place of Jesus Christ* (Hodder & Stoughton, 1909), p 101.

140a. Loisy, *The Gospel and the Church* (Fortress Press, 1976), p 13.

140b. E.g., righteousness, justification by faith, union with Christ, life in the Spirit.

141a. Dio Cassius, Hist. 65.15.

141b. B. W. Bacon, *The Gospel of Mark,* p 204.

142. See *A New Catholic Commentary on Holy Scripture* (Nelson, 1975), p 806.

143. E. Trocmé, *The Formation of the Gospel According to Mark,* p 74.

144. James M. Robinson, *The Problem of History in Mark* (SCM, London, 1971), p 10.

145. Ibid., p 11.

146. Norman Perrin would add a third, i.e., Hellenistic Jewish Mission Christianity: *The Expository Times,* August 1971, p 340.

147. See R. P. Martin, *The Four Gospels,* p 19.

148. C. H. Talbert, *What Is a Gospel?* (Fortress Press), p 19.

149. See Kümmel, p 330.

150. Robert C. Tannehill, "Tensions in Synoptic Sayings and Stories," *Interpretation,* April 1980, p 148.

151. A paraphrase of Dibelius' formulations by K. L. Schmidt quoted by J. M. Robinson in *Jesus and Man's Hope* (Pittsburgh, 1970), p 100.

152. R. P. Martin, *Mark,* p 144.

153. Note the criticisms of this statement in S. Neill, *The Interpretation of the New Testament,* p 241.

154. Translated in C. A. Braaten and R. A. Harrisville (eds), *The Historical Jesus and the Kerygmatic Christ* (Nashville, 1964).

155. B. Lonergan, *Method in Theology,* p 157.

156. Robert C. Roberts, *Rudolf Bultmann's Theology* (SPCK, London, 1977), p 323.

157. Bultmann, *Jesus and the Word,* p 79.

158. An interesting attempt to steer a middle course between the Charybdis of an uncritical attitude and the Scylla of a complete disregard of the mythical descriptions in the Bible is found in Paul Ricoeur, *The Symbolism of Evil* (Beacon Press, Boston, 1959). For Ricoeur a critical approach is useful in dispelling one's "first naiveté" which simply affirms the literal ac-

counts of the Bible. But we need to move on to a "second naiveté" which despite a critical awareness yet can appreciate the mythological language and is not just content to try to extract a meaning or message while rejecting the text itself.

159. Bultmann, *Kerygma and Myth*, p 4.

160. Kealy, *Who Is Jesus?* pp 209ff.

161. Bultmann, *The Theology of the New Testament*, Vol I, p 26.

162. Bultmann, *The History of the Synoptic Tradition*, p 347.

163. Bultmann, *Jesus and the Word*, p 6.

164. Bultmann, *The Historical Jesus and the Kerygmatic Christ* (Abingdon Press, 1964), pp 22–23.

165. R. P. Martin, *New Testament Foundations*, Vol I, p 39.

166. James M. Robinson, *The Problem of History in Mark*, pp 19ff.

167. Bultmann, *The History of the Synoptic Tradition*, p 350.

168. Ibid., p 258.

169. Streeter, *The Four Gospels*, p 562.

170. John Hawkins, *Horae Synopticae* (Oxford, 1899).

171. Gore's Commentary (SPCK, 1928), p 42f. See also C. E. Pryke, *Redactional Style in the Markan Gospel* (C.U.P., 1978).

172. According to W. Barclay's *The First Three Gospels*, p 132, Allen Menzies adds three other motives, the aetiological motive in which origins and causes of rites, practices and beliefs are given, the apologetic motive to defend the Church under attack, and the devotional motive to revive love which is going cold by going back to the beginning to see Jesus in action again.

173. V. Taylor, *The Gospel According to St. Mark*, p 76.

174. Cadbury, p 77.

175. Ibid., p 81.

176. Ibid., p 82.

177. *J.T.S.* (1966), pp 51–69. See M. Boucher, *The Mysterious Parable: A Literary Study*, (C.B.Q. 6, Washington, 1977) for a recent study of the parables of Mark.

178a. For a useful description of the studies of such writers as Wilder, Linnemann, Jüngel, Fuuk, Via, and Crossan, read W. S. Kissenger's history of the interpretation of the parables, *The Parables of Jesus* (Scarecrow Press, N.J. and London, 1979).

178b. *The Expository Times*, 1932, pp 396ff and *New Testament Studies*, 1953, pp 1ff. D. E. Nineham's criticism is found in *Studies in the Gospels* (1957), pp 223f and his *Mark*, p 22 and note 28. He insists that the order of events was of little significance in the apostolic preaching. In 1933 H. J. Cadbury in *The Beginning of Christianity*, F. J. Jackson and K. Lake (eds), Vol V, p 393, remarked: "the summaries . . . represent the latest part of Mark and specially reveal his editorial motives."

179. Dodd, *About the Gospels* (1950), p 22.

180. Dodd, *The Apostolic Preaching*, p 46.

181. Dodd, *The Expository Times*, 1932, p 399.

182. Ibid., p 400.

183. Lohmeyer says that a study of Mark would compel us to reconsider our ideas of the development of the Christian Church in its first forty years.

184. X. Leon-Dufour, *The Gospels and the Jesus of History* (Desclee, N.Y., 1968), pp 191f.

185. *Matthew, Luke and Mark* (Koinonia, 1977).

186. Quoted in Barclay, *The First Three Gospels,* p 128.

187. Cf. R. P. Martin, *Mark,* pp 148f.

188. Cf. Robert & A. Feuillet, *Introduction to the New Testament* (Desclee, N.Y., 1965), p 210.

189. V. Taylor, *The Gospel According to St. Mark,* p 24.

190. Patrick Henry, *New Directions in New Testament Study,* pp 225ff.

191. Quoted in J. A. T. Robinson, *Redating the New Testament,* p 30.

192. Kümmel, *The New Testament,* p 218. Frank Zimmermann, *The Aramaic Origin of the Four Gospels* (N.Y., Ktav, 1979) accepts C. C. Torrey's general thesis that the gospels as a whole were translated from Aramaic to Greek, adding some two hundred new examples and suggesting that the sayings and deeds of Jesus passed through three Aramaic phases (Galilean to Judaean to Eastern Aramaic) before the unknown Greek translator made his translation.

193. Robinson, p 12.

194. Ibid., p 343.

195. "The Messiah Jesus and John the Baptist," *The Expository Times,* 1931.

196. Reimarus, *Fragments,* C. H. Talbert (ed), 1970, p 137.

197. *New Testament Studies,* pp 126ff.

198. M. D. Goulder, *The Evangelists' Calendar* (SPCK, London, 1978).

199. *Jesus Transfigured* (Copenhagen, 1947), pp 283ff.

200. Quoted in Martin, *Mark,* pp 70, 160.

201. E. Trocmé, *The Formation of the Gospel According to Mark,* p 141.

202. J. M. Robinson & H. Koester (Fortress Press, Phil., 1971).

203. *New Testament Studies,* Vol IV, pp 1–24.

204. S. E. Johnson, *The Gospel According to Mark* (Adam & Charles Black, London).

205. Josephus, B. J. 6:5:2f.

206. Johnson, p 20.

207. Ibid., p 24.

208. Joachim Rohde, *Rediscovering the Teaching of the Evangelists* (1968), p 151. Kee, *J. B. L.,* pp 335f, criticizes Schreiber's redaction criticism study of Mark (Hamburg, 1967) as wholly arbitrary and lacking any discernible methodological controls. Not unlike Philo, Schreiber sees symbolic significance in the fact of the sun going down as the sick are brought to Jesus but rising on the occasion of his resurrection. In the death on the cross he

sees the divine word overcoming the powers of darkness so that "the Messiah suddenly breaks through the threatening silence" (15:57). Kee comments:

> At a time when gospel interpretation is beginning to recover from the distortion that resulted from reading Mark through the eyes of Paul, it is no advance now to read him through the eyes of John even as interpreted by Bultmann though Bultmann would not condone Schreiber's allegorical exegesis.

209. See C. H. Roberts in the *Cambridge History of the Bible,* Vol I, pp 48ff.

210. See H. A. Guy, *The Origin of the Gospel of Mark,* pp 155ff.

211. Manson, *The Teaching of Jesus* (Cambridge, 1931).

212. See M. Ward (ed), *Biblical Studies in Contemporary Thought,* p 100.

213. *Theology* IX, p 269.

214. See his summary in *Jesus and His Contemporaries* (SCM, London, 1973), p 19. In this latter work he divides into two categories the main ways of writing a life of Jesus. The first is typified by Strauss and Bultmann and sees the gospels as "symbolic expression of religious ideas." The second is typified by Renan and Dodd's *Founder of Christianity* which tries to produce "a psychological reconstruction of the central person in the drama." Both all too easily allow subjective preoccupations to distort their picture. Trocmé tries a new approach and searches the strata beneath the gospels. He is not so certain that we can reach reliable information about Jesus himself but concludes that we are able to attain the impression which individual disciples or groups had about Jesus and by identifying the different portraits of Jesus to make a partial synthesis of them and produce a coherent picture of Jesus.

215. Ibid., p 20.

216. Trocmé, *The Formation of the Gospel According to Mark,* p 80.

217. *Christ and the Spirit in the New Testament,* B. Linders and S. S. Smalley (eds) (Cambridge, 1973), pp 3–14.

218. S. Schulz, *Die Bedeutung des Markus fur die Theologiegeschichte des Urchristentums,* Studia Evangelica 2 (1964), pp 135–145.

219. Martin's description in *The Four Gospels,* p 221.

220. *Erwagungen zur Christalogie des Markusevangeliums,* in Festschrift R. Bultmann, E. Dinkler (ed), 1964.

221. *Die Function der alttestamenthichen Zitate und Ampielungen Markusevangelium* (Gutersloh, 1965).

222. E. Best, *The Temptation and the Passion: The Marcan Soteriology* (C.U.P. 1965).

223. Bowman, *The Gospel of Mark: The New Christian Jewish Passover Haggada* (Leiden, 1965).

224. D. Daube, in *The New Testament and Rabbinic Judaism* (London 1956) suggested some interesting rabbinic parallels that would make the

debates in Mark 12 to correspond to haggadic categories such as the four standard questions of the four sons in the Passover liturgy with the parable of the husbandmen as the Christian substitute for the blessing which preceded the questions.

225. R. H. Fuller, *A Critical Introduction to the New Testament* (Duckworth, London).

226. Fuller, *Preaching the New Lectionary* (Collegeville, 1974), pp xxif.

227. See Fuller, *The Foundations of New Testament Christology,* pp 108ff.

228. E. Schweitzer, *The Gospel According to Mark* (SPCK, London, 1970).

229. Consult the useful explanation *Good News for Everyone,* Eugene A. Nida (Collins, Glasgow, 1977); R. G. Bratcher & E. A. Nida, *Translator's Handbook on the Gospel of Mark* (1961); *So Many Versions?* Kubo & Specht (Zondervan, 1975).

230. *Interpretation,* October 1978, pp 389, 399.

231. H. Conzelmann, *An Outline of the Theology of the New Testament* (SCM, London).

232. Quoted from an article of Conzelmann in Martin's *Mark* (p 94, note).

233. In *Oikonomia,* O. Cullmann Festschrift, F. Christ (ed) (Hamburg).

234. *Jesus and the Twelve: Discipleship and Revelation* (Grand Rapids, 1968).

235a. *ZNTW* 59 (1968), pp 145–158; *Traditions in Conflict* (Phil., 1971).

235b. H. I. Marrou, *A History of Education in Antiquity,* pp 160–170, 277–281.

236. *The Role of Discipleship in Mark* (N.T.S., 1977), pp 377–401.

237. The latter remarks are taken from John H. Elliot's review in *C.B.Q.,* October 1977, p 600.

238. R. H. Fuller in his excellent commentary on the Sunday Lectionary, *Preaching the New Lectionary* (1977), describes its far-reaching ecumenical impact because of the sweep of its concepts and the thoroughness of its scholarship. Other churches, e.g., Presbyterian, Episcopal and Lutheran, all adapted lectionaries based on it.

239. *Markus, Lehrer der Gemeinde* (Stuttgart, 1969).

240. Analecta Biblica 38, Rome, 1969.

241. Quesnell, p 132.

242. *Cambridge History of the Bible,* Vol I, pp 270ff.

243. C. F. Evans, *Explorations in Theology,* Vol II (SCM, London, 1977), pp 36f.

244. F. Neirynck, *Duality in Mark* (Duclot, Louvain).

245. The Paternoster Press. Martin also has a useful popular com-

mentary on Mark, *Where the Action Is* (Regal Books, Glendale, California, 1977).

246. Note Martin's summary in his *The Four Gospels,* pp 214, 221f.

247. See the article in *Biblica 1972,* pp 91–100 and 101–104; cf also *Los papiros griegos de la cueva 7 de Qumran,* Biblioteca de Autores Christianos (Madrid, 1974).

248. English translation published by Orbis Books, N.Y. & SPCK, London, 1980.

249. Leonardo Boff, *Jesus Christ Liberator,* p 19.

250. Ibid., p 5.

251. Published by the Society of Biblical Literature Dissertation Series 10. Note also that Olivette Genest, *La Christ de la Passion* (Desclee, Tournai, 1978) applies the structuralist method of Roland Barthes to Mark's passion narrative (14:53—15:47). One interesting result is the structural parallelism between the hearing before the Sanhedrin (14:53–72), the Roman trial (15:1–20), the crucifixion (15:20–33) and the death (15:34–47) as follows—

(a) hearing,	mockery,	Peter,	exit.
(b) trial,	mockery,	Simon of Cyrene,	exit.
(c) crucifixion,	mockery,	thieves,	darkness.
(d) death,	word of centurion,		burial.

Thus the first element in each focuses on Jesus, the second gives an interpretation, the third the stand or response of others, the fourth an interlude. The centurion's confession parallels the three mockeries in each of which a title of Jesus is denied.

252. *Interpretation* (October 1978), pp 369ff.

253. *The Poetry of St. Mark in the Business of Criticism* (Oxford U. Press, 1959), p 102. See also Frank Kermode, *The Genesis of Secrecy* (Harvard U. Press) for a study of Mark as a work of literature.

254. Fortress Press. Kelber also published a popular commentary, *Mark's Story of Jesus,* also in Fortress Press (1979). A useful collection of studies on the Marcan passion has been edited by W. H. Kelber (Fortress Press, 1976). This gives what many would consider the extreme views of the Chicago school of Marcan redaction influenced by Norman Perrin, e.g., J. D. Crossan argues that Mark created the empty-tomb tradition. These scholars in general argue that Mark's passion narrative is a single composition throughout based on a multiplicity of traditional units, against other scholars who hold that there was a primitive narrative which Mark used. Another useful collection of Marcan articles edited by M. Sabbe, *L'evangile selon Marc* (Louvain, 1974), gives the papers of the 22nd Session of the Journées Bibliques, 1971 at Louvain.

255. See W. Davies, *The Gospel and the Land: Early Christianity and*

Jewish Territorial Doctrine (University of California Press, Berkeley, 1974), pp 241, 409ff.

256. W. H. Kelber, *Mark's Story of Jesus* (Fortress Press, 1979), p 11.

257. W. Lane, *The Gospel of Mark* (Marshall, Morgan & Scott, London).

258. V. Mauser, *Christ in the Wilderness: The Wilderness Theme in the Second Gospel and Its Basis in the Biblical Tradition* (Nashville, 1963).

259. W. R. Farmer, *The Last Twelve Verses of Mark* (C.U.P.). Note also Joseph Hug, *La finale de l'evangile de Marc (Mc 16:9–20)* (Paris, Gabalda, 1978). Hug analyzes the structure into vv 9–11, 12–13, 14–18, 19–20. Each is introduced by a temporal particle and has a threefold division of imitator, messenger and recipients of the message.

260. Published by *J.B.L.* (March 1966), pp 1–16.

261. E. Schillebeeckx, *Jesus, an Experiment in Christology* (Collins, English edition, 1979).

262. Ibid., pp 421f, 198f.

263. Perrin, *Rediscovering the Teaching of Jesus* (SCM, London, 1967), p 29.

264. *Mimesis,* p 36.

265. *Proclamation Commentaries* (Fortress Press). See his article "Mark as Interpreter of the Jesus Tradition," *Interpretation* (1978), pp 339ff.

266. See Kee, *Jesus in History,* second edition (Harcourt, N.Y., 1977), pp 32f.

267. Kee, *Interpretation,* 1978, p 365.

268a. J. P. Kealy, *Who Is Jesus of Nazareth?* (Dimension Books, N.J., 1978).

268b. Cf *The Sunday Times,* February 17, 1980, pp 33–34: Alec McCowen, "How St. Mark Became Big Box Office."

269. M. Hengel, *Acts and the History of Earliest Christianity* (SCM, London).

270. Marxsen, *Mark,* p 131.

271. D. E. Nineham, *Explorations in Theology* (SCM, London, 1977), pp 86f.

272. Ibid., p 89.

273. Ibid., p 97.

274. *The Way of All the Earth* (Sheldon Press, 1973).

275. Nineham, p 78.

276. Nikos A. Nissotis in *Jesus and Man's Hope* (Pittsburgh Theological Seminary, 1971), Vol II, p 122.

Author Index

Subject Index

Scripture Index